RACIAL AND ETHNIC DIVERSITY IN AMERICA

A Reference Handbook

Other Titles in ABC-CLIO's
CONTEMPORARY
WORLD ISSUES
Series

Books in the Contemporary World Issues series address vital issues in today's society such as genetic engineering, pollution, and biodiversity. Written by professional writers, scholars, and nonacademic experts, these books are authoritative, clearly written, up-to-date, and objective. They provide a good starting point for research by high school and college students, scholars, and general readers as well as by legislators, businesspeople, activists, and others.

Each book, carefully organized and easy to use, contains an overview of the subject, a detailed chronology, biographical sketches, facts and data and/or documents and other primary-source material, a directory of organizations and agencies, annotated lists of print and nonprint resources, and an index.

Readers of books in the Contemporary World Issues series will find the information they need in order to have a better understanding of the social, political, environmental, and economic issues facing the world today.

RACIAL AND ETHNIC DIVERSITY IN AMERICA

A Reference Handbook

Adalberto Aguirre, Jr.

A B C C L I O

Santa Barbara, California • Denver, Colorado • Oxford, England

Cataloging-in-publication data for this book is available from the Library of Congress.

ISBN 1-57607-983-X (alk. paper) ISBN 1-57607-984-8 (e-book)

07 06 05 04 03   10 9 8 7 6 5 4 3 2 1

This book is also available on the World Wide Web as an e-book. Visit abc-clio.com for details.

ABC-CLIO, Inc.
130 Cremona Drive, P.O. Box 1911
Santa Barbara, California 93116-1911

This book is printed on acid-free paper ∞.
Manufactured in the United States of America

I dedicate this book to my aunt,
Raquel Aguirre,
for giving me the spirit of inquiry
and a yearning for discovery

Contents

Preface

> If we are to achieve a richer culture, rich in contrasting values, we must recognize the whole gamut of human potentialities, and so weave a less arbitrary social fabric, one in which each diverse human gift will find a fitting place.
> —Margaret Mead

Racial and ethnic diversity is not going to disappear from U.S. society. Population statistics from the 2000 census show that nonwhite minorities make up almost one-third of U.S. society. As a result, as the United States enters the twenty-first century, it is significantly different than it was in its beginnings, when immigrants from Europe made up the core that shaped the character of U.S. society. One purpose of this book is to document how the character of diversity has changed in the United States. By examining changes in the racial and ethnic diversity of the United States, this book intends to engage the reader in a discussion regarding the context of social relations for racial and ethnic diversity in society.

I have attempted to construct a portrait of U.S. society that instructs the reader about its multicultural roots. Chapter 1 traces the beginnings of American society by identifying the role of European immigrants in shaping a social structure that excluded non-European immigrants and indigenous people of color. Chapter 2 highlights changes in the pool of immigrants in the United States during the nineteenth and twentieth centuries to document how the character of U.S. society has been shaped by people of color. Chapter 3 examines three outcomes of increased racial and ethnic diversity in the United States: racial profiling, hate crimes, and affirmative action. Ironically, an examination of the precarious context of diversity in U.S. society suggests that increased racial and ethnic diversity may not necessarily lead to the incorporation of plural identities in U.S. society.

Chapters 4 to 9 are intended to serve as starting points for the reader interested in pursuing further inquiry regarding racial and ethnic diversity in the United States. Chapter 4 is a chronology of people and events that have shaped the historical context for race and ethnicity in U.S. society. Chapter 5 presents biographical sketches of some of the scholars engaged in research on race and ethnicity. Some of these scholars have been pioneers in the study of race and ethnicity or critics of existing perspectives regarding racial and ethnic diversity. Chapter 6 contains quotations that illustrate the experiential nature of diversity. The chapter also contains statistical data that highlights the presence of racial and ethnic populations, including the foreign-born, in the United States. Chapter 7 identifies organizations that focus their activities on select ethnic and racial groups. The existence of such organizations clearly shows that race and ethnicity are dynamic and vibrant threads in the social fabric of U.S. society. Chapter 8 is a bibliography that complements the references in Chapters 1, 2, and 3. These print resources provide the reader with a range of issues and topics in the study of racial and ethnic diversity. Finally, Chapter 9 is a directory of nonprint resources, primarily videos. Fortunately, a fairly large number of videos are available on racial and ethnic diversity.

The ideas in the first three chapters of this book have benefited from my discussions with my graduate and undergraduate students. David Baker and Ruben Martinez have provided me with the opportunity to outline my thoughts on the topic of diversity and race and ethnic relations. They have always been kind and gracious in letting me get things "out of my head." Jacque Godsey and Shoon Lio were extremely resourceful in assisting me in identifying racial and ethnic organizations and with finding the available nonprint resources.

Adalberto Aguirre, Jr.

1

Early America

Here is not merely a nation, but a teeming nation of nations.
—Walt Whitman

The European settlers who arrived in North America found themselves not in a wilderness but in a land populated by a large and diverse American Indian population. There were as many as 5 million American Indians living in North America when the first European settlers arrived (Snipp 1989; Thornton 1987). In order to appreciate the diversity in the American Indian population and the complexity of that population's social organization, one must focus on the number of *groups* that made up the population. Although the term *tribe* is popularly used to refer to different components in the American Indian population, it is too simplistic because it obscures the linguistic and cultural diversity in the population. There were about two hundred groups in the American Indian population at the time the European settlers arrived in North America. Although the groups shared some social and cultural features, each was linguistically and culturally identifiable. Each group had built a specific relationship with the land they inhabited (Goodman 1985). For example, the groups who interacted with English settlers in the eastern region of North America had developed a complex set of social and economic activities based on hunting, farming, and fishing. The groups who interacted with Spanish settlers in the southwestern region of North America had developed societies based on hunting, agriculture, and sheepherding. Thus, the America that greeted the European settlers was populated by an American Indian population rich in its own linguistic, cultural, and social diversity.

1

The purpose of this chapter is to discuss the diversity in early America—that is, from 1500 to 1900—that resulted from the arrival of European settlers. There are two objectives for the chapter: One is to discuss the general features of European migration to North America, especially to what is now the United States. This discussion will serve as a framework for constructing a descriptive profile of racial and ethnic diversity in early America. The second objective is to discuss how European migration facilitated the development of an Anglo-Saxon core in the United States. It is important to understand the origin of the Anglo-Saxon core as a basis for interpreting the social context for diversity in twenty-first-century U.S. society, which is the focus of chapter 2.

The Spanish Exploration of North America

Christopher Columbus's search for a western route to Asia landed him in the Caribbean in 1492. The possessions he established there for Spain served as a staging area for the Spanish exploration of North America. Spanish explorers traveled and established settlements in the southwestern and southeastern regions of North America during the 1500s (Vigil 1980). Juan Ponce de León discovered Florida in 1513, and in 1518 Álvar Núñez Cabeza de Vaca began exploring the regions that later became the states of Texas, New Mexico, and Arizona. By 1540, Francisco Coronado had traveled up the Colorado River, and Hernando de Soto had explored the Mississippi River in 1541.

The conquest of Mexico by the Spanish in 1522 served as a catalyst for exploration of the southwestern region of North America. On the one hand, the Catholic church's interest in converting Indians to Christianity was a factor in opening up the southwestern region to Spanish exploration. The Spanish constructed settlements along the western region, in what is now California, from San Diego in the south to Monterey in the north. Each settlement was centered on a Catholic mission whose purpose was to Christianize the American Indian groups. On the other hand, tales of cities filled with gold pushed Spanish explorers into the southwestern region. Coronado set out from Mexico in 1540 in search of the Seven Cities of Cibola, whose streets were said to be paved with gold. Although he did not find the cities, his explorations led him to the Grand Canyon and to what is now Kansas.

While Spanish explorers were traveling overland from the

south into the western region of North America and by ship from the Caribbean to the eastern region of North America, the French were moving from the north into North America. Giovanni da Verrazano, an Italian explorer who sailed for the French, landed in North Carolina in 1524 and traveled from there up the eastern coast past New York harbor. In 1534, Jacques Cartier set sail from France seeking a sea corridor to Asia. His voyage, however, resulted in the exploration of the Saint Lawrence River, setting the basis for French claims to North America. Although French explorers traveled extensively through the eastern region of North America, they did not establish a noticeable presence, as the Spanish did. One reason for this failure was that the Spanish considered them a threat. For example, when French Huguenots attempted to settle the northern coast of Florida in the 1560s, they were attacked by Spanish forces led by Pedro Menéndez. In the process of fighting off the French Huguenots, Menéndez established what is considered to be the first European settlement in America: Saint Augustine, Florida.

Spain's success in exploring and colonizing the Americas attracted attention from other European nations. The wealth that Spain was drawing from its explorations of the Americas—gold, chocolate, silver, precious gems—alerted the other European nations to the riches to be had. England's emerging superiority as a military power on the seas increased interest in the Americas. Francis Drake's successes on the seas, especially his raids of Spanish ships carrying valuable cargo, also increased England's interest in seeking a presence in the Americas. Thus, in 1578 Elizabeth I commissioned Humphrey Gilbert to colonize lands in the New World that other European nations had not yet claimed. When Gilbert was lost at sea in 1583, his half brother, Walter Raleigh, took over his commission. In 1585, Raleigh establish the first British colony in North America on Roanoke Island off the coast of North Carolina. The colony, however, was abandoned after a few years. Twenty years would elapse after Raleigh's efforts before the British established another colony in North America.

The Spanish were thus a dominant force in the exploration and settling of North America in the 1500s. The system of missions they established in the western region of North America allowed them to build permanent settlements, introduce European customs and the Spanish language to American Indian groups, and establish the importance of the Catholic church. The dominant presence of the Spanish in the southwestern region of North America would play an important part in facilitating the adjustment of European settlers to the southwestern region.

European Immigrants in North America

Immigration from Europe to what is now the United States was a significant social force in the 1600s, with the infusion of English, French, and Dutch immigrants into North America. The immigrants arrived in a land where the Spanish had already established colonies and conquered the indigenous populations. The ocean voyages from Europe to the New World were lengthy, taking from six to twelve weeks depending on the weather, and travelers often died from starvation or disease on the way.

The majority of European immigrants looked at North America as a refuge from political oppression (Daniels 1990). The arbitrary rule of England's Charles I in the 1630s motivated people to move to North America. Similarly, the political instability created by the feuds of princes in German-speaking areas of Europe, especially those based on religious conflict, led people to move to North America. Immigrants from Europe also came to North America to pursue better living conditions and economic opportunity. For example, the economic problems that plagued England between 1620 and 1635 created a large class of peasants without work, skilled artisans had trouble finding work because of the Industrial Revolution, and an impoverished crop economy offered little hope to hungry people. For England, emigration to North America became an outlet for an expanding population that was growing increasingly unhappy and that could pose a significant threat to the political state. Furthermore, English colonies were both a resource providing raw materials to meet the demands of the Industrial Revolution and a new market for its manufactured goods.

In 1607, James I granted a group of merchants, operating as the Virginia Company, permission to establish a community at Jamestown, Virginia. A group of men interested in making their fortunes in the New World and men seeking political and religious freedom set out for the Chesapeake Bay in 1607. They chose a site far enough up the James River to avoid conflict with the Spanish. They encountered problems coping with the demands of a new land, which offered few comforts to persons only inter-

ested in treasure. Capt. John Smith emerged as a leader in helping the group survive and keeping the colony at Jamestown
together. However, after Captain Smith's return to England in
1609, the colony descended into anarchy, and more than 75 percent of the colonists died from disease.

Despite the situation at Jamestown, immigrants continued to
arrive from England. In 1612, the successful experiments conducted by John Rolfe on cross-breeding tobacco from the West
Indies with tobacco native to North America created a crop profitable for Virginia's economy and appealing to the European market. Virginia began shipping tobacco to England in 1614, and by
1625 tobacco had become Virginia's primary source of revenue.
The economic potential of tobacco attracted people interested in
acquiring property and money to Virginia. By 1650, the population of Virginia had reached 15,000. For many persons arriving in
the new land, Virginia became a stop on their way to inland areas,
especially the valleys along the James, York, and Rappahannock
Rivers. By 1685, the population of Virginia had increased to
60,000.

Although Virginia became a focal point for the economic
transformation of the new land, English settlers established other
colonies in the eastern region of North America. More than 1,000
Puritans arrived in the Massachusetts Bay area in 1630. They were
seeking protection from laws passed in England against those
critical of the Anglican church. By 1640, their numbers in and
around Boston had increased to 20,000. Other settlements
cropped up in nearby areas. A young clergyman named Roger
Williams purchased land from the Narragansett Indians in 1636
to establish what is now Providence, Rhode Island. Despite the
threat of Indian attacks, English settlers established colonies in
the Connecticut River Valley and along the New Hampshire and
Maine coasts.

The opportunity for riches attracted the interest of other
European countries (Babcock 1969; Swierenga 1985; Thernstrom,
Orlov, and Handlin 1980). In 1609, the Dutch East India Company
hired Henry Hudson to explore the land around what is now
New York City. Hudson explored the river that bears his name,
and his explorations opened the door for Dutch settlements in
North America. The Dutch, interested in establishing a fur trade,
formed a trading partnership with the Five Nations of the
Iroquois in order to have access to regions where furs were avail-
able. By 1617, the Dutch had built a fort at the junction of the

Hudson and Mohawk Rivers. The Dutch also started settling on the island of Manhattan in the early 1620s. In 1624, they purchased the island from the Indians for about twenty-four dollars and renamed it New Amsterdam.

In addition to the English and Dutch settlements in North America, the French established colonies during the 1600s around what are now Detroit, Michigan; Saint Louis, Missouri; Memphis, Tennessee; Natchez, Mississippi; and Mobile, Alabama. The larger French settlements were located in the lower Mississippi Valley, where fertile soil and a warm climate enabled settlers to farm and build plantations. By 1673, Robert Cavalier de La Salle had sailed down the Mississippi River to the Gulf of Mexico, claiming the land along the way for France. La Salle named the land Louisiana to honor Louis XIV.

Adding to the diversity introduced to North America by the English, French, and Dutch settlers were slaves from Africa, brought to North America in the 1600s (Curtin 1969). The success of tobacco as a profitable crop in Virginia created a demand for more labor—labor that would not decide to pursue its own riches and that could be controlled. Although initially, indentured servants from England had been used as labor in the tobacco industry, they were not a suitable source of labor because they would terminate their servitude to pursue their own opportunities. In 1662, in response to the cries for a stable source of labor, the British government granted a monopoly in the slave trade to the Royal African Slave Company to bring African slaves into North America. The slaves were regarded as an excellent source of labor because they could not terminate their servitude, they could increase and multiply their numbers, and they were capable of working in the hot weather. By 1671, black slaves made up about 5 percent of Virginia's population. By the end of the Civil War, as many as one-half million slaves had been imported from Africa to the United States.

The diversity that characterized North America by the end of the 1600s consisted of American Indians, black slaves, and English, French, Dutch, and Spanish settlers. The languages spoken by the different populations in North America were adding to the linguistic diversity already existing among indigenous peoples.

The Emerging Character of U.S. Society

By the start of the 1700s, English settlers were no longer the chief source of immigration to North America (Dinnerstein, Nichols, and Reimers 1996). The American population numbered about 250,000 in 1700. There were now noticeable numbers of Germans, Dutch, Swedes, French, Italians, Spaniards, and Portuguese living in North America. In addition, the collection of colonies that had been established in the eastern region gave America a distinctive character that highlighted its diverse roots.

The upper colonies were anchored by New England in the northeast. They developed industries that harnessed water power to run grain mills and sawmills, used the area's abundant timber to build ships, and developed an economy around the cod industry. The Massachusetts Bay Colony transformed Boston into an important port and city. Ships built in Massachusetts Bay represented almost half of the ships flying the British flag. New England was also a primary point of entry for slaves from Africa being brought to America.

In contrast to the upper colonies, the middle colonies were populated by persons from more diverse backgrounds. The people living in the middle colonies represented a variety of languages, trades, and national origins. The population along the Hudson River, for example, consisted of French, Germans, Dutch, Norwegians, Italians, Portuguese, Scots, and Irish. The middle colonies became noted for their industries: shoemaking, cabinetmaking, weaving, and farming. The center of the middle colonies was Philadelphia.

The southern colonies consisted of rural settlements in Virginia, Maryland, North and South Carolina, and Georgia. Their distinctive feature was large plantations supported by slave labor. Charleston, South Carolina, was the most prominent port for trade and served as a profitable economic trading center for tobacco, rice, and cotton. By 1750, there were more than 100,000 people living in the colonies of North and South Carolina.

By the end of the 1700s, America was an ethnically and linguistically diverse society. The English, however, remained the most powerful group in the colonies. Groups that were unwilling to come into conflict with the English, such as the Germans and Scots-Irish, moved to the remote regions of the colonies, where they built farms and prospered. By the 1730s, the Shenandoah

Valley was populated by farmers. Thus, by the late 1700s, the character of what became the United States had been shaped by a variety of colonies dominated by the powerful influence of the English.

A renewed wave of immigrants arrived from Britain in the 1800s. The first British population census was conducted in 1801. It showed that Britain had a population of more than 10 million people and led to speculation that the population had doubled since 1750. Increasing demand to feed a growing population led to large-scale, scientific farming. However, the move to such farming left many agricultural workers jobless. Many of those without work decided to leave for other countries, especially the United States. In 1830, 15,000 people had boarded ships at Liverpool, bound for the United States. By 1842, the number of people leaving from Liverpool had increased to more than 200,000.

While the British were trying to find a way to feed a growing population, the Irish were trying to save their crops from destruction (Brown 1966). In 1845, the potato crop failed, affecting about 4 million people who depended on the crop as their primary staple. Stored reserves offered some relief from the crop's failure. However, the blight returned in 1846 and 1847, resulting in the death of more than a million people. The Great Potato Famine, as the failure of the potato crop became known, was a catalyst for Irish migration to the United States. More than 90,000 Irish left for the United States in 1846. Over the years, the number increased dramatically, culminating in more than 200,000 Irish leaving for the United States in 1850. About one-fourth of Ireland's population had emigrated to the United States by the end of 1854.

Political conflict was a factor in drawing German immigrants to the United States in the 1880s (Faust 1909). The failed German revolution in 1848 resulted in more than a million persons leaving Germany to settle in the United States between 1848 and 1858. The majority of those leaving Germany for the United States were poor and suspicious of the government's ability to solve Germany's economic problems. New York City and Chicago became popular destinations for German immigrants. By 1860, more than 100,000 Germans lived in New York City and about 130,000 lived in Chicago.

Immigration from France to the United States also increased during the 1800s (Olson 1979). Many of those leaving France for the United States were fleeing the political upheaval that resulted from the failed 1848 revolution in France. By 1851, more than 20,000 French immigrants had arrived in the United States. The French quickly made their presence known in the United States by establishing a network of French newspapers in New York City and Philadelphia. French immigrants were attracted to three cities in the United States: New York City, Chicago, and New Orleans.

The 1800s were thus a period of continued immigration from Europe. The countries serving as primary sources of immigrants during the 1800s were Britain, France, Germany, and Ireland. Other European countries, such as Norway, Sweden, and the Netherlands, were also sources for immigrants to the United States; however, the numbers of immigrants from these countries were small compared to the numbers arriving from Britain, Germany, France, and Ireland. Immigration from Europe continued until World War I, with persons arriving in the United States from additional countries such as Italy, Hungry, Russia, and Austria. Earlier immigration from Europe had peaked by 1900, but the arrival of new immigrants in the United States after World War I would alter the character of United States society once more.

The Anglo-Saxon Core

The preceding discussion serves as background for the general observation that the United States is "a nation of immigrants" (Handlin 1973). In an attempt to retain their ethnic identity and ties to their home countries, European immigrants established schools in their communities in the language of their home countries. As a result, foreign-language schools became commonplace in most states. The most common non-English languages used for instruction were German, Swedish, Danish, Norwegian, Italian, French, Spanish, and Czech (Kloss 1977). The diversity of the backgrounds of the European immigrants in the United States was also reflected in the different religious traditions that emerged in the United States: Protestant, Catholic, Eastern Orthodox, Quaker, Presbyterian, and Jewish.

Despite the diversity in the population of European immigrants, some groups within the population were more instrumental than others in shaping the character of U.S. society. The influence wielded by English immigrants was clearly a factor in forging an identity rooted in the English language and customs, which served as a core culture for the assimilation of other European immigrants. The core culture forged by English immigrants is often referred to as the "Anglo-Saxon" core in U.S. society. In an early observation of the Anglo-Saxon core, Alexis de Tocqueville, writing in *Democracy in America*, noted,

> The emigrants who came at different periods to occupy the territory now covered by the American Union differed from each other in many respects; their aim was not the same, and they governed themselves on different principles. These men had, however, certain features in common, and they were all placed in an analogous situation. The tie of language is, perhaps, the strongest and the most desirable that can unite mankind. All the emigrants spoke the same tongue; they were all offsets from the same people. (Tocqueville [1835, 1840] 1984, 40)

Tocqueville made his observations about life and society in the early United States during his visit from May 1831 through February 1832. His reference to "the same tongue" probably refers to the prevalent use of English in the new republic. To Tocqueville, it may have appeared as if European immigrants, despite their diverse backgrounds, had adopted the English language as the basis for a shared identity. More importantly, his observation suggests that European immigrants had forged a national identity to fit the character of the new republic. In a broader context, Tocqueville's observation suggests that social forces were at work in the new republic that facilitated the construction of a U.S. character rooted in Anglo-Saxon values.

One social force at work in the new republic had to do with the relative numerical size of the European groups immigrating to the United States. Historically, the largest European groups immigrating to the United States were the English, Irish, and Germans. Table 1.1 shows the numbers of foreign-born persons in the United States between 1850 and 1900. One can observe that immigrants born in England, Germany, and Ireland constituted a significant proportion of the foreign-born population. It has been suggested that these three immigrant groups served as the seed for the formation of an Anglo-Saxon core in the new republic (Daniels 1990; Kivisto 1995). That is, the influence of the English in the new republic increased the assimilation by other European groups to the language and culture of the English settlers. In turn,

Table 1.1
Region and Country or Area of Birth of the U.S. Foreign-Born Population: 1850–1900

	1850	1860	1870	1880	1890	1900
Total	2,244,062	4,138,697	5,567,229	6,697,943	9,249,547	10,341,276
England	278,675	431,692	550,924	662,676	908,141	840,513
France	54,069	109,870	116,402	106,971	113,174	104,197
Germany	583,774	1,276,075	1,690,533	1,966,742	2,784,894	2,663,418
Ireland	961,519	1,611,304	1,855,827	1,854,571	1,871,509	1,615,459
Italy	3,679	11,677	17,157	44,230	182,580	484,027
Scandinavia	18,075	72,582	241,685	440,262	933,249	1,134,733
Scotland	70,550	108,518	140,835	170,136	242,231	233,524
Spain	3,113	4,244	3,764	5,121	6,185	7,050
Wales	29,868	45,763	74,533	83,302	100,079	93,586

Source: Campbell J. Gibson and Emily Lennon, "Historical Census Statistics on the Foreign-Born Population of the United States: 1850–1990." Population Division, U.S. Census Bureau, working paper no. 29, Washington, DC, 1999.

assimilation to a common core rooted in English language and culture increased the likelihood that European groups would intermarry, resulting in households consisting of couples from diverse backgrounds. As a consequence, ethnic boundaries between European immigrant groups became more permeable in the new republic.

The increased permeability of ethnic boundaries between European immigrant groups facilitated their identification with a common identity. This common identity shared by European immigrant groups was rooted in another social force in the new republic: the identification of European immigrant groups on the basis of *whiteness.* That is, the assimilation and acculturation of European immigrant groups to a core culture revolved around their identification as "white" (Alba 1990; Waters 1990). Not only did whiteness become a marker of one's identity with the Anglo-Saxon core, but it also served to distance European settlers from other populations in the United States, namely, nonwhite populations. As a result, European immigrants saw themselves as a "new ethnic group" in the new republic: white, English-speaking Americans (Vargas 1998).

The diverse backgrounds of European immigrants were instrumental in shaping an identity in the new republic that reduced ethnic-group differences. Given the numbers of immigrants from England and their involvement in such major enterprises as commerce, mercantilism, and banking, it is not surprising that English language and culture served as the basis for the emergence of an Anglo-Saxon core in the new republic. In addition, European immigrants tended to see each other as "white," thereby further reducing ethnic-group boundaries between them and vesting the Anglo-Saxon core with images of superiority. As a result, the "new" Americans saw themselves as superior to those not part of the Anglo-Saxon core.

Marginalized Populations in the New Republic

The popular notion that the United States is a "nation of immigrants" often ignores "the 'uprooted' from Africa, Asia, and Latin America . . . that also helped to make 'the American People'" (Takaki 1993, 6). The "immigrant" origins of U.S. society are often associated with Europeans. Even though American Indians, Asians, black slaves, and Mexicans were part of the founding of the United States, they are excluded from the "founding immigrant myth" of the United States because they were not considered part of the Anglo-Saxon core. In a sense, European settlers regarded them as "others," not as part of the "we" they perceived themselves as being. As a result, these "other" populations were marginalized and were regarded by the European settlers as people and communities to be colonized and exploited for labor.

Table 1.2 shows the numbers of American Indians, Asians, Mexicans, and blacks present in the U.S. population between 1850 and 1900. Despite their presence, they are often missing from a discussion of diversity in early U.S. society. In addition to serving as markers for the relative size of the populations, the numbers in Table 1.2 also raise a question about these four populations: if they were present in early U.S. society, why were they excluded from the formation of the mainstream? One approach to answering this question is to examine the social context for each population in U.S. society.

American Indians

The consequences of contact with European settlers were devastating for American Indians (Snipp 1989; Thornton 1987). Europeans exposed American Indians to diseases—smallpox, cholera, diphtheria, measles, typhoid, and scarlet fever—that killed American Indians in vast numbers. To satisfy their hunger

Table 1.2
Race and Ethnicity of the U.S. Population, 1850–1900

	White	Black	American Indian	Asian	Mexican[3]
1850	19,553,068	3,638,808[1]	NA	NA	13,317
1860	26,922,537	4,441,830[2]	44,021	34,933	27,466
1870	33,589,377	4,880,039	25,731	63,254	42,435
1880	43,402,970	6,580,793	66,417	105,613	68,399
1890	54,983,890	7,470,040	58,806	109,514	77,853
1900	66,809,196	8,833,994	237,196	114,189	103,393

[1]Free = 434,495, Slave = 3,204,313
[2]Free = 488,070, Slave = 3,953,760
[3]Reported as foreign-born
Source: Campbell J. Gibson and Emily Lennon, "Historical Census Statistics on the Foreign-Born Population of the United States: 1850–1990" (Population Division, U.S. Census Bureau, working paper no. 29, Washington, DC, 1999); Campbell J. Gibson and Kay Jung, "Historical Census Statistics on Population Totals by Race, 1790 to 1990, and by Hispanic Origin, 1790 to 1990, for the United States, Regions, Divisions, and States" (Population Division, U.S. Census Bureau, working paper no. 56, Washington, DC, 2002).

for land and resources, European settlers displaced American Indians from their lands, often relocating them to land not suitable for hunting or agriculture that resulted in many Indians starving to death. American Indians also suffered large numbers of casualties in their skirmishes with European settlers over land rights, and many lost their lives serving as slave labor in the colonies.

If one assumes that there were 5 million Americans Indians at the time of first contact with Europeans (Snipp 1989), the numbers in Table 1.2 reflect a devastating drop in the American Indian population: There were slightly more than one-quarter million American Indians in the United States in 1900. By the start of the twentieth century, the American Indian population in the United States had been decimated by conquest and exploitation to about 5 percent of its original size. In displacing American Indians from their lands, European settlers had, in effect, erased them from the social and cultural fabric of the emerging new republic.

Blacks

Blacks were brought involuntarily from Africa to the colonies to serve as slave labor to fuel the economic interests of European settlers. Life in the colonies was harsh and demanding for black slaves (Elkins 1959; Fogel and Engerman 1974; Genovese 1965; Stampp 1956). They were treated like animals, subjected to harsh punishments, and used as commodities in barters or trades. Black slave women were used by white owners as mistresses, were mated with black males in order to increase an owner's slave-holdings, and were separated from their own children. In short, black slaves were a tool Europeans used to implement and expand their economic interests in the new republic. From the beginning, black slaves were excluded from the Anglo-Saxon core. As Table 1.2 shows, the number of black persons in the U.S. population more than doubled between 1850 and 1900. However, the population data for 1850 to 1860 in Table 1.2 show that about 90 percent of blacks in the United States were slaves. Black persons identified as "free" were those who served as indentured servants, who had been set free by their masters, or who had managed to purchase their freedom. The important point is that until their emancipation, the experience of black persons in the new republic was almost entirely limited to their role as slaves. Black persons were thus marginalized in U.S. society because they were regarded not as persons but as property.

Asians

The figures in Table 1.2 show that the Asian population in the United States more than tripled between 1860 and 1900. The majority of people in the Asian population during this period were Chinese. Noticeable numbers of immigrants from Japan did not start arriving until the late 1800s. The first major arrival of immigrants from China in San Francisco occurred at almost the same time as the discovery of gold in California in 1848 (Kitano and Daniels 1988). Although small numbers of immigrants from China arrived on the eastern shore of the United States, most arrived in California. Most of the immigrants from China arrived as sojourners; that is, they planned to return to China after a period of three to five years, hopefully with riches (Takaki 1989).

The discovery of gold encouraged persons to emigrate from China to the United States. The majority of Chinese immigrants arrived as indentured or bonded servants. Chinese laborers became a primary source of labor for gold mining, for the building of the transcontinental railroad, and for domestic chores. The general treatment of immigrants from China on the West Coast was not much different from that of black slaves in the South (Perea, Delgado, Harris, and Wildman 2000; Takaki 1989). Chinese immigrants were exploited for their labor and were constrained to occupations marginal to the Anglo-Saxon core. In addition, because Asians lived mostly on the West Coast, they were marginalized from East Coast social forces that were shaping mainstream U.S. society.

Mexicans

The number of foreign-born persons who identified their country of origin as Mexico increased dramatically between 1850 and 1900. Although the number of Mexicans migrating to the United States prior to 1900 was small, the figures for 1850 through 1890 in Table 1.2 is questionable because the 1848 Treaty of Guadalupe Hidalgo, ending the Mexican War, gave about 75,000 Mexicans living in the southwestern region of the United States the choice of staying or leaving (Perea, Delgado, Harris, and Wildman 2000). In addition, there is some question as to how many of the "Mexicans" residing in the southwestern region of the United States—the states of California, Arizona, New Mexico, Colorado, and Texas—were mestizos or American Indians (Acuña 1988). Setting aside the issue of how these persons were classified, Mexicans were a noticeable presence in the United States, primarily in the southwestern region of the country.

The condition of Mexicans in the Southwest is complicated. Prior to the arrival of European settlers from the eastern region of the United States, Mexicans had established many communities in the Southwest with Mexican land grants. The arrival of European settlers in the Southwest, especially in response to the discovery of gold in California, altered the condition of the Mexicans there. Reginald Horsman (1981) argues that the contact between European settlers and Mexicans in the Southwest was the first expression of the settlers as an Anglo-Saxon race. The European settlers' perception of themselves as an Anglo-Saxon race served as the basis for an ideology that they used to justify the domination and exploitation of Mexicans. As a result, European settlers saw themselves as changing the destiny of the Southwest by voiding Mexican land grants and taking political control over the land. The introduction of private land ownership was a tool for taking away land from a people whose system of ownership was based on communal land ownership.

Mexicans were thus displaced from their own land by European settlers. The communities and society that Mexicans had built in the Southwest fell victim to a system of social and cultural values brought by European settlers, a system that stressed individualism, economic exploitation, and colonization of those not part of the Anglo-Saxon core. It is not surprising, then, that Mexicans have not been seen as having a part in shaping the character of U.S. society. They were marginalized in U.S. society and silenced by an Anglo-Saxon core that privileged European immigrants.

Conclusion

The new land that later became the United States had a highly diverse society. The arrival of European immigrants augmented an American Indian population already living there and an established Spanish, American Indian, and Mexican presence in the southwestern region of the continent. In spite of its exploitative and dehumanizing features, slavery also contributed to the diverse character of early American society by introducing African cultures, languages, and traditions into the new land. However, the social, political, religious, and economic forces that stimulated persons to emigrate from Europe to North America resulted in the marginalization of American Indians, blacks, Asians, and Mexicans in the formation of the United States.

Despite their diverse backgrounds, European immigrants were able to identify with each other as a "new race." They assimilated to a central set of values and beliefs, rooted in English customs and the English language, that identified them as the Anglo-Saxon core, and they regarded themselves as destined to create the history and society of the new republic. Those persons perceived by them as not part of the Anglo-Saxon core were regarded as inferior, suitable only for labor, and unworthy of incorporation into the society European immigrants were designing. American Indians, blacks, Asians, and Mexicans became casualties of the European immigrants' interest in colonizing the new republic. In the process of colonizing the new republic, European settlers silenced and marginalized those persons excluded from the Anglo-Saxon core.

Finally, by the beginning of the twentieth century, the diversity of European immigration had folded into a U.S. character solidly rooted in Anglo-Saxon values. The diverse character of U.S. society would not become an issue again until the second half of the twentieth century. As we shall see in Chapter 2, the diversity that fueled U.S. society in the second half of the twentieth century differed from the diversity that had shaped early U.S.

society. For one thing, in the second half of the twentieth century, growing numbers of immigrants came from non-European countries. Immigrants from Mexico, Central America, and Asia became noticeable in the United States. The dominance of the Anglo-Saxon core in U.S. society served to strengthen immigrant identities in U.S. society. That is, the new immigrants resisted assimilation to the Anglo-Saxon core and infused U.S. society with multicultural values.

References and Suggested Readings

Acuña, Rodolfo. 1988. *Occupied America: A History of Chicanos.* 3rd ed. New York: Harper and Row.

Aguirre, Adalberto, Jr., and Jonathan Turner. 2001. *American Ethnicity: The Dynamics and Consequences of Discrimination.* 3rd ed. New York: McGraw-Hill.

Alba, Richard. 1990. *Ethnic Identity: The Transformation of White America.* New Haven, CT: Yale University Press.

Babcock, Kendric. 1969. *The Scandinavian Element in the United States.* New York: Arno Press.

Brown, Thomas. 1966. *Irish-American Nationalism.* Philadelphia: J. B. Lippincott.

Curtin, Philip. 1969. *The Atlantic Slave Trade.* Madison: University of Wisconsin Press.

Daniels, Roger. 1990. *Coming to America: A History of Immigration and Ethnicity in American Life.* New York: HarperCollins.

Dinnerstein, Leonard, Roger Nichols, and David Reimers. 1996. *Natives and Strangers: A Multicultural History of Americans.* New York: Oxford University Press.

Elkins, Stanley. 1959. *Slavery: A Problem in American Institutional and Intellectual Life.* Chicago: University of Chicago Press.

Faust, Albert. 1909. *The German Element in the United States, with Special Reference to Its Political, Moral, Social, and Educational Influence.* 2 vols. Boston: Houghton Mifflin.

Fogel, Robert, and Stanley Engerman. 1974. *Time on the Cross.* Boston: Little, Brown.

Genovese, Eugene. 1965. *The Political Economy of Slavery.* New York: Vintage Books.

Gibson, Campbell. 1998. "Population of the 100 Largest Cities and Other Urban Places in the United States: 1790–1990." Population Division, U.S. Census Bureau, working paper no. 27. Washington, DC.

Gibson, Campbell, and Kay Jung. 2002. "Historical Census Statistics on Population Totals by Race, 1790 to 1990, and by Hispanic Origin, 1790 to 1990, for the United States, Regions, Divisions, and States." Population Division, U.S. Census Bureau, working paper no. 56. Washington, DC.

Gibson, Campbell, and Emily Lennon. 1999. "Historical Census Statistics on the Foreign-Born Population of the United States: 1850–1990." Population Division, U.S. Census Bureau, working paper no. 29. Washington, DC.

Goodman, James. 1985. "The Native American." In *Contemporary America: A Geographical Appraisal*, ed. Jesse McKee, 31–53. Dubuque, IA: Kendall/Hunt.

Gordon, Milton. 1964. *Assimilation in American Life*. New York: Oxford University Press.

Handlin, Oscar. 1973. *The Uprooted*. Boston: Little, Brown.

Horsman, Reginald. 1981. *Race and Manifest Destiny: The Origins of American Racial Anglo-Saxonism*. Cambridge, MA: Harvard University Press.

Hutner, Gordon, ed. 1999. *Immigrant Voices: Twenty-Four Narratives on Becoming an American*. New York: Signet Classic.

Kitano, Harry, and Roger Daniels. 1988. *Asian Americans: Emerging Minorities*. Englewood Cliffs, NJ: Prentice Hall.

Kivisto, Peter. 1995. *Americans All: Race and Ethnic Relations in Historical, Structural, and Comparative Perspective*. Belmont, CA: Wadsworth.

Kloss, Heinz. 1977. *The American Bilingual Tradition*. Rowley, MA: Newbury House.

Olson, James. 1979. *The Ethnic Dimension in American History*. New York: St. Martin's Press.

Perea, Juan, Richard Delgado, Angela Harris, and Stephanie Wildman. 2000. *Race and Races: Cases and Resources for a Diverse America*. St. Paul, MN: West Group.

Snipp, C. Matthew. 1989. *American Indians: The First of This Land*. New York: Russell Sage Foundation.

Stampp, Kenneth. 1956. *The Peculiar Institution: Slavery in the Ante-Bellum South*. New York: Vintage Books.

Swierenga, Robert, ed. 1985. *The Dutch in America: Immigration, Settlement, and Cultural Change.* New Brunswick, NJ: Rutgers University Press.

Takaki, Ronald. 1989. *Strangers from a Different Shore: A History of Asian Americans.* Boston: Little, Brown.

———. 1993. *A Different Mirror: A History of Multicultural America.* Boston: Little, Brown.

Thernstrom, Stephan, Ann Orlov, and Oscar Handlin, eds. 1980. *Harvard Encyclopedia of American Ethnic Groups.* Cambridge, MA: Belknap Press.

Thornton, Russell. 1987. *American Indian Holocaust and Survival: A Population History since 1492.* Norman: University of Oklahoma Press.

Tocqueville, Alexis de. [1835, 1840] 1984. *Democracy in America.* New York: Mentor Books.

U.S. Bureau of the Census. 1960. *Historical Statistics of the United States, Colonial Times to 1957.* Washington, DC.

———. 1975. *Historical Statistics of the United States: Colonial Times to 1790.* Washington, DC.

———. 1996. *Population of the States and Counties of the United States: 1790–1990.* Washington, DC: U.S. Government Printing Office.

Vargas, Sylvia. 1998. "Deconstructing Homo[geneous] Americanus: The White Ethnic Immigrant Narrative and Its Exclusionary Effect." *Tulane Law Review* 72: 1493–1596.

Vigil, James. 1980. *From Indians to Chicanos: The Dynamics of Mexican American Culture.* Prospect Heights, IL: Waveland Press.

Waters, Mary. 1990. *Ethnic Options: Choosing Identities in America.* Berkeley and Los Angeles: University of California Press.

2

Twenty-First-Century U.S. Society

Just as we welcome a world of diversity, so we glory in an America of diversity—an America all the richer for the many different and distinctive strands of which it is woven.

—Hubert H. Humphrey

As the United States entered the twentieth century, U.S. society consisted of a fairly large population of persons who were either European immigrants to the United States or the descendants of European immigrants, and a small population of nonwhite persons. For the purpose of illustration, consider the population data in Table 1.2. (Keep in mind that the data in that table may not be completely representative of the population due to reporting inaccuracies or misidentification of a person's racial or ethnic background.) According to Table 1.2, white persons made up about 88 percent and nonwhite persons made up about 12 percent of the U.S. population in 1900. Blacks made up about 95 percent of the nonwhite population. That is, in 1900, the U.S. population consisted of a large white population and a sizable nonwhite population made up primarily of black persons.

The population of white persons in the United States continued to grow in the twentieth century with the arrival of European immigrants. However, whereas the pre-1900 wave of European immigrants moved freely to the United States, immigrants from Europe began to encounter immigration restrictions in the twentieth century (Bennett 1963). In 1917, Congress passed legislation requiring immigrants to pass a literacy test. The Immigration Act

21

of 1917 had two purposes: The literacy test was designed both to restrict immigration from Italy and the Slavic east, where literacy was not widespread, and to benefit immigration from northern and western Europe, where literacy was more widespread.

The Johnson Act of 1921 created a quota system, restricting immigration by nationality. Specifically, the act limited the number of immigrants by nationality to 3 percent annually of the number of persons of that nationality living in the United States in 1910. The 1910 U.S. census was used to establish numerical quotas instead of the 1920 census because it included fewer immigrants from southern and eastern Europe. As a result, immigration from southern and eastern Europe was severely restricted. The Immigration Act of 1917 and the Johnson Act of 1921 were designed to restrict immigration from southern and eastern Europe because these immigrants were perceived by the older and more established European immigrants as "incapable of assimilation and . . . biologically inferior to the Nordic stock out of western and northern Europe" (Hraba 1994, 21; see also Handlin 1957).

Immigrants from southern and eastern Europe were not the only ones encountering restrictions (Daniels 1997). Immigration restrictions against Asians that developed late in the nineteenth century in California were strengthened in the twentieth century by the U.S. government. In 1882, Congress passed the Chinese Exclusion Act prohibiting the immigration of Chinese laborers to the United States and denying Chinese aliens in the United States the opportunity to acquire U.S. citizenship. In 1907, the United States and Japan negotiated the Gentleman's Agreement, which limited immigration from Japan to resident aliens or relatives of resident aliens. In 1917, Congress created the Asiatic Barred Zone to keep immigrants from Asia out of the United States. Similarly, the Quota Act of 1924 restricted immigration from China and Japan by imposing numerical quotas designed to decrease the number of immigrants from China and Japan over time.

The emergence of restrictive immigration legislation in the twentieth century, coupled with the Great Depression and the U.S. involvement in the Spanish American War, World War I, and World War II, resulted in decreasing numbers of immigrants from Europe and Asia. Interestingly, between the end of World War I and passage of the Quota Act of 1924, the number of Mexican laborers recruited by sugar beet companies in the United States increased (McWilliams 1968) and kept increasing up to the Great

Depression. During the Great Depression, however, Mexican immigrants were victims of nativist public sentiment and social policies that sought their deportation to Mexico (Hoffman 1974). Immigration from Mexico would not increase again until the 1940s, when Congress implemented the Bracero Program to recruit Mexican laborers to fill in the labor gaps created by U.S. citizens' going to war and to satisfy the growing demand for labor in an expanding agricultural industry in the United States (Grebler, Moore, and Guzman 1970).

In summary, although the numbers of immigrants from Europe steadily increased in the nineteenth century, their numbers decreased in the first three decades of the twentieth century in response to restrictive immigration policies and the Great Depression. Similarly, immigration from China and Japan faced restrictive immigration laws that began in the late nineteenth century and that were designed to exclude Chinese and Japanese from U.S. society and to prevent them from becoming U.S. citizens. In contrast, immigration of Mexican laborers and their importation to satisfy U.S. agricultural interests increased during the first three decades of the twentieth century, until the Great Depression. In response to nativist public attitudes and social policies that portrayed Mexican immigrants as taking social services and jobs away from Americans, they, as well as Mexican Americans, were subjected to deportation proceedings during the Great Depression.

Immigration would not become a social force for racial and ethnic diversity in the United States until the 1960s. The Immigration Act of 1965 repealed national origin quotas and opened the door for immigrants from countries outside Europe. In 1980, Congress passed the Refugee Act, and as a consequence, large numbers of immigrants from Vietnam, Cambodia, and Laos arrived in the United States. Passage of the Immigration Reform and Control Act (IRCA) of 1986 increased the numbers of immigrants from Mexico and Central America. As a result, the last four decades of the twentieth century witnessed a shift in the social forces fueling diversity from European immigrants to immigrants from Latin America, Asia, the Caribbean, and Africa (Swerdlow 2001). According to Audrey Singer, "During the first 2 decades of the century, 85 percent of the 14.5 million immigrants admitted to the United States originated in Europe, largely Southern and Eastern Europe. This is a sharp contrast to the 14.9 million admitted in the last two decades, an equally large percentage of whom were from the countries of Asia, Latin America, the Caribbean and Africa" (2002, 4).

The purpose of this chapter is to construct a descriptive profile of the racial and ethnic diversity in the U.S. population. According to population data from the 2000 U.S. census, the racial and ethnic composition of the U.S. population is as follows: white, 75.1 percent; Hispanic/Latino, 12.5 percent; black/African American, 12.3 percent; Asian and Pacific Islander, 3.7 percent; and American Indian/Alaska Native, 0.9 percent. This chapter will focus on these five populations. For interpretive purposes, the racial and ethnic populations are defined as follows (definitions based on Aguirre and Turner 2001):

White: The largest racial population in the United States is made up of descendants of European immigrants from countries such as England, Germany, Ireland, Wales, Italy, Scotland, France, the Netherlands, Sweden, and Norway. It was noted in Chapter 1 that immigrants from England were more influential than other immigrant groups in shaping the U.S. character, and thus persons in this population are often identified as WASPs (white, Anglo-Saxon Protestants). According to the 2000 U.S. census (U.S. Bureau of the Census 2003), the largest European American ancestry groups, by percent of the total U.S. population, are German (17 percent), Irish (12 percent), English (10 percent), Italian (6 percent), and French (4 percent).

Hispanic/Latino: According to the 2000 census, the largest group in the Hispanic/Latino population (66.1 percent of that category) consists of persons who trace their ancestry to Mexico (Therrien and Ramirez 2000). Other groups in the Hispanic/Latino population are Central and South Americans (14.5 percent), Puerto Ricans (9.0 percent), and Cubans (4.0 percent).

Black/African American: Persons in this category trace their ancestry to Africa and to African slaves brought to the United States to work on the tobacco and cotton plantations.

Asian and Pacific Islander: Persons in this category trace their ancestry to countries in the Far East, Southeast Asia, and the Indian subcontinent (Barnes and Bennett 2002). According to the 2000 census, the largest groups in this population are Chinese (23 percent), Filipino (20 percent), Asian Indian (16 percent), Korean (10 percent), Japanese (10 percent), and Vietnamese (10 percent).

American Indian and Alaska Native: Persons in this category have origins in any of the original peoples of North and South America, including Central America, and maintain tribal identity or community attachment (Ogunwole 2002). According to the 2000 census, the American Indian tribal groupings with 100,000 or more persons are Cherokee, Navajo, Latin American Indian, Choctaw, Sioux, and Chippewa.

Shifting Racial and Ethnic Composition

There has been a shift in the racial and ethnic composition of U.S. society. Entering the twentieth century, the U.S. population consisted primarily of white persons. Although whites remain the numerical majority in the United States, the percentage of the population of people of other racial and ethnic groups grew in the second half of the twentieth century. As Table 2.1 shows, the proportion of racial and ethnic minority persons in the U.S. population increased 14.1 percent between 1960 and 2000, from 15.2 percent in 1960 to 29.3 percent in 2000. In contrast, the white population in the U.S. population decreased by 13.5 percent between 1960 and 2000, from 88.6 percent in 1960 to 75.1 percent in 2000. As a result, the United States has arrived at the twenty-first century much more diverse than it was when it entered the twentieth century.

The data in Table 2.1 show that the United States population became increasingly diverse between 1960 and 2000. This increase can be analyzed from two perspectives: how the racial and ethnic composition of the U.S. population has changed relative to the white population between 1960 and 2000, and how racial and ethnic populations have increased their numbers between 1960 and 2000.

Table 2.2 presents the numerical size of racial and ethnic populations in the United States between 1960 and 2000. The non-white population—blacks, American Indians, Asians, and Hispanics—was numerically equivalent to 17 percent of the white population in 1960 and 39 percent in 2000. Relative to the white population, then, the nonwhite population increased 22 percent between 1960 and 2000. Thus, the United States arrives at the twenty-first century with a nonwhite population almost equivalent to 40 percent of the white population of the United States.

As shown in Table 2.1, the white population, relative to the total U.S. population, decreased by 13.5 percent between 1960 and 2000. In contrast, the black population increased 1.8 percent between 1960 and 2000, American Indians increased 0.6 percent,

Table 2.1
Racial and Ethnic Populations as a Percent of the Total U.S. Population, 1960–2000

	White	Black	Indian	Asian	Hispanic	Total Nonwhite[1]
1960	88.6%	10.5%	0.3%	0.5%	3.9%	15.2%
1970	87.5%	11.1%	0.4%	0.8%	5.2%	17.5%
1980	83.1%	11.7%	0.6%	1.5%	6.4%	20.2%
1990	80.3%	12.1%	0.8%	2.9%	9.0%	24.8%
2000	75.1%	12.3%	0.9%	3.6%	12.5%	29.3%
Percent change, 1960–2000	−13.5%	1.8%	0.6%	3.1%	8.6%	14.1%

Notes: [1]Total nonwhite = black + American Indian + Asian + Hispanic
Source: Frank Bean and Marta Tienda, *The Hispanic Population of the United States* (New York: Russell Sage Foundation, 1987); Campbell Gibson and Kay Jung, "Historical Census Statistics on Population Totals by Race, 1790 to 1990, and by Hispanic Origin, 1970 to 1990, for the United States, Regions, Divisions, and States" (Population Division, U.S. Census Bureau, working paper no. 56, Washington, DC, 2002); U.S. Bureau of the Census, *The Population Profile of the United States: 2000* (on-line; available: www.census.gov/main/www/cen2000.html.)

Table 2.2
Racial and Ethnic Populations in the United States, 1960–2000

	White	Black	Indian	Asian	Hispanic
1960	158,831,732	18,871,831	551,669	980,337	6,993,604
1970	177,748,975	22,580,289	827,255	1,538,721	10,567,020
1980	188,371,622	26,495,025	1,420,400	3,726,440	14,603,683
1990	199,686,070	29,986,060	1,959,234	7,273,663	22,354,159
2000	211,460,626	34,658,190	2,475,956	10,242,998	35,305,818
Percent change, 1960–2000	33%	84%	349%	945%	405%

Source: Bean and Tienda 1987; Gibson and Jung 2002; U.S. Bureau of the Census 2002a.

Asians increased 3.1 percent, and Hispanics increased 8.6 percent. Relative to the total U.S. population, Asians and Hispanics had the largest increases in their populations between 1960 and 2000. Thus, one can observe that the increasing level of diversity in the U.S. population was driven by rising numbers of Hispanics and Asians between 1960 and 2000.

It is not surprising that the numbers of Asians and Hispanics in the U.S. population have increased if one considers the importance of immigration in the increase (U.S. Bureau of the Census, 2002a, 2002d). The number of immigrants in the U.S. population tripled between 1960 and 2000, from 9.7 million to 28.4 million (Camarota 2001). The immigrant share of the total U.S. population increased significantly in the second half of the twentieth century, and immigrants represented 11 percent of the total U.S. population in 2000. To put this in perspective, the representation of immigrants in the U.S. population peaked at 14.8 percent in 1890 (Camarota 2002). If the immigrant population continues to increase at its current pace, then immigrants will surpass the 1890 figure in the first decade of the twenty-first century.

Hispanics and Asians make up the largest proportion of the immigrant population in the United States. Hispanics were 19 percent of the immigrant population in the United States in 1970 and 51 percent in 2000 (Lollock 2001; Schmidley 2001). Asians were 9 percent of the immigrant population in 1970 and 26 percent in 2000. Together, Asians and Hispanics made up 76 percent of the immigrant population in 2000 (U.S. Bureau of the Census, 2002b). The increased Hispanic and Asian share of the U.S. immigrant population may explain the growing numbers of Asians and Hispanics in the United States between 1960 and 2000. It is clear that their increased share of the immigrant pool has increased their overall representation in the U.S. population. The increased Hispanic and Asian share of the U.S. immigrant population also suggests that immigration to the United States is becoming less diverse. That is, the diversification of the U.S. population appears to be driven primarily by the increasing number of Hispanics and Asians.

Social Indicators

One approach to examining the social condition of racial and ethnic populations in the United States is to observe how they fare along such major social indicators as education outcomes, poverty rates, income levels, and occupational groupings (Blank 2001). These social indicators serve as a window through which we may observe how racial and ethnic groups are represented in major social sectors relative to the white population in the United States. In addition, different racial and ethnic populations' social relations in U.S. society can be evaluated by contrasting their outcomes on these social indicators.

Educational Attainment

Table 2.3 summarizes educational outcomes for the U.S. population by racial and ethnic group. A slightly higher percentage of

Table 2.3
Educational Attainment of Persons 25 Years and Older by Race and Ethnicity, 2000

	White	Black	Asian	Hispanic
High school graduate	34.1%	35.3%	22.1%	27.9%
College graduate	27.0%	18.4%	35.7%	12.3%
Two-year degree	8.4%	6.9%	7.0%	5.0%
Four-year degree	18.6%	11.5%	28.7%	7.3%
Master's degree	6.5%	4.2%	9.4%	2.2%
Doctoral degree	1.3%	0.3%	3.1%	0.5%
Professional degree	1.7%	0.6%	2.7%	0.7%

Source: *Chronicle of Higher Education Almanac 2002–2003* (August 30, 2002).

black persons (35.3 percent) than of white persons (34.1 percent) earned high school degrees in 2000. The figures for Asians and Hispanics were 22.1 percent and 27.9 percent, respectively. Regarding college degrees, a higher percentage of Asians (35.7 percent) than of whites (27.0 percent), blacks (18.4 percent), or Hispanics (12.3 percent) earned college degrees in 2000. A higher percentage of whites (8.4 percent) than of other racial and ethnic populations earned two-year college degrees, and a higher percentage of Asians (28.7 percent) than of other racial and ethnic populations earned four-year college degrees. And a higher percentage of Asians than of whites, blacks, or Hispanics earned master's, doctoral, and professional degrees.

School dropout rates are another indicator of educational progress. For example, 28 percent of Hispanics aged 16 to 24 were school dropouts in 2000 (Kaufman, Alt, and Chapman 2001). The figures for dropout rates for other racial populations are white, 7 percent; black, 13 percent; and Asian/Pacific Islander, 4 percent. That is, Hispanics are four times as likely and blacks are almost twice as likely as whites to drop out of school. In contrast, Asians/Pacific Islanders are almost half as likely as whites to drop out of school. The high dropout rate for Hispanics correlates with their low high school and college graduation rates compared to those of other racial populations (see Table 2.3).

Poverty Level

As Table 2.4 shows, blacks and Hispanics are more than twice as likely to be poor than are whites or Asians. Similarly, Hispanic and black families are more than twice as likely to be poor than are white or Asian families. A striking feature of the data in Table

Table 2.4
People and Families Living in Poverty by Race and Ethnicity, 2000

	People	Families
White	9.5%	7.1%
Black	22.5%	19.3%
Asian	9.9%	7.8%
Hispanic	21.5%	19.2%

Source: Proctor, Bernadette, and Joseph Dalaker, *Poverty in the United States: 2001* (Current Population Report P60-219). Washington, DC: U.S. Census Bureau, 2002.

2.4 is the similarity in poverty levels between the white and Asian populations and between the black and Hispanic populations. Poverty may be a social factor that plays a greater role for blacks and Hispanics than it does for either whites or Asians in defining the social relations of persons and families in U.S. society. For example, a high level of poverty among black families increases the numbers of black children living in poverty, and it may also increase the proportion of those children living in "extreme" poverty (Children's Defense Fund 2003).

In 2000, 31 percent of persons under the age of 18 in the black population were living in poverty (Proctor and Dalaker 2002). The figures for other populations are white, 9 percent; Hispanic, 28 percent; and Asian, 13 percent. That is, almost one-third of black and Hispanic youth under the age of 18 are living in poverty. From another perspective, the majority of poor children under the age of 18 are either black or Hispanic. The percentage of poor white children under the age of 18 is consistent with the figures for poverty among white families (see Table 2.4). In contrast, the percentages of poor black, Hispanic, and Asian children under the age of 18 are greater than the figures for the poverty level in families for each respective racial and ethnic population.

Although education is regarded as a social force that can reduce a person's or family's risk of being poor, it does not remove the poverty differential among whites, and blacks, and Hispanics. For example, one can observe from the figures in Table 2.5 that in households where the head of household does not have a high school degree, slightly more than one-third of black households are in poverty, compared to 28 percent of Hispanic households and 19 percent of white households. Similarly, where the head of household has a high school degree but no college, black households are three times as likely as white households to be

Table 2.5
Households in Poverty by Race or Hispanic Origin and Education, 2000

Head of Household	White	Black	Hispanic
Not a high school graduate	19%	34%	28%
High school graduate	7%	21%	16%
Some college	4%	15%	10%
College degree or more	2%	4%	7%

Source: 2000 U.S. Statistical Abstract available at www.census.gov.

poor, and Hispanic households are more than twice as likely as white households to be poor. For households in which the head of household has completed some college but has not received a college degree, black households are more than three times as likely as white households to be poor, and Hispanic households are more than twice as likely as white households to be poor. For households in which the head of household has completed a college degree or more, Hispanic households are more than three times as likely as white households to be poor, and black households are twice as likely as white households to be poor. One observation that can be drawn from the data in Table 2.5 is that increasing educational levels among heads of households is associated with decreasing levels of household poverty across racial and ethnic populations. For whites, graduation from high school is associated with a single-digit poverty level. However, single-digit poverty levels among blacks and Hispanics are only found in households where the head of household has completed a college degree or more. As a result, it appears that black and Hispanic households need higher levels of educational completion than do white households to reduce household poverty, especially to a single-digit percentage.

Income Levels

The median income for the Asian population ($57,313) was higher than the median income for the white ($45,142), black ($30,495), or Hispanic ($34,094) populations (see Table 2.6). Comparatively speaking, the median income in the Asian population was 127 percent of the median income for the white population, and the figures for the same comparison for Hispanic and black populations are 76 percent and 68 percent, respectively. Black income is 53 percent and Hispanic income is 59 percent of Asian income. Interestingly, the percentage of black and Hispanic incomes rela-

Table 2.6
Median Income by Race and Ethnicity, 2000

	Nonwhite Income	Median Income as Percentage of White Income
White	$45,142	—
Black	$30,495	68%
Asian	$57,313	127%
Hispanic	$34,094	76%

Source: DeNavas-Walt, Carmen, and Robert W. Cleveland, *Money Income in the United States* (Current Population Report P60-218). Washington, DC: U.S. Census Bureau, 2002.

Table 2.7
Median Income by Educational Attainment for Persons 25 Years Old and Older, by Race and Ethnicity, 2000

	Total Population	White	Black	Hispanic	Asian
High school graduate	$19,979	$20,325	$17,657	$17,693	$18,781
College graduate					
Two-year degree	$27,492	$28,061	$25,853	$24,629	$27,974
Four-year degree	$36,715	$37,211	$34,438	$31,394	$33,165
Master's degree	$47,467	$47,727	$42,290	$39,177	$59,337
Doctoral degree	$62,354	$64,337	$50,072	$48,277	$56,038
Professional degree	$67,461	$70,490	$50,818	$46,894	$60,580

Source: U.S. Census Bureau, Annual Demographic Survey, 2000 Income, available at http://ferret.bls.census.gov/macro/032001/perinc/toc.htm.

tive to white income is higher than the percentage of black and Hispanic incomes relative to Asian income. In addition, white median income is 79 percent of Asian median income.

Returns on Education

Another indicator of how racial and ethnic minorities are doing in U.S. society is income by educational attainment. Table 2.7 provides a summary of median income by level of education and racial and ethnic population. The table shows that white median income is higher than that of the total U.S. population across all educational levels and that the median incomes of blacks and Hispanics are lower than those of the total U.S. population across all educational levels. Except among high school graduates, black median income is higher than that of Hispanics. In addition, Asian median income is generally higher than the median incomes of blacks and Hispanics. Interestingly, Hispanic median income lags behind the median incomes of whites, blacks, and Asians. An examination of the relative differences in earnings by racial and ethnic populations shows that the difference between black and Hispanic incomes is less than the difference between either black or Hispanic income and white income.

The data in Table 2.7 allow one to compare income differentials by race, ethnicity, and educational attainment and especially to contrast minority income with white income. For example, for high school graduates, Asian income is 92 percent of white income, whereas Hispanic and black incomes are 87 percent of white income. For college graduates, both for two-year and four-year degrees, Asian income is 94 percent, black income is 92 percent, and Hispanic income is 86 percent of white income. For persons with graduate degrees, Asian income is 96 percent, black income is 78 percent, and Hispanic income is 74 percent of white income. Comparatively speaking, increasing levels of educational attainment reduce the income differential between Asians and whites. With the exception of persons with two-year and four-year college degrees, increasing levels of educational attainment increase the income differential between blacks and whites. Interestingly, the income differential between Hispanics and whites increases with increasing levels of educational attainment.

In the discussion of educational outcomes summarized in Table 2.3, it was noted that Asians have, in general, higher educational outcomes than other racial and ethnic populations. In particular, the percentage of Asians attaining college graduate and graduate/professional degree levels exceeds that of the white population. However, the data in Table 2.7 showed that for Asians, increasing educational outcomes are not associated with increasing income levels relative to the white population and, especially at the postsecondary levels, are not associated with higher incomes that reduce the income differential between Asians and whites. That is, the economic returns from increased educational attainment are lower for Asians than they are for whites (a discussion of this observation is found in Woo 2000).

Occupational Levels

Regarding the occupational representation of racial and ethnic populations in the United States, one can make the following observations from the data in Table 2.8: (1) a higher percentage of Asians than of whites, blacks, or Hispanics have managerial and professional specialty occupations; (2) Hispanics are not as likely as whites, blacks, or Asians to have technical, sales, and adminis-

Table 2.8

Occupation of the Employed Population 16 Years and Older by Race and Ethnicity, 2000

	White	Black	Asian	Hispanic
Managerial and professional specialty	33.2%	21.7%	39.3%	14.0%
Technical, sales, and administrative support	30.3%	29.0%	28.1%	24.6%
Service occupations	11.8%	22.6%	14.9%	19.4%
Precision-production, craft, and repair	10.9%	7.8%	5.7%	14.4%
Operator, fabricator, and laborer	11.6%	16.1%	11.3%	22.0%
Farming, forestry, and fishing	2.3%	0.8%	0.6%	5.7%

Source: Population Division, Racial Statistics Branch and Ethnic and Hispanic Statistics Branch, *Current Population Survey*. Washington, DC: U.S. Census Bureau, March 2000.

trative support occupations; and (3) a higher percentage of blacks than of whites, Asians, or Hispanics have service occupations. The data in Table 2.8 also show that a lower percentage of Asians than of whites, blacks, or Hispanics have precision-production, craft, and repair occupations; a higher percentage of Hispanics than of whites, blacks, or Asians have operator, fabricator, and laborer occupations; and a higher percentage of Hispanics than of whites, blacks, or Asians have farming, forestry, and fishing occupations.

A comparison of earnings by occupation among racial and ethnic populations provides one with information about unequal outcomes in the labor market. It has already been noted that blacks and Hispanics, in general, have lower educational outcomes than whites or Asians (see Table 2.3). If a higher level of education increases a person's chances of obtaining a higher-paying occupation, then, on average, whites and Asians should have higher occupational earnings than blacks or Hispanics. In addition, since Asians have higher educational outcomes than whites, especially at the postsecondary levels, then their earnings should be higher than those of whites.

According to Deborah Reed and Jennifer Cheng (2003), wage gaps among white, black, Hispanic, and Asian workers are a result of educational differences. For example, among U.S.-born full-time workers in California, Hispanic men earned $.81 for every dollar earned by white men, black men earned $.74 for every dollar earned by white men, and Asian men earned $1.04 for every dollar earned by white men. Among U.S.-born full-time women workers in California, Hispanic women earned $.79 for every dollar earned by white women, black women earned $.86 for every dollar earned by white women, and Asian women earned $1.15 for every dollar earned by white women. These wage gaps are consistent with the expectation that, given the educational outcomes of each racial and ethnic population, Asian earnings would be higher than white earnings, and black and Hispanic earnings would be lower than white or Asian earnings.

What happens to wage gaps if one removes educational and thus occupational differences among racial and ethnic populations? According to Reed and Cheng, removing differentials in education outcomes between Hispanic workers and white workers increases the earnings of Hispanic men and women to $.93 for every dollar earned by white workers. In order for Hispanic workers to earn wages comparable to those of white workers, they would also need to work in the same occupations as whites. For black workers, removing the differential in education outcomes between black workers and white workers would have a negligible effect on increasing wages for black workers. However, if black workers worked in the same occupations as white workers, then their wages would increase substantially: Black men would earn $.84 for every dollar earned by white men and black women would earn $.95 for every dollar earned by white women. Ironically, because U.S.-born Asian workers have higher education outcomes than white workers and thus are more likely to work in higher-paying occupations, matching their education outcomes to those of white workers reduces the wage differential that favors Asian workers relative to white workers.

Quality of Life Indicators

Well-being in society is determined by factors that reflect how persons interact with disruptive social forces or events. In particular, how a society's youth interact with disruptive social forces or events can help evaluate the society's health. Looking at the social health of minority youth helps one understand the relations between race and ethnicity and U.S. society. For example, according to the data in Table 2.9, for children aged 10 to 14, the black homicide rate is more than three times the white homicide rate, and the Hispanic homicide rate is slightly more than twice the white homicide rate. For 15 to 19 year olds, the black homicide rate is more than nine times and the Hispanic homicide rate is more than three times the white homicide rate. For 20 to 24 year olds, the black homicide rate is almost ten times and the Hispanic homicide rate is slightly more than three times the white homicide rate.

Table 2.9
U.S. Death Rates[1] by Homicide by Age, Race, and Hispanic Origin, 2000

	10–14 Year Olds			15–19 Year Olds			20–24 Year Olds		
	White	Black	Hispanic	White	Black	Hispanic	White	Black	Hispanic
Homicide[2]	0.5	1.8	1.1	3.9	29.1	14.0	5.6	55.6	18.1

Notes: [1]Rates are based on an annual basis per 100,000 population in specified age group. [2]Assault by discharge of firearms.
Source: Minino, Arialdi, Elizabeth Arias, Kenneth Kochanek, Sherry Murphy, and Betty Smith, "Deaths: Final Data for 2000," *National Vital Statistics Reports* 50, no. 15 (2002): 1–120.

In addition to being at risk for becoming victims of homicide, minority youth are more likely than white youth to be incarcerated. According to the U.S. Department of Justice (2000), almost 75 percent of inmates in state correctional institutions are black or Hispanic. Of inmates under the age of 18 in state correctional institutions, 60 percent are black, 19 percent are white, 13 percent are Hispanic, and 8 percent are Asian or American Indian. In general, for every 100,000 people in the United States, 3,535 blacks, 1,177 Hispanics, and 462 whites are incarcerated (Miller 2002). The proportionate distribution of incarcerated persons by race and ethnicity shows that blacks are overrepresented in the inmate population relative to whites and Hispanics.

An analysis of the inmate population by race, ethnicity, and age shows that blacks have higher rates of incarceration relative to other racial and ethnic groups; in particular, 12 percent of black males in their twenties and thirties are in prison or jail (U.S. Department of Justice 2002). For example, of the 1.96 million offenders incarcerated in the United States, 31 percent are black males between the ages of 20 and 39. In relationship to their number in the general population, 13 percent of black males aged 25 to 29 are in prison or jail, compared to 4 percent of Hispanic males and about 2 percent of white males. The percentage of black males aged 45 to 54 in prison or jail (3.4 percent) was almost twice the highest rate among white males (1.9 percent, for white males aged 30 to 34).

A Descriptive Portrait

The social indicators discussed in this chapter construct a complex yet fragmented portrait of the social relations for racial and ethnic populations in the United States. Although racial and ethnic populations are not faring as well as the white populations, compared to each other, some racial and ethnic populations are faring better than others. This discussion of social indicators serves as a framework for making general observations about blacks, Hispanics, and Asians in U.S. society.

The Black Population

The education outcomes of the black population lag behind those of the white population, as do income-by-education outcomes. Relative to whites, blacks are underrepresented in white-collar (for example, professional and managerial) occupations and over-represented in blue-collar (such as service and laborer) occupations. The combined effect of education outcomes and occupation create a context in which equalizing occupational levels rather than education outcomes between black and white workers significantly reduces wage differentials between them; that is, black wages increase relative to white wages.

One-fifth of black persons and families are living in poverty. The level of poverty among blacks may create a nested context that results in large numbers of black children growing up in poverty. Increasing education outcomes do not reduce poverty levels in black households as they do in white households. Ironically, the only group of black families for whom the poverty level is reduced to single digits is the group whose heads of household have completed a college degree or more. A more distressing observation is that almost one-fifth of black households living in poverty are headed by a householder with a college degree or more.

The black population's quality of life is at risk, and to a noticeably higher degree than that of other racial and ethnic populations. The homicide rate for 10 to 24 year olds places black youth at a significant risk in society. Most noticeably, the homicide rate for blacks aged 20 to 24 is ten times that of whites and three times that of Hispanics. The black population's quality of life is also at risk given the high numbers of blacks in jails and prisons. The majority of inmates (60 percent) under the age of 18 in state correctional institutions are black, and 31 percent of the offenders incarcerated in the United States are black men between the ages of 20 and 39.

Hispanic Population

Hispanic education outcomes lag behind those of the white population, and Hispanic incomes lag behind those of whites with comparable years of education. The majority of Hispanics work in blue-collar occupations, and Hispanics are underrepresented in white-collar occupations. Removing the differential in education outcomes between Hispanic and white workers closes the wage gap between them.

Poverty among Hispanic persons and families is at the same level. The percentage of Hispanics living in poverty is twice as high as whites, and the percentage of Hispanic families living in poverty is three times as high. Increased education outcomes among Hispanic heads of household are not associated with decreasing levels of household poverty. Household poverty is reduced to single digits when heads of household have completed a college degree or more. Similar to the situation of black households, almost 20 percent of Hispanic households living in poverty have heads of household who have some level of college education.

The Hispanic population's quality of life is at risk because of the following factors: First, Hispanics aged 10 to 24 are at greater risk than whites of the same age of becoming victims of homicide. The homicide rates for Hispanics aged 15 to 19 and 20 to 24 is more than three times the homicide rate for whites in the same age groups. Second, there are twice as many Hispanic males as white males aged 25 to 29 incarcerated in the United States. In addition, 13 percent of inmates under the age of 18 in state correctional institutions are Hispanic.

Asian Population

Education outcomes in the Asian population clearly surpass education outcomes in the white, black, and Hispanic populations. Despite having higher education outcomes than whites, Asian incomes lag behind those of whites at the same levels of education. The high education outcome for Asians is one possible explanation for the fact that the majority of Asians work in white-collar occupations. However, although the wage differential between Asian workers and white workers benefits Asians, matching Asian and white workers on education outcomes reduces the wage differential.

Economically, the Asian population fares just as well as the white population and noticeably better than the black or Hispanic populations. The percentages of Asian persons and families living in poverty are comparable to those of the white population. The percentages of Asian persons and families living in poverty are less than half those of black and Hispanic persons and families living in poverty. Asians have a higher median income than whites, blacks, and Hispanics

Blacks, Hispanics, and Asians are making uneven progress on various social indicators. Asians are faring better than either blacks or Hispanics. Although Asians fare better than whites on some indicators, such as education, those outcomes are not translated to other outcomes in the same way they are in the white population; for example, for Asians, higher education outcomes do not translate into higher income outcomes to the same extent they do for whites. Black and Hispanic quality of life is at greater risk than white or Asian quality of life. The level of poverty, homicide rate among youth, and representation in the inmate population for blacks and Hispanics place them at risk in U.S. society. It would appear that the social relations that blacks and Hispanics experience in U.S. society are characterized by social forces that constrain their quality of life.

The Racialization of the U.S. Population

Another approach to understanding the diversity in the U.S. population is to examine how persons identify themselves racially. The 2000 census provides a tool for doing so. In a departure from previous censuses of the U.S. population, the questions on race and Hispanic origin were revised on the 2000 census in order to better document the diversity in the country's population (Grieco and Cassidy 2001). The revised questions on race and Hispanic origin allow one to observe the extent of racial self-identification, especially multiracial self-identification, in the U.S. population. For example, 2.4 percent of the U.S. population, or 6.8 million persons, reported on the 2000 census that they were of more than one race, with the majority (93 percent) reporting that they were of two races. The 2000 census used five race categories: white, black or African American, American Indian and Alaska Native, Asian, and Native Hawaiian and Other Pacific Islander. Persons could respond to the question on

Table 2.10
Two-Race Combinations (as a percent of the U.S. Population), 2000

	White	Black/African American	Asian	American Indian/Alaska Native
White	—	—	—	—
Black/African American	11.5%	—	—	—
Asian	12.7%	1.6%	—	—
American Indian/Alaska Native	15.9%	2.7%	0.8%	—
Native Hawaiian/Pacific Islander	1.7%	0.4%	2.0%	0.1%

Source: Jones, Nicholas A., and Amy Symens Smith, *The Two or More Races Population: 2000* (Census 2000 Brief). Washington, DC: U.S. Census Bureau, 2001.

race by selecting either "race alone" or "race in combination." Almost 98 percent of the respondents identified themselves as being of one race. The majority of these respondents identified themselves as white (75.1 percent), followed by black (12.3 percent), Asian (3.6 percent), American Indian (0.9 percent), and Native Hawaiian/Pacific Islander (0.1 percent).

As Table 2.10 shows, the combinations of race most frequently reported in the 2000 census were white and American Indian/Alaska Native, 15.9 percent; white and Asian, 12.7 percent; white and black/African American, 11.5 percent; and black/African American and American Indian/Alaska Native, 2.7 percent. These four categories accounted for 43 percent of the population reporting being of two or more races (Grieco and Cassidy 2001). In the responses to the "race in combination" categories, the race cited most often in combinations was white (77 percent), followed by black/African American (13 percent), Asian (4.2 percent), American Indian/Alaska Native (1.5 percent), and Native Hawaiian/Pacific Islander (0.3 percent). Specific characteristics of how each race population responded to the "race in combination" category are discussed below.

White Population

The majority of persons in the U.S. population (75.1 percent) identified themselves as only white (Grieco 2001b). The race combinations reported most often by white persons were white and American Indian/Alaska Native (20 percent), white and Asian (16 percent), and white and black/African American (14 percent).

Black/African American Population

About 12.3 percent of the U.S. population, or 34.7 million persons, identified themselves as only black/African American (McKinnon 2001). The race combinations reported most often by black/African American persons were black/African American and white (45 percent), black/African American and American Indian/Alaska Native (10 percent), and black/African American and white and American Indian/Alaska Native (6 percent).

Asian Population

About 3.6 percent of the U.S. population, or 10.2 million persons, identified themselves as only Asian (Barnes and Bennett 2002). The race combinations reported most often by Asian persons were Asian and white (52 percent), Asian and Native Hawaiian/Pacific Islander (8 percent), and Asian and black/African American (6 percent).

American Indian/Alaska Native Population

About 0.9 percent of the U.S. population, or 2.5 million persons, identified themselves as only American Indian/Alaska Native (Ogunwole 2002). The race combinations reported most often by American Indian/Alaska Native persons were American Indian/Alaska Native and white (66 percent), American Indian/Alaska Native and black/African American (11 percent), and American Indian/Alaska Native and white and black/African American (7 percent).

Native Hawaiian/Pacific Islander Population

About 0.1 percent of the U.S. population, or 399,000 persons, identified themselves as only Native Hawaiian/Pacific Islander (Grieco 2001a). The race combinations reported most often by Native Hawaiian/Pacific Islander persons were Native Hawaiian/Pacific Islander and Asian (29 percent), Native Hawaiian/Pacific Islander and white (24 percent), and Native Hawaiian/Pacific Islander and Asian and white (19 percent).

Hispanic Origin

I wish to make a caveat regarding the Hispanic population: "Hispanic origin" is not one of the race categories employed in the 2000 census. The task of separating the responses of Hispanic persons to the race questions becomes complex because the majority of Hispanic persons identified themselves as "white" (Grieco 2001b). According to the 2000 census data, the majority of persons identifying themselves as "white and Hispanic (white Hispanics)" and who reported more than one race identified themselves as "white and some other race" (80 percent), followed by "white and American Indian/Alaska Native" (6 percent), "white and black/African American" (5 percent), and "white and Asian" (3 percent).

Other Considerations

The vast majority of persons in the U.S. population (almost 98 percent identify themselves as belonging to only one race (Grieco and Cassidy 2001). Only about 2 percent of persons in the U.S. population identify themselves as being of two or more races; that is, they identify themselves as multiracial. Unsurprisingly, the majority of persons who identify themselves as multiracial claim "white" as one component in their multiracial identity. What implications does this have for understanding diversity in U.S. society?

First, one needs to consider which racial component of their multiracial identity persons identify with. If persons claiming "white" as one component in their multiracial identity identify as "white," then the numerical size of the white population increases. (Bear in mind that 2 percent of the U.S. population is approximately 6.8 million persons.)

There may be social forces that encourage multiracial persons to claim to be "white." If multiracial persons encounter resistance to the expression of their multiracial identity, then one needs to question U.S. society's attitudes toward and perceptions of multiracial persons. Consider that, because numbers of racial and ethnic minority populations in the United States are growing, there will be more contact between them and the white population. If this is the case, then the number of persons who identify as multiracial will grow in the twenty-first century. However, in order for us to understand how they contribute to the diversity in U.S. society, it will be necessary to study those social forces that either promote or resist the expression of multiracial identities.

Conclusion

As the United States enters the twenty-first century, it is more diverse in its racial and ethnic composition than it was at the start of the twentieth century. Whereas immigrants from Europe were the primary force shaping the racial complexion of U.S. society in the twentieth century, increasing numbers of immigrants from non-European countries, coupled with the numerical increases in minority populations in the United States, shaped the racial complexion of U.S. society in the second half of the twentieth century. The United States thus enters the twenty-first century with almost one-third of its population consisting of racial and ethnic minority persons. From another perspective, the United States enters the twenty-first century with more than 80 million racial and ethnic minority persons in its population.

We have noted that racial and ethnic populations are making uneven progress in U.S. society. Blacks and Hispanics, in particular, are at greater risk in their quality of life than are whites or Asians. The noticeably large numbers of blacks and Hispanics in the penal population and living in poverty are significant at-risk factors. In addition, a high homicide and incarceration rate among black and Hispanic youth only serves to exacerbate the at-risk status of the populations. It is alarming that blacks and Hispanics enter the twenty-first century with significant segments of their population in so precarious a position.

The Asian population fares much better on certain social indicators than do whites, blacks, and Hispanics. Although the education outcomes of the Asian population certainly help portray the population as the "model minority," Asians do not receive the same economic returns that whites receive. As a result, they are in the same situation as blacks and Hispanics: Asian income lags behind white income for the same level of educational completion. The economic returns on education are a dilemma for Asians. If increasing levels of education increase access to high-paying occupations or higher incomes, then Asians should be earning the same as or more than whites earn at the same level of education. However, the fact that Asian incomes lag behind white incomes at the same level of education suggests that other factors or social forces may be involved. In particular, it lends support to the argument that Asians encounter a "bamboo curtain" in the occupational world that places them in an unequal position relative to whites (for an extensive discussion of this issue, see Aguirre and Turner 2001).

Finally, there is a small portion (2 percent) of persons in U.S. society who identify themselves as multiracial. Although the number of these persons is small, they should not be ignored because they open a window on another view of diversity in twenty-first-century U.S. society. It is still too early to guess what role they may play in the future, but we may speculate that the number of persons identifying themselves as multiracial will increase in the twenty-first century. If the number of racial and ethnic minority persons continues to increase in the twenty-first century, then contact between racial and ethnic populations and the white population will increase. Potentially, then, increased contact will result in more persons—for example, births in multiracial households—with a multiracial identity. What if *diversity* in the twenty-first century reflected the multiracial complexity of U.S. society rather than the presence of several distinct racial and ethnic populations in U.S. society?

References

Aguirre, Adalberto, Jr., and Jonathan Turner. 2001. *American Ethnicity: The Dynamics and Consequences of Discrimination.* 3rd ed. New York: McGraw-Hill.

Barnes, Jessica, and Claudette Bennett. 2002. "The Asian Population: 2000." Census 2000 brief. Washington, DC: U.S. Census Bureau.

Bean, Frank, and Marta Tienda. 1987. *The Hispanic Population of the United States.* New York: Russell Sage Foundation.

Bennett, Marion. 1963. *American Immigration Policies: A History.* Washington, DC: Public Affairs Press.

Blank, Rebecca. 2001. "An Overview of Trends in Social and Economic Well-Being, by Race." In *America Becoming: Racial Trends and Their Consequences,* ed. Neil Smelser, William Wilson, and Faith Mitchell, vol. 1, 21–39. Washington, DC: National Academy Press.

Camarota, Steven. 2001. *Immigrants in the United States—2000: A Snapshot of America's Foreign-Born Population.* Washington, DC: Center for Immigration Studies.

————. 2002. "Census Releases Immigrant Numbers for 2000: Analysis by CIS Finds Size, Growth Unprecedented in American History." Washington, DC: Center for Immigration Studies.

Children's Defense Fund. 2003. *Number of Black Children in Extreme Poverty Hits Record High: Analysis Background.* Washington, DC: Children's Defense Fund.

Daniels, Roger. 1997. *Not Like Us: Immigrants and Minorities in America, 1890–1924.* Chicago: Ivan R. Dee Publishing.

Gibson, Campbell, and Kay Jung. 2002. "Historical Census Statistics on Population Totals by Race, 1790 to 1990, and by Hispanic Origin, 1970 to 1990, for the United States, Regions, Divisions, and States." Population Division, U.S. Census Bureau, working paper no. 56. Washington, DC: Government Printing Office.

Grebler, Leo, Joan Moore, and Ralph Guzman. 1970. *The Mexican-American People: The Nation's Second Largest Minority.* New York: Free Press.

Grieco, Elizabeth. 2001a. "The Native Hawaiian and Other Pacific Islander Population: 2000." Census 2000 brief. Washington, DC: U.S. Census Bureau.

————. 2001b. "The White Population: 2000." Census 2000 brief. Washington, DC: U.S. Census Bureau.

Grieco, Elizabeth, and Rachel Cassidy. 2001. "Overview of Race and Hispanic Origin: 2000." Census 2000 brief. Washington, DC: U.S. Census Bureau.

Handlin, Oscar, 1957. *Race and Nationality in American Life.* Boston: Little, Brown.

Hoffman, Abraham. 1974. *Unwanted Mexican Americans in the Great Depression: Repatriation Pressures, 1929–1939.* Tucson: University of Arizona Press.

Hraba, Joseph. 1994. *American Ethnicity.* 2nd ed. Itasca, IL: F. E. Peacock.

Kaufman, Phillip, Martha Alt, and Christopher Chapman. 2001. "Dropout Rates in the United States: 2000." *Education Statistics Quarterly* 3: 41–46.

Lollock, Lisa. 2001. "The Foreign Born Population in the United States: March 2000." Washington, DC: U.S. Census Bureau.

McKinnon, Jesse. 2001. "The Black Population: 2000." Washington, DC: U.S. Census Bureau.

McWilliams, Carey. 1968. *North from Mexico: The Spanish-Speaking People of the United States.* New York: Greenwood Press.

Miller, Leslie. 2002. "Increase in U.S. Prison Inmates Slowed in 2001." *Salt Lake Tribune,* July 31, B1.

Minino, Arialdi, Elizabeth Arias, Kenneth Kochanek, Sherry Murphy, and Betty Smith. 2002. "Deaths: Final Data for 2000." *National Vital Statistics Reports* 50, no. 15: 1–120.

Ogunwole, Stella. 2002. "The American Indian and Alaska Native Population: 2000." Census 2000 brief. Washington, DC: U.S. Census Bureau.

Proctor, Bernadette, and Joseph Dalaker. 2002. "Poverty in the United States: 2001." Washington, DC: U.S. Census Bureau.

Reed, Deborah, and Jennifer Cheng. 2003. *Racial and Wage Gaps in the California Labor Market.* San Francisco: Public Policy Institute of California.

Schmidley, A. Dianne. 2001. *Profile of the Foreign-Born Population in the United States: 2000.* Washington, DC: U.S. Census Bureau.

Singer, Audrey. 2002. *America's Diversity at the Beginning of the Twenty-First Century: Reflections from Census 2000.* Washington, DC: Brookings Institution.

Swrdlow, Joel. 2001. "Changing America." *National Geographic,* September, 42–61.

Therrien, Melissa, and Roberto Ramirez. 2000. *The Hispanic Population in the United States: March 2000.* Current Population Reports, P20-535. Washington, DC: U.S. Census Bureau.

U.S. Bureau of the Census. 2002a. *Coming from the Americas: A Profile of the Nation's Foreign-Born Population from Latin America (2000 Update).* Washington, DC: U.S. Census Bureau.

———. 2002b. *Coming to America: A Profile of the Nation's Foreign-Born (2000 Update).* Washington, DC: U.S. Census Bureau.

———. 2002c. *The Population Profile of the United States: 2000.* On-line; available: http://www.census.gov/main/www/cen2000.html.

———. 2002d. *A Profile of the Nation's Foreign-Born Population from Asia (2000 Update).* Washington, DC: U.S. Census Bureau.

———. 2003. American Factfinder. On-line; available: http://factfinder.census.gov; accessed May 26, 2003.

U.S. Department of Justice. 2000. *Profile of State Prisoners under Eighteen, 1985–97.* Washington, DC: Office of Justice Programs.

———. 2002. *Prison and Jail Inmates at Midyear 2001.* Washington, DC: Bureau of Justice Statistics.

Woo, Deborah. 2000. *Glass Ceilings and Asian Americans: The New Face of Workplace Barriers.* Walnut Creek, CA: AltaMira Press.

3

The Precarious Context
for Diversity

What we have to do . . . is to find a way to celebrate our
diversity and debate our differences without fracturing our
communities.

—Hillary Rodham Clinton

A voice announces in the movie trailer for *Gangs of New York*
that America was born in the streets. By focusing on warfare
between the "natives" and the "foreign invaders," the movie
captures the adversity faced by nonmainstream immigrants in
the early United States. The movie provides a visual depiction of
the social forces that can motivate people to express hostility and
hatred toward persons identifiably different from themselves.
Ironically, the battle between the "natives" and "foreign
invaders" remains a recurring theme in discussing the context for
diversity in twenty-first century U.S. society. A key concept for
understanding the precarious context for diversity in U.S. society
is *identifiability*, as is violently demonstrated in *Gangs of New York*.

Consider that one can share membership with other persons
in a community. If everyone in the community is the same as
everyone else, then the community is undifferentiated, or not
diverse. Some religious communities, such as the Quakers and
the Amish, promote "sameness" among members as a fundamental principle for belonging in the community. However, if
community members are distinguished (for example, by such features as race or ethnicity), then one can say that the community is
differentiated, or diverse. Such differentiation often results in the

47

identification of "groups" that have a certain feature or even a combination of features in common. As a result, *diversity* and *identifiability* are tied synergistically together in a process of establishing community membership and social identity. One outcome of the synergistic association between diversity and identifiability is that increasing awareness of diversity in society implies that the number of persons exhibiting the certain features, or combinations of those features, enhances their identifiability.

In Chapter 1, we examined racial and ethnic diversity in early America. That diversity had Eurocentric roots that shaped an Anglo-Saxon core in U.S. society. The Anglo-Saxon core, in turn, expanded its influence over racial and ethnic minorities that did not share its Eurocentric roots. As a result, American Indians, Mexicans, Asians, and African slaves in early America became victims of the Anglo-Saxon core's intent to create a hegemonic society based on its Eurocentric roots. Thus, the racial and ethnic diversity that shaped the Anglo-Saxon core in early American society was able to forge a community rooted in one feature, European roots, which made nonmembers of the Anglo-Saxon core highly identifiable. In turn, the increased identifiability of those persons made their position in early American society more precarious.

In Chapter 2, we examined diversity in twentieth- and twenty-first-century U.S. society as shaped by waves of immigrants who did not mirror the European immigrants who had formed early American society. As the number of immigrants from non–western European countries increased, the identifiability of those persons increased. We noted in Chapter 2 that attempts were made to reduce the numbers of immigrants from non-European countries, for example, by passing restrictive immigration legislation. The Anglo-Saxon core resisted—and as we will see in this chapter, continues to resist—increased diversity that might overshadow its influence in U.S. society. Thus, the diversity that resulted from immigration in twentieth- and twenty-first-century U.S. society differed from the diversity that had shaped early American society: That diversity was hegemonic, forming an Anglo-Saxon core along Eurocentric roots. In contrast, the diversity that shaped twentieth- and twenty-first-century U.S. society was nonhegemonic because the new immigrants were coming from a greater variety of countries different than the countries from which the earlier European immigrants came.

Given the discussion in Chapters 1 and 2, one can observe that there are at least two phases in the shaping of a diverse population in U.S. society: In a first phase, the Anglo-Saxon core promoted a "benign and circumscribed cultural pluralism based on national origin groups" (Fredrickson 1998: 860). That is, diversity in U.S. society into the twentieth century was depicted as pluralism shaped by the cultural preferences and identities of white ethnic groups. In a second phase, the increased numbers of immigrants from non-European countries promoted a cultural pluralism rooted in differentiated identities that were marked as different from the Anglo-Saxon core (Glazer 1997). That is, diversity in the twenty-first century is shaped by discriminatory practices that increase the identifiability of racial and ethnic populations in U.S. society.

The purpose of this chapter is to discuss the challenges faced by racial and ethnic diversity in U.S. society. *Diversity* is treated as a dynamic social force in society, one that is constantly changing its presence in society and its association with societal institutions. To facilitate discussion, the chapter is divided into the following sections: The first section focuses on the relationship between immigration and diversity, especially immigration reform in response to nativist concerns. The second section discusses racial profiling as a social process that reinforces the at-risk status of racial and ethnic minorities in society. The third section focuses on the use of affirmative action to increase diversity in social institutions such as public universities.

This chapter focuses on the "new" challenges brought about in society from the increasing diversity of new social space. That is, diversity is (1) altering the character of society by redrawing boundaries around race and ethnicity, (2) promoting racial and ethnic identities that challenge negative images, and (3) introducing itself into social spaces void of racial and ethnic populations. Implicit in the discussion in this chapter is the observation that racial and ethnic minorities' *identifiability* increases their risk of facing obstacles and challenges in U.S. society. For example, not only is diversity more noticeable in U.S. society at the beginning of the twenty-first century, but diversity also increases the identifiability of persons within racial and ethnic populations in the United States. Thus, one purpose of this chapter is to instruct the reader regarding the types of challenges faced by racial and ethnic populations, challenges that derive from their enhanced identifiability in U.S. society.

Table 3.1
Americans' Responses to Diversity

It is important to consider how Americans perceive immigrants in discussions of diversity. For example, when Americans are asked their perception of how immigrants contribute to diversity, they respond as follows:

The diversity created by immigrants in the United States (percent agreeing):
    45 percent—strengthens American culture[1]
    38 percent—weakens American culture
    36 percent—strengthens American character[2]
    50 percent—weakens American character

Regarding the effects of diversity on U.S. social institutions such as schools, Americans have responded as follows to the question:

How important is increased diversity in the public school student population as a cause for increased violence in the public schools?[3]
    58 percent—important
    11 percent—not at all important

[1]Gallup Poll (March 26, 2001)
[2]NBC News and *Wall Street Journal* Poll (March 1, 1999)
[3]Gallup Poll (May 11, 1999)

Immigration and Diversity

We have seen in Chapters 1 and 2 that immigration has been an important force in establishing diversity in the U.S. social fabric. Unsurprisingly, U.S. society has promoted itself as a *nation of immigrants*. But even though diversity in U.S. society has been fueled by immigration, Americans are uncertain of the benefits brought to society by diversity created by immigration. For example, according to the poll results summarized in Table 3.1, Americans have conflicting perceptions of the diversity created by immigration in U.S. society. On the one hand, they perceive diversity as strengthening U.S. culture. This perception may be supported by the generalized notion in society that the United States is composed of diverse populations whose presence is celebrated as part of the nation's cultural heritage, for example, in such observances as Black History Month, Saint Patrick's Day, Hispanic Heritage Month, and Columbus Day.

On the other hand, Americans perceive the diversity created by immigration as weakening the U.S. character. This perception may be supported by the generalized notion in society that immigrants are unwilling to learn English, refuse to adopt U.S. culture, and put a strain on public services. As such, the diversity created by immigration challenges Americans' expectations that immigrants will assimilate and acculturate to U.S. culture in order not to become burdens on society. The perception that the diversity created by immigration weakens the U.S. character has the potential of fueling nativist sentiments that seek to control immigrant populations in the United States. In order to show how nativist attitudes pose a challenge to diversity, we discuss the passage of Propositions 187 and 227 in California.

The Context for Nativist Attitudes

I wish to state a caveat regarding the use of the term *nativism* in this chapter: John Higham defines *nativism* as "intense opposition to an internal minority on the ground of its foreign (i.e., 'un-American') connections . . . [which] translates . . . into a zeal to destroy the enemies of a distinctively American way of life" (1955, 4). In order to survive as a social force in society, nativism, in the form of perceptions and attitudes, identifies targets—that is, persons or groups—who can be blamed for society's problems or misfortunes. These persons or groups thus become scapegoats for nativist concerns (Calabresi 1994). For example, during the 1980s recession in the United States, workers in the U.S. automotive industry expressed nativist concerns that competition by the Japanese and by Asians in general was the reason for declining sales of U.S. automobiles. One outcome of the nativist concerns expressed by U.S. auto workers was passage by Congress of higher import fees for Japanese automobiles sold in the United States.

Nativist reaction to immigrants has deep roots in U.S. society. The Know-Nothing movement of the 1850s used *nativism* successfully in its political efforts to bring about restrictive immigration laws and laws that would prevent the foreign-born from holding political office (Carlson 1989). Immigration laws were passed in the latter part of the nineteenth century to prevent persons from entering the United States if they were perceived as lunatics or idiots, thus alleviating nativist fears that they would contaminate the "morals" of U.S. society (Jaret 1999).

During World War I, German immigrants and German Americans became targets of nativist attacks that often resulted in public flogging and lynching (Perea 1992). During the early twentieth century, parochial schools in the United States became the target of nativists, who complained that parochial schools' education of immigrants posed a threat to U.S. culture and the

English language by preventing immigrants from assimilating in U.S. society (Ross 1994). The nativist fear that immigrants would take land away from native-born Californians resulted in passage of the Alien Land Law in 1913, which prohibited aliens who were ineligible for citizenship from owning real property in California (Ferguson 1947; McGovney 1947).

Nativism promoted fears in U.S. society that the diversity created by immigration was either a threat to U.S. cultural values or a threat to the U.S. character, which happened to be expressible only in English. Charles Jaret summarizes the nativist fear of diversity thus: "(a) The new immigration is bringing in too many people with cultures and values that differ from and conflict with that of the 'American mainstream' or its established lifestyle groups; and (b) this plethora of diversity will create a disaster in the form of cultural strife and fragmentation, which may weaken or destroy one of history's greatest civilizations" (1999, 31–32). As a result of nativist fears, diversity is not perceived as a building block in U.S. society; rather, it is perceived as tarnishing U.S. culture and character.

Diversity under Attack

The image of an "immigrant culture" that characterizes and romanticizes immigrants' contributions to creating a diverse U.S. society is under attack in California because this "immigrant culture" is no longer European in origin; it is Third World in origin. Historically, the "immigrant culture" has served as a bridge for European immigrants' absorption into U.S. society. For the "new" immigrants, most of whom are from Mexico, Central America, and Latin America, their identifiability as Third World residents has emphasized their *difference* in U.S. society and has stirred dormant nativist fears that they are a threat to U.S. society. In particular, the "new immigration" stirred nativist concerns that immigrants threatened a Californian society historically rooted in a Eurocentric ideology.

From its beginning, nativist fears were a driving force in shaping the character of Californian society. The ceding of California to the United States in 1848 was a catalyst for Anglo immigration into California. As the Anglo population increased in numbers during the 1850s, it petitioned Washington, D.C., for legislation that would bar American Indians from owning land, especially mines, and from residing near Anglo settlements

(Scafidi 1999). An Anglo-controlled legislature passed laws in the 1850s that banned Chinese immigration, prohibited Chinese laborers from competing with Anglo laborers for work, and prevented Chinese from owning land (McClain 1984). During the 1850s, Anglos challenged in court the land grants held by Mexican families in California (Cameron 1998). The creation of a commission by Congress in 1851 to review land grants in California was the first step in displacing Mexican families from their land (Barrera 1979). Thus, nativism in early Californian society was anti-immigrant and antiminority, and it created a climate of fear in order to buffer Californian society from diversity.

Mexican immigrants in Californian society have been frequent targets of nativist sentiment. During the Great Depression, nativists portrayed Mexican immigrants, as well as Mexican Americans, as threats to the state's and country's economy. They were cast as parasites on social welfare programs and accused of depriving "true" Americans of jobs during the economic depression. In response to public outcry, the Immigration and Naturalization Service (INS) deported thousands of Mexican immigrants and Mexican Americans to Mexico (Hoffman 1974; McWilliams 1968). By 1940, more than a million Mexican-origin persons had been deported from the United States. Most of those deported, about 60 percent, had been born in the United States (Balderrama and Rodriguez 1995).

Ironically, with the entry of the United States into World War II and the resulting reduction in the number of workers available for the U.S. labor pool, the nativist sentiment that had supported the deportation of Mexican-origin persons during the depression became focused on encouraging Mexican laborers to work in the agricultural fields of the southwestern United States. The creation of the Bracero Program by Congress in 1942 allowed thousands of Mexican laborers to enter the United States as legal, seasonal workers in a growing U.S. agricultural-industrial complex (Aguirre and Turner 2001).

Not surprisingly, twelve years later, in 1954, nativist concerns that Mexican immigrants were again displacing American workers served as a catalyst for the INS's launching of Operation Wetback to apprehend Mexican laborers in the United States who had not entered legally as braceros. Operation Wetback was an attempt by the U.S. government to appease nativist fears that Mexicans were streaming uncontrollably across the border in order to take jobs away from Americans. By 1959, the INS had deported 3.8 million persons to Mexico (Grebler, Moore, and Guzman 1970). Operation Wetback reinforced the perception held by Mexicans and Mexican Americans living in the United States that theirs was a marginal and tenuous presence.

In the 1940s, Mexican American youth became the target of nativist fears in California. The "zoot-suit" riots that took place in Los Angeles during the 1940s involved attacks by U.S. military personnel on Mexican-origin youth dressed in zoot suits (Mazon 1984). Although not worn exclusively by Mexican-origin youth, the zoot suit was a distinctive style of dress often associated with deviant subcultures. It was popularized in U.S. culture by jitterbug fans. In general, the zoot suit was a suit with an exaggerated cut consisting of a long coat, with or without a vented back and with wide lapels, and high-rise trousers with wide legs pegged at the ankle. Anglos looked at zoot-suited Mexican-origin youth as deviants and as threats to U.S. patriotism. Their perceived subculture kindled nativist fears that they were unpatriotic during wartime and, as a result, posed a threat to U.S. society. On June 3, 1943, U.S. military personnel set out to remove "unpatriotic" persons from Los Angeles by launching unprovoked violent and physical attacks on zoot-suited Mexican-origin youth.

We can thus make the general observation that nativism was an important social force in shaping perceptions of the diversity created by immigration. In particular, nativist sentiments controlled the extent of diversity represented in Californian society. Tomas Almaguer says of the social context that fostered nativist sentiment in California's white population, "The cultural division of the world into different categories of humanity led white, European Americans in California to arrogantly privilege themselves as superior to non-European people of color" (1994, 7). White, European-origin immigrants, consequently, built an infrastructure of social institutions to promote and protect their own interests. Nativist movements in California arose when nonwhite immigrants were perceived as posing a threat to the infrastructure, and especially when nonwhite immigrants were perceived as asserting that diversity should be incorporated into the social fabric.

Nativism in Twenty-First-Century Californian Society

The number of immigrants in Californian society increased dramatically during the 1990s. By the end of the 1990s, immigrants made up 26 percent of California's population (Camarota 2001). Almost one-fourth of the immigrant population in the United States lived in California by the end of the 1990s (Schmidley and Alvarado 1998). In addition, almost 30 percent of the persons in the immigrant population were born in Mexico (Aguirre 2002; Muller 1993; Parker 1994; Vernez 1994). Is it coincidence that during the 1990s, as immigrants, especially Mexican immigrants, increased their representation in Californian society, they became the targets of nativist attacks?

In November 1994, California voters approved Proposition 187, the Save Our State (SOS) initiative, by a vote of 59 percent to 41 percent. There are five major sections to the proposition: (1) Illegal aliens are barred from the state's public education system, and education institutions are required to verify the legal status of students and their parents. (2) Providers of publicly paid, non-emergency health services are required to verify the legal status of persons seeking their services. (3) Persons seeking cash assistance and other benefits are required to verify their legal status before receiving services. (4) Service providers are required to report suspected illegal aliens to the California Attorney General's Office and to the INS. (5) It is a state felony to make, distribute, or use false documents that conceal one's legal status to obtain public benefits or employment (Garcia 1995; Schuler 1996).

Four years later, in June 1998, Proposition 227, the English Language in Public Schools initiative, was approved by California voters by a vote of 61 percent to 39 percent. Proposition 227 dismantled bilingual education in California's public schools by requiring that all students be taught academic subjects in English; non-English-speaking children at public schools must be taught in sheltered immersion programs, or programs that can use non-English languages to move children into English-only instruction as quickly as possible. The proposition also made school personnel, especially teachers, liable for attorney's fees and damages if they do not follow an English-only curriculum and if they fail to report *suspect* immigrant children to the proper school authorities (Gullixson 1999; Johnson 1999).

As nativist responses to Mexican immigrants in California,

Propositions 187 and 227 were based on three assumptions about Mexican immigrants in Californian society: (1) that Mexican immigrants in California are a burden on the state's public services, (2) that immigrant children and children born to immigrants in California are a drain on the state's educational resources, and (3) that Mexican immigrants are not interested in establishing permanent residency in the United States. Interestingly, Californian voters regarded Propositions 187 and 227 as immigration-reform measures. That is, they regarded the propositions as vehicles for constraining the diversity introduced in Californian society by immigrants.

Proposition 187 created a "state-run system to verify the legal status of all persons seeking public education, health care and other public benefits, and add[ed] public education to the list of services for which unauthorized aliens are ineligible" (Martin 1995, 255). Proposition 227 reinforced Proposition 187 by requiring school personnel to report and identify suspected immigrant children, and it encouraged outsiders (for example, the parents of schoolchildren) to identify school personnel not teaching an English-only curriculum. Both propositions targeted immigrants as a suspect category, thus increasing their identifiability in Californian society. Proposition 187 made immigrants suspect in the delivery of public services, and Proposition 227 stigmatized immigrant children in public education. Both propositions were thus nested in the nativist fear that the diversity created by immigrants was out of control in Californian society.

One noticeable outcome of Proposition 187 is that it has facilitated the emergence of a social climate that implicitly supported measures to control the movement of Mexican immigrants into the United States. For example, vigilante groups organized by white ranchers and landowners became commonplace along the U.S.-Mexican border. Since the passage of Proposition 187, there have been more than twenty-five incidents in Arizona's Cochise County that have resulted in the death or injury of Mexican immigrants (Contreras 2000). In some instances, white vigilante groups have detained Mexican immigrants at gunpoint at the U.S.-Mexican border, sometimes leading them back into Mexican territory (MacCormack 2002). In an especially violent occurrence in San Diego County in California, a band of white adolescent males were arrested for shooting Mexican immigrants with pellet guns and beating them with lead pipes (Thornton 2000).

The point is not that Proposition 187 resulted in the emergence of white vigilante groups who targeted Mexican immigrants; after all, white vigilante groups have been present in the United States since its inception (Chalmers 1987). The point is that Proposition 187 exacerbated a social climate that treated Mexican immigrants as threats to U.S. society.

Finally, the events of September 11, 2001, intensified the nativist response to Mexican immigrants. Vigilante groups—such as Civil Homeland Defense, American Border Patrol, and Ranch Rescue—operating along the U.S.-Mexican border escalated their operations to apprehend and detain Mexican immigrants. According to Chris Simcox, founder of Civil Homeland Defense, Mexican immigrants are "enemies who are wrecking our economy" (quoted in Baum 2003, 9). The events of September 11 served as a catalyst for the movement of volunteers armed with Web cams, infrared night scopes, and guns to the U.S.-Mexican border in order to stem the tide of Mexican immigrants who posed a "terrorist" threat to U.S. society.

Unsurprisingly, the U.S. decision to attack Iraq also served to intensify the nativist response to Mexican immigrants. American Border Patrol and Civil Homeland Defense have admitted using physical force, and sometimes firing weapons, in order to apprehend Mexican immigrants crossing into the United States. These two vigilante organizations argue that the U.S. Constitution gives them the "civil authority" to protect the country from terrorists during wartime. After the U.S. invasion of Iraq, Civil Homeland Defense issued a warning to Mexicans: "Do not attempt to cross the border illegally; you will be considered an enemy of the state; if aggressors attempt to forcefully enter our country they will be repelled with force if necessary" (quoted in Ibarra 2003, A1).

Profiling Diversity

What are the costs of identifiability to racial and ethnic minorities in U.S. society? We noted in the preceding discussion that identifiability was a factor in stirring nativist concerns regarding the diversity created by immigration. We also noted that in California, the increasing identifiability of immigrants, especially in workplaces and schools, served as a catalyst for the passage of legislation designed to curtail the diversity created by immigration. In this section, we focus on a general question: Does a person's identifiability as a member of a racial or ethnic population carry a cost? That is, is racial or ethnic identity a liability in U.S. society? I will attempt to answer this question by constructing an interpretive framework for two activities in society that target racial and ethnic identity: racial profiling and hate crimes.

Racial Profiling

Racial profiling is a term used to identify law enforcement practices that use race or ethnicity as the basis for discretionary judgments. In general, race and ethnicity are used to profile minority persons in a variety of contexts in their public lives: shopping, driving, applying for bank loans, buying real estate, and being placed in public school educational tracking (Austin 1994; Eisenman 2001; Fennessy 1999; Graves 2001; Main 2000–2001). Profiling on the basis of race or ethnicity, especially in traffic stops, has generated the catchphrase "driving while black" (DWB) or, in the case of Latinos, "driving while brown." Law enforcement personnel use the identifiability of black or brown persons as either drivers or passengers of automobiles as a basis for profiling minority persons. For example, black and Hispanic motorists stopped by the police are twice as likely as white motorists to have their vehicle and their person searched (U.S. Department of Justice 2001). In addition, black and Hispanic persons are more likely to be victims of force used against them by police. In general, law enforcement agencies rationalize their use of race as a profiling tool by arguing that minorities commit more crimes than whites, that the social impact of crimes committed by minorities is greater than those committed by whites, and that minorities are more likely than whites to possess weapons and illegal contraband (Rudovsky 2002).

According to a Harris opinion poll, most white persons (55 percent) do not oppose racial profiling, whereas most minority persons (55 percent) oppose it (cited in Fetto 2002). One possible explanation for these results is that white persons do not oppose racial profiling because they do not perceive themselves as potential victims of racial profiling, whereas minority persons do see themselves as potential victims. The poll results might also indirectly support the general observation that white persons see diversity as posing challenges to the U.S. social order. For example, as Table 3.1 shows, a majority of Americans (58 percent) think increased diversity in the public schools is an important cause of increased violence in the schools. In general, these observations can be interpreted as suggesting that racial profiling should be practiced in order to control the harmful effects of diversity in everyday life.

Racial profiling is so prevalent in U.S. society that, in an ironic twist, Pre-Paid Legal Services, Inc., in Ada, Oklahoma, offers black and Hispanic motorists an insurance policy that covers them as potential victims of racial profiling. The company markets a plan called Legal Shield that provides telephone access to a lawyer twenty-four hours a day. Clients are provided with a card they can present to a police officer if they are stopped. The card tells the officer, "If it is your intention to question, detain or arrest me, please allow me to call an attorney immediately" (O'Brien 2000). The assumption behind Legal Shield is that police officers will be less likely to detain persons on the basis of racial profiling if they know that persons have immediate access to an attorney. Since its inception in 1999, Legal Shield has enrolled more than 100,000 members.

Outside of law enforcement, racial profiling is used to control the movement and presence of racial and ethnic minority persons. For example, in *City of Chicago v. Morales* (119 S. Ct. 1849 [1999]), the U.S. Supreme Court ruled that a gang-loitering ordinance passed by Chicago in 1992 was overly broad and vague. The ordinance empowered police to disperse groups of two or more persons if they were standing in public space, such as on a sidewalk or street corner, and if the police suspected them of gang activity. Persons refusing to disperse were subject to arrest and six months in prison. According to Dorothy Roberts, the ordinance was written in language that was "deliberately expansive to allow the police to clean up the streets based on their suspicions of gang membership rather than waiting for a crime to take place" (1999, 775). The gang-loitering ordinance was in effect for three years and resulted in more than 40,000 arrests. The majority of the persons arrested were either black or Latino residents of inner-city neighborhoods in Chicago.

Racial and ethnic minority persons are often profiled as potential shoplifters by store personnel. In *Robinson v. Town of Colonie* (878 F. Supp. 387, 392 [N.D.N.Y. 1995]), employees of a T. J. Maxx clothing store called police to remove a "suspicious" black couple, Mr. and Mrs. Robinson, from the store. The couple's behavior looked "suspicious" to store employees because they were trying on clothes. Police were called to the store by employees when the Robinsons refused to leave the store after employees accused them of stealing. When Mrs. Robinson asked why they were being asked to leave the store, a police officer replied, "They don't need a reason. If you don't want to leave you will be arrested for trespass" (Fennessy 1999, 550). Although there was no evidence showing that the Robinsons had shoplifted, a police officer testified in court that a series of prior shoplifting incidents involving black persons had made store employees suspicious of the Robinsons. The police officer also testified that store employees felt that the Robinsons had been involved in the prior shoplifting incidents. No evidence was presented showing the Robinsons' involvement in the prior shoplifting incidents.

And another example of racial profiling: On October 10, 2000, the publisher of the *Sacramento Valley Mirror*, Tim Crews, created a stir when he revealed the contents of a U.S. Forest Service memo. The memo directed U.S. Forest Service officers to detain Hispanics driving through Mendocino National Forest as *potential* drug smugglers. It stated, "If a vehicle stop is conducted and no marijuana is located and the vehicle has Hispanics inside at a minimum we would like all individuals FI'd [field interrogated]" (quoted in Bulwa 2000, A4). In this example, the generalized profiling of all Hispanics as drug smugglers served as the basis for the U.S. Forest Service's strategy to curb drug smuggling by detaining only Hispanics for field interrogation.

The preceding examples illustrate the precarious position of minority persons in U.S. society when race and ethnicity are used as the basis for judgments about their activities. Although one might argue that it makes sense to target those persons more likely to commit crimes, this practice sets aside concerns regarding the harmful effects of racial profiling. The logic of racial profiling is built on three harmful assumptions: (1) that racial and ethnic minority persons are potential deviants or criminals, (2) that they are different from members of mainstream (white) society and thus should be subjected to closer public scrutiny, and (3) that their actions and behaviors have costlier outcomes than those of persons belonging to mainstream (white) society. In short, the diversity introduced by race and ethnicity in U.S. society is regarded as a social problem.

If one accepts the logic underlying the practice of racial profiling, one has failed to consider that the structuration of social relations for minorities in U.S. society is designed to fabricate deviant images of minority persons. That is, the social relations characterizing the life experience of minority persons in U.S. society are shaped by social forces, such as prejudice and discrimination, that constrain their participation to social contexts, such as poor, crime-ridden neighborhoods, that impugn their social identity with stereotypes of deviance (Aguirre and Turner 2001; Appiah 2000; Delgado and Stefancic 1992). For example, the depiction by the television and movie industry of black and Latino youth as inner-city gang members whose only form of economic activity is selling drugs criminalizes their social identity in U.S. society. Norman Denzin (1998) argues that the "hood and barrio" movies of the 1990s created an image of violent minority youth, an image that served to privilege whiteness in U.S. society. In this context, racial profiling is both the means and the end for legitimating the deviant images associated with racial and ethnic identity. (For an example of how racial profiling affects the quality of life of minority persons and their communities, see Romero 2001.)

The deviant images associated with racial and ethnic identities in society facilitate the operation of interpretative assumptions that racialize the behavior of minority persons by providing interpretive filters that target as significant only behavior that is profiled as deviant. That is, the behavior of racial and ethnic minority persons is "racialized" because the assumptions are rooted in the deviant images attributed to minority persons; as a result, "minority" behavior can only be interpreted as "minority" behavior. Racial and ethnic diversity is, because of these assumptions, racialized. In turn, diversity must be profiled because it is identifiable in society. In the end, the identifiability of diversity becomes a liability for racial and ethnic minority persons.

Finally, one note regarding identifiability and racial profiling, especially of Mexican-origin persons in the United States. In order to understand the nexus of Mexican-origin social identity and racial profiling in the United States, one must examine *United States v. Brigoni-Ponce* (422 U.S. 873 [1975]). In *Brigoni-Ponce* the U.S. Supreme Court ruled that the Border Patrol's stopping of vehicles based only on the "perceived" Mexican ancestry of the vehicle's occupants violated the Fourth Amendment. The Supreme Court noted in its ruling that Border Patrol agents may stop persons "only if they are aware of specific attributable facts, together with rational inferences from the facts, that reasonably warrant suspicion that the vehicles contain aliens who may be illegally in the country" (*Brigoni-Ponce*, 884). In his writing of the Court's opinion, Justice Lewis F. Powell Jr. constructed the context for using social identity as a basis for profiling Mexican-origin

persons: "The likelihood that any given person of Mexican ancestry is an alien is high enough to make Mexican appearance a relevant factor, but standing alone it does not justify stopping all
Mexican-Americans to ask if they are aliens" (*Brigoni-Ponce*,
886–887).

Despite its ruling that Mexican ancestry, or Mexican identity,
alone is not sufficient to justify stopping Mexican Americans, the
Court did suggest in *Brigoni-Ponce* that there is a "likelihood" that
Mexican-origin persons are aliens. Based on a review of immigration cases after *Brigoni-Ponce*, Kevin Johnson (2000) argued that
Brigoni-Ponce opened the door for the U.S. Border Patrol to
increase its use of Mexican appearance as the sole basis for stopping Mexican-origin persons. The Court's ruling in *Brigoni-Ponce*
served as a tool legitimating the processing of Mexican identity
by organizations that are instrumental in constructing and promoting perceptions of people based on group characteristics in
public life. In this case, the Court created the opportunity for the
U.S. Border Patrol to use Mexican identity as a tool for profiling
Mexican-origin persons.

The dilemma posed by *Brigoni-Ponce* is that it identifies social
contexts, such as immigration stops, in which Mexican identity
can be used to classify "suspects." According to David Strauss,
Brigoni-Ponce ruled that "law enforcement officers may use
Mexican American ancestry as a 'relevant factor' . . . in determining whether there is reasonable suspicion that a person is an
undocumented alien. . . . it seems reasonably clear that *Brigoni-
Ponce* represents a category of cases in which the courts would
allow race or national origin to be used as a basis for classifica-
tion. . . . Thus the prohibition on the use of racial generalizations
is not as absolute as the cases suggest" (1995, 9n. 38). The ruling
in *Brigoni-Ponce* creates an overly inclusive category for Mexican-
origin persons that is premised on the expectation that "Mexican
ancestry" is associated with a negative evaluation, for example,
that a person is an undocumented alien.

Twenty-five years after *Brigoni-Ponce*, the generalized use of
Mexican ancestry in establishing reasonable suspicion for stops
by law enforcement agencies remains controversial in the courts
(Romero 2000; Sterngold 2000). Ruling in a case similar to *Brigoni-
Ponce*, the U.S. Court of Appeals for the Ninth Circuit ruled in
United States v. Montero-Camargo (208 F.3d 1122 [9th Cir. 2000])
that the U.S. Border Patrol could not consider "Hispanic appear-
ance" in making immigration stops. The court argued that popu-

lation changes had taken place in the southwestern states since *Brigoni-Ponce* resulting in the noticeable presence of Mexican-origin persons. The court noted that in some areas of California and Texas, Mexican-origin persons had become the single largest group. Thus, the court noted in its ruling that "in an area in which a large number of people share a specific characteristic, that characteristic casts too wide a net to play any part in a particularized suspicion determination" (*Montero-Camargo*, 1134). In other words, the increased number of Mexican-origin persons in the U.S. population makes Hispanic appearance of little use to law enforcement agencies in their efforts to determine who is an undocumented alien. As a result, the court wrote in its ruling, "Hispanic appearance is, in general, of such little probative value that it may not be considered as a relevant factor where particularized or individualized suspicion is required" (*Montero-Camargo*, 1135).

The ruling in *Montero-Camargo* is especially interesting because it identifies the harm of profiling persons simply on the basis of Hispanic appearance. For example, the court noted in its ruling that

> stops based on race or ethnic appearance send the underlying message to all our citizens that those who are not white are judged by the color of their skin alone. Such stops also send a clear message that those who are not white enjoy a lesser degree of constitutional protection—that they are in effect assumed to be potential criminals first and individuals second. It would be an anomalous result to hold that race may be considered when it harms people, but not when it helps them. (*Montero-Camargo*, 1135)

The court appears to be making a significant statement about institutional practices and social relations that result in some persons being treated less equally or equitably than others.

Hate Crimes

Hate crimes are among the most damaging forms of racial and ethnic discrimination in the United States (Bell 2002; Winborne and Cohen 1999). Some hate crimes have received national attention because they have illustrated the deep roots of bigotry in U.S. culture. For example, on the evening of June 19, 1982, Vincent

Chin, a twenty-seven-year-old Chinese American, met some friends at a Detroit bar to celebrate his upcoming wedding. Two white automobile factory workers started harassing him verbally, calling him "Jap" and saying he was the cause for the loss of jobs in the automobile industry. The automobile workers chased Chin out of the bar into the parking lot, where they beat him with a baseball bat. He died of his injuries.

In another case that drew national attention and resulted in an outcry about racism in the United States, three white men chained an African American man, James Byrd Jr., to a pickup truck and dragged him to his death on a country road outside Jasper, Texas, on June 7, 1998 (Weiss 1998). According to documents presented at the trial of one of the white men, Byrd's face was spray-painted, and he was dragged behind the pickup truck until he was decapitated. Despite the seriousness of the crimes committed against Byrd, his death was parodied by white men in blackface on a float titled "Black to the Future 2098," in the 1998 Columbus Day Parade in New York City. One of the white men in blackface on the float "hung briefly from its rear bumper in apparent parody of the killing of James Byrd" (Harden 1998, A6). Not long after the Columbus Day Parade incident, Byrd's grave site was vandalized: Someone removed the nameplate on his tombstone (Gamino 1998).

According to the FBI's annual statistics on hate crimes, the number of incidents motivated by racial bias against racial and ethnic minorities decreased between 1995 and 2000, from 4,831 to 4,433. According to Tanya Schevitz (2002), the total number of hate crimes committed annually increased 21 percent between 2000 and 2001, from 8,063 to 9,730. The data in Table 3.2 on incidents motivated by racial bias in 1995 and 2000 show the following: (1) Blacks are the largest group of victims of racial-bias hate crimes, 61 percent in 1995 and 65 percent in 2000. (2) Incidents directed against American Indians/Alaska Natives increased 44 percent between 1995 and 2000. (3) Incidents directed against persons based on their ethnicity or national origin increased 13 percent between 1995 and 2000. (4) Incidents directed against multiracial individuals increased 11 percent between 1995 and 2000. Regarding hate crimes based on the victims' ethnicity or national origin, Polly Hughes (2002) argues that hate crimes against Hispanics have increased dramatically since September 11, 2001, especially in states with large Hispanic populations. Comparatively speaking, although racial-biased hate crimes decreased

Table 3.2
Hate Crimes in the United States, 1995 and 2000

	Incidents[1]		Offenses[2]		Victims	
	1995	2000	1995	2000	1995	2000
Total Race	4,831	4,433	6,170	5,300	6,438	5,532
Antiwhite	1,226	910	1,511	1,093	1,554	1,125
Antiblack	2,988	2,937	3,805	3,482	3,945	3,609
Anti–American Indian/Alaskan Native	41	59	59	64	59	66
Anti–Asian/Pacific Islander	355	282	484	322	496	347
Ethnicity/national origin	814	921				
Multiracial	221	245				

[1]Reported number of acts motivated by race, ethnicity, and national origin
[2]Reported number of bias-motivated acts by category (e.g., anti-Black, anti-White, etc.)
Source: U.S. Statistical Abstract (http://www.census.gov/statab/www)

8 percent between 1995 and 2000, violent crime decreased 26 percent between 1995 and 2000 (again according to the FBI, www.fbi.gov). As a result, hate crimes have become a growing area of concern in society.

The terrorist attack on the World Trade Center on September 11, 2001, increased the identifiability of persons who looked Middle Eastern as potential terrorists. Congress responded to the terrorist threat by passing the USA Patriot Act (The Uniting and Strengthening America by Providing Appropriate Tools Required to Intercept and Obstruct Terrorism Act) less than two months later. The USA Patriot Act was passed by Congress in order to safeguard the security of the United States (see Chapter 6). However, implicit in the act's framework was the assumption that persons would have to be profiled based on their apparent race or ethnicity in order to identify potential terrorists or threats to the national security. Historically, the United States has utilized immigration policy—such as the Alien Act (1798), the Alien Enemies Act (1798), and the Immigration Act of 1924—to exclude immigrants, mostly nonwhites, who are profiled as threats to the country's stability (Saito 1997). The USA Patriot Act is consistent with the use of legislation to protect the country from insurgents and terrorists, who were often immigrants deemed "undesirable."

One result of the terrorist attack on September 11 and passage of the USA Patriot Act was the association of "foreignness" with terrorism. We have noted in this chapter that the association of *difference* (for example, foreignness) with immigrants in California served as a catalyst for the passage of state propositions designed to limit immigrants' participation in Californian society. Similarly, the concern with identifying potential terrorists has resulted in the indiscriminate profiling of racial and ethnic minorities (Vu 2002). For example, Arab Americans became easy targets of racial profiling by the U.S. airline industry and its passengers. Arab American passengers were often asked to wait by the boarding gate in order to undergo further screening by security personnel, their carry-on luggage was tagged with special labels stating "positive ID," and passengers asked flight attendants for different seats if they felt unsafe sitting near a Middle Eastern–looking passenger; "in some cases passengers asked flight attendants to remove them from the airplane, thus giving meaning to the phrase 'Flying While Arab'" (Baker 2002, 1375).

The events of September 11 and the country's implementation of laws to counter terrorism made the position of diversity in U.S. society more precarious. Although the immediate focus after September 11 was on Arabs and Muslims, the context for using *difference* as a strategy for singling out racial and ethnic minorities was already firmly established in the social fabric. Prior to September 11, black churches in the South were frequent targets of terrorist acts. More than eighty black churches were burned, firebombed, or vandalized during the 1990s because the black community was identified as a threat to the white community (Simms Parris 1998). Immigrants from Mexico were subjected to attacks from white-supremacist groups and vigilante groups of white ranchers intent on policing the U.S.-Mexican border (Thornton 2000; Walker 1993). Asian Americans were victims of hate and bigotry, especially from white militant groups (National Asian Pacific American Legal Consortium 2001). Even prior to September 11, then, hate crimes against racial and ethnic groups were frequent occurrences in U.S. society.

The events of September 11 demonstrated how quickly ethnic and racial identity could be profiled as a threat in the United States and how profiling could result in acts of violence (such as hate crimes) against racial and ethnic minorities. Hate crimes against Arabs and Muslims increased more than 1,600 percent after September 11 (Schevitz 2002). According to Human Rights Watch (2002), Arabs and Muslims in the United States, including persons perceived to be Arab or Muslim, became victims of a severe wave of backlash violence that included murder, beatings, arson, the vandalization of mosques, shootings, and verbal threats. Since September 11, more than 2,000 hate crimes, including at least seven murders, have been committed against Arabs, Muslims, and those perceived to be either Arab or Muslim. For example:

- On September 29, 2001, Abdo Ali Ahmed, a fifty-one-year-old Yemeni Arab, a Muslim and father of eight, was shot and killed while working at his convenience store in Reedley, California. The cash in two registers was left untouched.
- On September 15, 2001, Adel Karas, a forty-eight-year-old Arab, a Coptic Christian and father of three, was shot and killed at his convenience store in San Gabriel, California. Again, no money was taken from the cash register.
- On November 19, 2001, four teenagers burned down the Gobind Sadan, a multifaith worship center in Oswego, New York, because they believed the worshippers were supporters of Osama bin Laden.
- On September 23, 2001, the Saint John's Assyrian American church was set on fire in Chicago. The church's pastor believes that the person who he thinks set the fire had asked a local resident whether the church was a mosque.
- On August 24, 2002, federal authorities in Tampa Bay, Florida, discovered a plan by a doctor to bomb and destroy approximately fifty Mosques and Islamic cultural centers in south Florida.

One group that became victims of the profiling of Middle Eastern–looking persons as terrorists or as un-American were South Asians. The National Asian Pacific American Legal Consortium (2001) and its affiliates have documented nearly 250 bias-motivated incidents targeting South Asians particularly in the three-month period following the terrorist attacks on September 11. For example:

- At least two South Asian Americans were murdered as part of the September 11 backlash. Almost immediately following the terrorist attacks on September 11, a Sikh American gas-station owner was shot and killed in Mesa, Arizona. Frank Roque, the main suspect in the murder, was also charged with three counts of drive-by shooting: into the home of an Afghani American and at two

Lebanese gas-station attendants. As he was arrested, Roque screamed, "I stand for America all the way! I'm an American. Go ahead. Arrest me and let those terrorists run wild!" (Delgado, St. John, and Gordon 2001).

- A Pakistani grocer was shot and killed in Dallas, Texas. There was no evidence of a robbery. Although law enforcement officials suspected the grocer was the target of a hate crime, the incident was classified as a random act of violence.

- In Northridge, California, a Sikh American was preparing to close his liquor store when two men confronted him. The men asked him, "Are you [Osama] bin Laden?" The Sikh American was unable to convince the two men that he was not bin Laden, and the two men beat him with metal pipes.

- South Asian persons were not the only targets of violence. Business establishments that were perceived as Middle Eastern were also targeted. Bottles and rocks were thrown at an Afghan restaurant in Fremont, California. A Sikh temple was vandalized and spray-painted with graffiti in Stockton, California.

These post–September 11 attacks have occurred throughout the United States. The majority of the violent attacks on South Asian Americans have focused on Sikh Americans, Indian Americans, and Pakistani Americans, who were targeted because they were perceived to be Arab or Muslim. Sikh Americans, a religious group whose members are mostly of South Asian descent, were particularly singled out because the men wear turbans and beards, characteristics associated with the image of Osama bin Laden.

The context of hate and violence that developed after September 11 targeted racial and ethnic minorities as looking "like the enemy" and subjected them to attack as a result. This context was an extension of a fragile social fabric that had already been bruised by the Rodney King beating, the deaths of James Byrd Jr. and Vincent Chin, the beating of Mexican immigrants by white-supremacist groups, and the burning of black churches.

Affirming Diversity

A continuing challenge for diversity in U.S. society is its incorporation into societal institutions. Although the U.S. population has become more racially and ethnically diverse in the twenty-first century, societal institutions have been slow to respond to the increased presence of diversity in society. U.S. society has entered the twenty-first century burdened with baggage from the latter half of the twentieth century and is filled with institutionalized forms of discrimination that impair the life chances of racial and ethnic minority populations. Institutionalized forms of discrimination result in opportunity structures for racial and ethnic minorities that are inferior to those available to the white population. As a result, racial and ethnic minorities have yet to attain educational, economic, and political parity in U.S. society (Aguirre and Turner 2001; Graham 1994; Massey and Denton 1993).

The second half of the twentieth century in the United States was consumed with numerous social and civil rights struggles focused on promoting equal opportunity for racial and ethnic minorities. These struggles acknowledged that racial and ethnic diversity was being ignored by mainstream societal institutions (Morris 1984; Ramirez and Rumminger 2000–2001). One policy intervention that had its inception in the 1960s and that was regarded by policymakers as a useful tool for promoting opportunity for racial and ethnic minorities became known as affirmative action. The term *affirmative action* originated in President John F. Kennedy's 1961 executive order establishing the President's Committee on Equal Employment Opportunity (Woodhouse 2002). The concept of affirmative action has its roots in the passage of the Civil War amendments that abolished slavery and secured equal rights, that is, Amendments Thirteen, Fourteen, and Fifteen. Broadly conceived, the term *affirmative action* refers to "measures or practices that seek to terminate discriminatory practices by permitting the consideration of race, ethnicity, sex, or national origin in the availability of opportunity for a class of qualified individuals who have been the victims of historical, actual, or recurring discrimination" (Aguirre and Martinez 2003, 9).

The courts' difficulty in defining the scope and practice of affirmative action is a problem for implementing measures and policies that seek to promote strategies for improving the quality of life for racial and ethnic minorities (Perea et al. 2000).

Affirmative action measures that have sought to improve working conditions, opportunities for career advancement, and access to educational institutions for racial and ethnic minorities either have made limited progress or have been challenged in the courts as depriving white persons of their rights (Aguirre 2000; Springer 2003; Wellman 1997). Educational institutions have especially become contested terrain for affirmative action initiatives. For example, because educational institutions are integral to providing persons with the social capital necessary for determining their level and extent of participation in society, it is important to understand the context for racial and ethnic diversity in education. In the following pages, we will review the emergence of the diversity rationale in higher education.

Before proceeding with a discussion of the diversity rationale and affirmative action, we need to focus on how Americans feel about affirmative action. According to the data shown in Table 3.3, the majority of Americans are opposed to the use of affirmative action measures for diversifying student bodies in public universities. They are less sure whether affirmative action programs are necessary in order to make companies have racially diverse workforces. On the surface, this is not surprising, since what goes on in the workplace often occurs away from the public's eyes (Aguirre 2003; Allison 1999). At a deeper level, Americans' concern with affirmative action in public universities identifies education as *contested terrain* in U.S. society. Most people see education as a vehicle for improving one's social position in life and as a level playing field that gives every student the same chances of being successful. Affirmative action, however, may be perceived as a measure that tilts the playing field by providing more opportunity to some, for example, racial and ethnic minorities, than to others, for example, white persons (Bollinger 2002; Platt 1997). Education, especially higher education, may serve as the battlefield for determining how diversity will fare in twenty-first-century U.S. society. As a result, we focus on affirmative action in higher education as one of the challenges diversity faces in U.S. society.

The Diversity Rationale

The U.S. Supreme Court significantly shaped the contemporary legal context for affirmative action in higher education through its decision in *University of California v. Bakke* (438 U.S. 265 [1978])

Table 3.3
Affirmative Action and Diversity

How do we promote diversity within U.S. social institutions? Affirmative action is a vehicle for including underrepresented groups, such as racial and ethnic minorities. However, Americans are opposed, as the following poll results show, to the use of affirmative action in public universities and in the workforce.

Public universities can use race as a factor in diversifying student bodies:[1]
   26 percent—favor
   65 percent—oppose
Affirmative action programs are necessary to make companies have racially diverse worforces:[2]
   46 percent—necessary
   48 percent—not necessary

[1] *Wall Street Journal* Poll (January 28, 2003); [2] CBS News Poll (September 15, 2000)

(Aguirre and Martinez 2003). In *Bakke,* Alan Bakke, a white male, challenged the validity of a special admissions program at the University of California–Davis School of Medicine after having twice been denied admission. The medical school filled sixteen of its hundred slots in its entering class through a special admissions program only open to minority applicants, who were compared among themselves and not to the overall applicant pool. Bakke's college grade point average and MCAT scores were among the highest of all of the applicants' and higher than those of all of the minority applicants admitted into the medical school through the special admissions program. In *Bakke,* the U.S. Supreme Court affirmed the California Supreme Court's decision that the special admissions program had violated the equal protection clause of the Fourteenth Amendment. The Court directed that the plaintiff be admitted to the School of Medicine but reversed the judgment prohibiting the defendant from considering race in its future admissions.

Justice Powell wrote in his opinion regarding *Bakke* that "ethnic diversity is only one element in a range of factors a university properly may consider in attaining the goal of a heterogeneous student body" (quoted in Parloff 2002). However, he wrote in the same opinion that quotas "would hinder rather than further attainment of genuine diversity." Following Justice Powell's opinion, an admissions program that considers a range of factors, race being one of them, is admissible even if race were to tip the scales in the pool of qualified applicants. However, also following that opinion, a school may not "refuse to compare applicants of different races or establish a strict quota on the basis of race" (Perea et al. 2000, 732). Interestingly, the U.S. Supreme Court outlawed racial quotas in higher education but appears to condone the use of race as a selective factor (Philip 2002). Justice Powell's opinion creates a dilemma for institutions of higher education seeking to implement admissions policies that take race into consideration but that do not formulate quotas based on race. Institutions of higher education have interpreted Justice Powell's opinion in *Bakke* as identifying a *diversity rationale* that allows them to use race as a selective factor in admissions as long as racial quotas are not promoted.

Bakke has shaped a precarious context for diversity initiatives in higher education. On the one hand, the U.S. Supreme Court has reasoned that race may serve a purpose in the admissions process; however, race may not be used as a corrective measure, such as by establishing quotas. As such, race can be used in the admissions process to diversify the student population, but it may not be used as a vehicle for diversifying the institutional character of higher education. That is, although race may be used to enhance the "representativeness" of students to mirror diversity in society, it may not be used to implement institutional or organizational strategies that use diversity to change the institutional character and organizational culture in higher education institutions.

On the other hand, *Bakke* makes it difficult for higher education to develop diversity initiatives that respond to the changes taking place in the composition (for example, in race and ethnicity) of U.S. society. The Court's decision in *Bakke* suggests that race plays an important part in shaping diversity measures that are linked with access to social opportunity in U.S. society. However, the decision mirrors U.S. society's reluctance to alter the structure of social opportunity in order to remove barriers for minority (nonwhite) populations.

Twenty-five years later, the diversity rationale noted in Justice Powell's opinion is at the forefront. The legal challenges to the University of Michigan's use of affirmative action in its law school admissions (*Grutter v. Bollinger)* and in its main undergraduate college (*Gratz v. Bollinger*) created an opportunity for the U.S. Supreme Court to decide how affirmative action will be practiced in the twenty-first century. Will the Court's decision in June 2003 that universities can consider race a factor in admissions settle the debate regarding the application of a diversity rationale? Will the Court's decision bring closure to the acrimonious debates about affirmative action in public life?

Gratz v. Bollinger (122 F. Supp. 2d 811 [E.D. Mich. 2000]) (Undergraduate)

In 1997, Jennifer Gratz and Patrick Hamacher filed a class-action suit on behalf of themselves and all others similarly situated against the University of Michigan alleging that the university's College of Literature, Science, and the Arts had violated Title VI of the Civil Rights Act of 1964, which prohibits recipients of federal funds from discriminating on the basis of race, and the equal protection clause of the Fourteenth Amendment by using race as a factor in admissions decisions. The court ruled in favor of the plaintiffs and declared the admissions programs in existence from 1995 through 1998 unconstitutional on the basis that they were not narrowly tailored to meet the interest of diversity under the standard of strict scrutiny. However, the court found the admissions programs in existence in 1999 and 2000 to be constitutional.

Grutter v. Bollinger (137, F. Supp. 2d 821 [U. S. Dist. 2001]) (Law School)

In 1997, Barbara Grutter filed suit against the University of Michigan Law School after having been denied admission in June of that year. Grutter alleged that she was discriminated against on the basis of her race (Caucasian—"a disfavored racial group") and that the law school had violated the Fourteenth Amendment and Title VI of the Civil Rights Act of 1964. In 1998, the University of Michigan sought to have this case designated a companion to *Gratz*. However, in a series of odd procedures involving an Order of Disqualification and Transfer by the chief judge of the District Court and the nullification of an opinion by a two-judge panel, the cases were ultimately deemed not to be companion cases (16 F. Supp. 2d 797 [E. D. Mich. 1998]).

In *Grutter,* the court found in favor of the plaintiff and against the law school. The court declared that the law school's use of race in its admissions decisions violated the equal protection clause of the Fourteenth Amendment and Title VI of the Civil Rights Act of 1964, and it prohibited the law school from using race as a factor in its admissions decisions. The University of Michigan requested a stay of injunction and was denied by the District Court. On May 14, 2002, a sharply divided U.S. Court of Appeals for the Sixth Circuit voted 5 to 4 to overturn the lower court's ruling that the admissions policy used by the University of Michigan's law school illegally discriminated against white applicants.

On June 23, 2003, the U.S. Supreme Court ruled that the University of Michigan Law School's race admissions policy was constitutional. However, the Court rejected the university's use of race in undergraduate admissions (Hurley 2003; Jones 2003). Justice Sandra Day O'Connor, in writing for the 5–4 majority in *Grutter v. Bollinger*, noted that by upholding the University of Michigan Law School's race-conscious admissions policy, the Court was endorsing Justice Lewis Powell Jr.'s opinion in *Bakke* that "student body diversity is a compelling state interest that can justify the use of race in university admissions" (quoted in Mauro, 2003, 4). However, Justice O'Connor also noted in writing for the majority in *Grutter* that affirmative action programs must be narrowly tailored and of limited duration because "we expect that twenty-five years from now, the use of racial preferences will no longer be necessary to further the interest approved today" (quoted in Mauro, 2003, 4).

Chief Justice William Rehnquist wrote for the 6–3 majority in *Gratz v. Bollinger* rejecting the University of Michigan's use of race in undergraduate admissions that the university's use of race in its undergraduate admissions, in which minorities received an automatic 20 points toward the 100 points needed for admission, was "not narrowly tailored" (quoted in Mauro, 2003, 4). Justice Rehnquist also noted in writing the majority opinion that "the fact that the implementation of a program capable of providing individualized consideration might present administrative challenges does not render constitutional an otherwise problematic system" (quoted in Mauro, 2003, 4). Justice Rehnquist's comment suggests that perhaps race can be considered in undergraduate admissions if it is part of an individualized assessment of each applicant, and that individualized assessment should not be replaced by institutional practices that avoid challenging the admissions process in higher education. The Court's decisions in *Gratz* and *Grutter* do not quite resolve the conflicting portrait of affirmative action in U.S. society. On the one hand, the Court has recognized the importance of diversity. By upholding *Grutter* the Court recognizes that diversity is best served in society by making educational institutions more responsive to racial and ethnic minority populations. On the other hand, by rejecting *Gratz* the Supreme Court suggests that practices such as affirmative action focused on promoting institutional diversity must be narrowly tailored. As such, diversity is best served by practices that are designed to survive challenges and not to avoid them.

It is still too early to tell how affirmative action will be interpreted or applied given the Supreme Court's decisions in *Gratz* and *Grutter*. We can, however, offer some observations about what the Court's decisions suggest. First, as we have noted in Chapters 1 and 2 of this book, diversity is increasing, and will not disappear, from the U.S. social fabric. The Court's decisions serve to reinforce the importance of addressing the needs of racial and ethnic diversity in the United States. Second, the Court's decisions suggest that it may be time to implement practices, such as affirmative action, that remedy the exclusion of racial and ethnic minorities from educational institutions. As racial and ethnic minority populations increase in numbers, it becomes imperative that the youth in those populations be offered opportunities to participate in educational institutions. Third, the Court's decisions suggest that affirmative action can be practiced to remove discriminatory and segregationist social forces in U.S. higher education. As such, the decisions open the door to diversity by using it as a weapon against discrimination.

Challenges to Diversity in Higher Education

In order to complete our discussion of the diversity rationale in higher education, the following pages contain a summary and review of legal cases that have focused on diversity issues in higher education.

Johnson v. University of Georgia (106 F. Supp. 2d 1362 [S.D. Ga. 2000])

In 1999, Jennifer Johnson filed suit against the University of Georgia after she was denied admission to the freshman class for fall 1999. Her complaint was later consolidated with the complaints of Aimee Bogrow and Molly Ann Beckenhauer, who were also denied admission in 1999. Johnson was offered admission to the University of Georgia after she had filed her lawsuit, but she declined to enroll at that time. The plaintiffs alleged that they were denied admission on the basis of race (Title VI) and gender (Title IX of the Education Act of 1973). The University of Georgia gave automatic preference in admissions to male applicants. The District Court for the Southern District of Georgia ruled in favor of the plaintiffs. The decision was upheld by the U.S. Court of Appeals for the Eleventh Circuit (263 F. 3d 1234 [U.S. App. 2001]).

Smith v. University of Washington (2000 WL 177045 [2000])

In 1997, Katuria Smith, Angela Rock, and Michael Pyle (collectively "Smith") filed a class-action suit against the University of Washington Law School alleging that they and other white applicants had been denied admission on the basis of racially discriminatory admissions policies. In this case, the court followed the majority opinion rendered in *Bakke* and held that the law school's admissions program could consider race in the promotion of educational diversity, a compelling governmental interest, and that the program met the demands of strict scrutiny of race-conscious measures. In 2001, the U.S. Supreme Court declined to hear the appeal despite the contradiction between this ruling and that in *Hopwood*. The Court held that the issue was moot since the University of Washington had discontinued using race, ethnicity, and national origin as factors in the admissions process following passage of Initiative 200. Initiative 200, the Washington State Civil Rights Initiative, was approved by voters in 1998. Modeled after California's Proposition 209, Initiative 200 prohibited the state from granting preferential treatment on the basis of race, sex, or national origin in public education, public contracting, and public employment.

Hopwood v. Texas (861 F. Supp. 551 [W. D. Tex. 1994])

In 1992, Cheryl J. Hopwood and three other white plaintiffs filed suit against the University of Texas Law School alleging that they were denied admission as a result of procedures granting preferences to black and Mexican American applicants. The court deferred to the U.S. Supreme Court's precedent in *Bakke* and declined to declare the school's use of racial preferences in its admissions process unconstitutional (*Hopwood v. State of Texas*). Instead, the court applied strict scrutiny to the law school's admissions process and found that the use of racial preferences for the purpose of achieving a diverse student body served a compelling state interest under the Fourteenth Amendment. The court also found that the use of racial classifications for overcoming the present effects of past discrimination served a compelling government interest. However, the court ultimately found that the law school's use of separate admissions procedures for minorities and nonminorities prevented any meaningful comparative evaluation among applicants of different races and was not narrowly tailored to achieve those compelling interests. Consequently, the court declared that the law school's 1992 admissions procedures violated the Fourteenth Amendment. In effect, the court ruled that the admissions procedures favored only black and Mexican American applicants.

The U.S. Court of Appeals for the Fifth Circuit reversed and remanded the lower court's decision in part. It declared that the law school's use of racial preferences served no compelling state interests under the Fourteenth Amendment and directed the law school not to use race as a factor in admissions. The remanded part of the decision had to do with whether or not the plaintiffs would have been admitted to the law school in the absence of admissions procedures that took into account an applicant's race or ethnicity. The U.S. Supreme Court declined to hear appeals of the circuit court's decision, acknowledging that the 1992 admissions program had been discontinued and would not be reinstated.

Finally, there are other affirmative action initiatives that have attracted public interest and scrutiny (Selingo 2003). For example, in 1998, as a response to *Hopwood v. Texas*, the State of Texas created a "percentage plan" that guarantees any student ranked in the top 10 percent of his or her graduating high school class admission to any public institution of higher education (Selingo 2002). California and Florida also approved their own percentage plans (Ahern 2002; "U. of Florida to Open Its Doors to Top 5 Percent of Each High-School Graduating Class" 2002). The California plan guarantees admission to one of the University of California campuses to the top 4 percent of graduating high school seniors, and the Florida plan guarantees admission to the top 20 percent of graduating seniors to one of the state's public colleges or universities. Colorado and Pennsylvania also considered percentage plans. Colorado has not yet approved such a plan, and Pennsylvania has abandoned the percentage plan and is considering using student performance on a statewide standardized test.

Although percentage plans are heralded by politicians and higher education leaders as a sound alternative to affirmative action, their effectiveness in promoting diversity in higher education is questionable (for example, see Bowen and Rudenstine 2003; Trounson 2003). In an effort to gauge the effectiveness of percentage plans, the U.S. Commission on Civil Rights (2000) undertook a study of percentage plans in higher education. The commission's report criticizes percentage plans for their inability to promote diversity in higher education, especially at the flagship institutions and in graduate and professional schools. Moreover, the report interprets percentage plans as an experimental response to the attacks on affirmative action and a reflection of the states' failure to provide equal learning opportunities for poor Latino and African American students. Only time will tell whether or not percentage plans promote diversity in higher education at levels beyond the limited outcomes produced by affirmative action. Moreover, the question of disparate impact will probably remain at the forefront of the debate on percentage plans. In particular, percentage plans will be ineffective in diversifying higher education if they result in the sorting of minority students into institutions at the lower end of the higher education stratification system.

Discussions of affirmative action are uncomfortable for a number of reasons. The discussion of affirmative action identifies the unwillingness of U.S. society to alter its institutions to accommodate an increasingly diverse and multicultural society. The (white) majority in U.S. society has yet to see the benefits of incorporating diverse and multicultural mind-sets into societal institutions. The discussion of affirmative action portrays the (non-white) minority as a threat to the privileges enjoyed by the (white) majority. The minority is depicted as having excluded itself through its own lack of effort and initiative from the social opportunity enjoyed by the majority; thus in the majority's eyes, the minority is its own victim. The discussion of affirmative action has a tragic outcome for the minority because it documents the unintended benefits of affirmative action for the majority. Consider that the notion of reverse discrimination advanced by the majority often outweighs the direct and harmful effects of racism experienced by the minority. In the end, the most noticeable unintended benefit of affirmative action for the majority is the court's use of affirmative action to silence the minority's cry for social justice.

Conclusion

Can diversity survive within a context of adversity in U.S. society? We have noted that the diversity created by immigration is often perceived as problematic. Perhaps one reason for the perception that the diversity created by immigration is loaded with social problems is because the persons making up the new diversity are immigrants from Mexico and Central and South

America. For example, an examination of the state-by-state data summarized in Chapter 6 reveals that Hispanics and Asians have increased their numbers within the United States. In most states during the 1990s, Hispanics and Asians increased their numbers at a greater rate than the state's population as a whole increased. Hispanics, in particular, were the only population in the 1990s whose numbers increased in twenty states by more than 100 percent.

Increasing racial and ethnic diversity may be a factor in an increase of hate crimes against racial and ethnic minorities. The growth in the numbers of racial and ethnic minorities in U.S. society has increased their identifiability in society, and this greater identifiability, in turn, may increase the perception that they are threats to U.S. culture and character. For example, the tragic events of September 11 framed the precarious position of diversity in U.S. society. They illustrated how foreignness could quickly be identified as a threat; that is, they showed how easy it is to profile racial and ethnic minorities, who often became the innocent victims of violence and hatred after September 11.

Perhaps the most serious challenge diversity faces in the twenty-first century is its incorporation into societal institutions. Affirmative action serves as a vehicle for providing racial and ethnic minorities with opportunities to increase their representation within societal institutions. Given the general perception that education is a means to improving a person's social position, it is not surprising that education is contested terrain for affirmative action. The U.S. Supreme Court's decisions in *Gratz* and *Grutter* will shape the context for diversity in U.S. society. The Court's decision has affirmed that diversity is a contributing factor to U.S. society and is therefore a compelling interest for states.

Finally, the topics discussed in this chapter—immigration, racial profiling, hate crimes, and affirmative action—highlight the precarious position of diversity in the social fabric. Each of these topics illustrates the importance of identifiability in shaping the social relations of racial and ethnic minorities. Ironically, the identifiability of diversity may be its greatest liability. The "new immigration" will challenge U.S. society's ability to alter its culture and character to mirror the increasing diversity of the population. Thus, the topics we have discussed in this chapter are those that will dominate the American public's imagination and discourse in the twenty-first century.

References

Aguirre, Adalberto, Jr. 2000. "Academic Storytelling: A Critical Race Theory Story of Affirmative Action." *Sociological Perspectives* 43: 319–339.

———. 2002. "Propositions 187 and 227: A Nativist Response to Mexicans." In *California's Social Problems,* ed. Charles Hohm and James Glynn, 2nd ed., 303–324. Thousand Oaks, CA: Pine Forge Press.

———. 2003. "Linguistic Diversity in the Workforce: Understanding Social Relations in the Workplace." *Sociological Focus* 36: 65–80.

Aguirre, Adalberto, Jr., and Ruben Martinez. 2003. "The Diversity Rationale in Higher Education: The Precarious Context for Affirmative Action." Unpublished manuscript.

Aguirre, Adalberto, Jr., and Jonathan Turner. 2001. *American Ethnicity: The Dynamics and Consequences of Discrimination.* 3rd ed. New York: McGraw-Hill.

Ahern, Louise. 2002. "UC Opens Door Wider." *Riverside* [Calif.] *Press-Enterprise,* May 16, B5.

Allison, Maria. 1999. "Organizational Barriers to Diversity in the Workplace." *Journal of Leisure Research* 31: 78–91.

Almaguer, Tomas. 1994. *Racial Fault Lines: The Historical Origins of White Supremacy in California.* Berkeley and Los Angeles: University of California Press.

Appiah, Anthony. 2000. "Stereotypes and the Shaping of Identity." *California Law Review* 88: 41–53.

Austin, Regina. 1994. "A Nation of Thieves: Securing Black Peoples' Rights to Shop and Sell in White America." *Utah Law Review* (1994): 147–177.

Baker, Ellen. 2002. "Flying While Arab: Racial Profiling and Air Travel Security." *Journal of Air Law and Commerce* 67: 1375–1405.

Balderrama, Francisco, and Raymond Rodriguez. 1995. *Decade of Betrayal: Mexican Repatriation in the 1930s.* Albuquerque: University of New Mexico Press.

Barrera, Mario. 1979. *Race and Class in the Southwest: A Theory of Racial Inequality.* Notre Dame, IN: University of Notre Dame Press.

Baum, Dan. 2003. "Patriots on the Borderline." *Los Angeles Times Magazine,* March 16, 9–10.

Bell, Jeannine. 2002. *Policing Hatred: Law Enforcement, Civil Rights, and Hate Crime.* New York: New York University Press.

Bollinger, Lee. 2002. "Seven Myths about Affirmative Action in Universities." *Willamette Law Review* 38: 535–547.

Bowen, William, and Neil Rudenstein. 2003. "Race-Sensitive Admissions: Back to Basics." *Chronicle of Higher Education,* February 7, B7–B10.

Bulwa, Demian. 2000. "Memo: Interrogate Hispanics." *San Francisco Examiner,* October 13, A4.

Calabresi, Guido. 1994. "Scapegoats." *Quinnipiac Law Review* 14: 83–89.

Camarota, Steven. 2001. *Immigrants in the United States—2000: A Snapshot of America's Foreign-Born Population.* Washington, DC: Center for Immigration Studies.

Cameron, Christopher. 1998. "One Hundred Fifty Years of Solitude: Reflections on the End of the History Academy's Dominance of Scholarship on the Treaty of Guadalupe Hidalgo." *Southwestern Journal of Law and Trade in the Americas* 5: 83–107.

Carlson, A. Cheree. 1989. "The Rhetoric of the Know-Nothing Party: Nativism as a Response to the Rhetorical Situation." *Southern Communication Journal* 54: 364–384.

Chalmers, David. 1987. *Hooded Americanism: The First Century of the History of the Ku Klux Klan.* Durham, NC: Duke University Press.

Contreras, Guillermo. 2000. "Conflict on the Border." *Albuquerque Journal,* May 21, A1.

Delgado, Ray, Kelly St. John, and Rachel Gordon. 2001. "Ex-S.F. Cabbie, a Sikh, Slain in Arizona." *San Franciso Chronicle,* September 17, A1.

Delgado, Richard, and Jean Stefancic. 1992. "Images of the Outsider in American Law and Culture: Can Free Expression Remedy Systemic Social Ills?" *Cornell Law Review* 77: 1258–1297.

Denzin, Norman. 1998. "Reading the Cinema of Racial Violence." *Perspectives on Social Problems* 10: 31–60.

Eisenman, Russell. 2001. "Demographic Profiling." *Policy Evaluation* 7: 4–11.

Fennessy, James. 1999. "New Jersey Law and Police Response to the Exclusion of Minority Patrons from Retail Stores Based on the Suspicion of Shoplifting." *Seton Hall Constitutional Law Journal* 9: 549–608.

Ferguson, Edwin. 1947. "The California Alien Land Law and the Fourteenth Amendment." *California Law Review* 35: 61–90.

Fetto, John. 2002. "The Usual Suspects: Americans Are Divided on the Issue of Racial Profiling." *American Demographics* 24: 14.

Fredrickson, George. 1998. "America's Diversity in Comparative Perspective." *The Journal of American History* 85: 859–875.

Gamino, Denise. 1998. "James Byrd's Grave Disturbed by Vandals." *Cox News Service*, December 17. Accessed on Lexis-Nexis.

Garcia, Ruben. 1995. "Critical Race Theory and Proposition 187: The Racial Politics of Immigration Law." *Chicano-Latino Law Review* 17: 118–154.

Glazer, Nathan. 1997. *We Are All Multiculturalists*. Cambridge, MA: Harvard University Press.

Graham, Hugh. 1994. "Race, History, and Policy: African Americans and Civil Rights since 1964." *Journal of Policy History* 6: 12–39.

Graves, Matt. 2001. "Purchasing While Black: How Courts Condone Discrimination in the Marketplace." *Michigan Journal of Race and Law* 7: 159–194.

Grebler, Leo, Joan Moore, and Ralph Guzman. 1970. *The Mexican-American People: The Nation's Second Largest Minority*. New York: Free Press.

Gullixson, Kirsten. 1999. "California Proposition 227: An Examination of the Legal, Educational, and Practical Issues Surrounding the New Law." *Law and Inequality* 17: 505–536.

Harden, Blaine. 1998. "Giuliani Suspends Two N.Y. Firemen for 'Display of Racism' at Parade." *Washington Post*, September 12, A6.

Higham, John. 1955. *Strangers in the Land: Patterns of American Nativism, 1860–1925*. New Brunswick, NJ: Rutgers University Press.

Hoffman, Abraham. 1974. *Unwanted Mexican Americans in the Great Depression: Repatriation Pressures, 1929–1939*. Tucson: University of Arizona Press.

Hughes, Polly. 2002. "Big Rise in Hate Crimes." *Houston Chronicle*, June 15, 38.

Human Rights Watch. 2002. *We Are Not the Enemy: Hate Crimes against Arabs, Muslims, and Those Perceived to Be Arab or Muslim after September 11*. New York: Human Rights Watch.

Hurley, Laurence. 2003. "Split Supreme Court Upholds Race as a Factor." *Daily Record*, June 24, 1.

Ibarra, Ignacio. 2003. "Battle of Border Enforcers Heats Up." *Arizona Daily Star*, March 27, A1.

Jaret, Charles. 1999. "Troubled by Newcomers: Anti-Immigrant Attitudes and Action during Two Eras of Mass Immigration to the United States." *Journal of American Ethnic History* 18: 9–39.

Johnson, Catherine. 1999. "The California Backlash against Bilingual Education: *Valeria G. v. Wilson* and Proposition 227." *University of San Francisco Law Review* 34: 169–195.

Johnson, Kevin. 2000. "The Case against Race Profiling in Immigration Enforcement." *Washington University Law Quarterly* 78: 675–736.

Jones, Barbara. 2003. "Local Law Schools Welcome Affirmative Action Ruling." *Minnesota Lawyer* (June 30): 1.

MacCormack, John. 2002. "Border Vigilante Handed Five Years: Vet Shot Migrant from Behind." *San Antonio Express-News,* November 16, 5B.

Main, Amanda. 2000–2001. "Racial Profiling in Places of Public Accommodation: Theories of Recovery and Relief." *Brandeis Law Journal* 39: 289–316.

Martin, Philip. 1995. "Proposition 187 in California." *International Migration Review* 29: 255–263.

Massey, Douglas, and Nancy Denton. 1993. *American Apartheid: Segregation and the Making of the Underclass.* Cambridge, MA: Harvard University Press.

Mauro, Tony. 2003. "High Court Upholds Affirmative Action, with Limitations." *Legal Intelligencer* (June 24): 4.

Mazon, Mauricio. 1984. *The Zoot-Suit Riots: The Psychology of Symbolic Annihilation.* Austin: University of Texas Press.

McClain, Charles. 1984. "The Chinese Struggle for Civil Rights in Nineteenth Century America: The First Phase, 1850–1870." *California Law Review* 72: 529–568.

McGovney, Dudley. 1947. "The Anti-Japanese Land Laws of California and Ten Other States." *California Law Review* 35: 7–60.

McWilliams, Carey. 1968. *North from Mexico: The Spanish-Speaking People of the United States.* New York: Greenwood Press.

Morris, Aldon. 1984. *The Origins of the Civil Rights Movement: Black Communities Organizing for Change.* New York: Free Press.

Muller, Thomas. 1993. *Immigrants and the American City.* New York: New York University Press.

National Asian Pacific American Legal Consortium. 2001. *Backlash: 2001 Audit of Violence against Asian Pacific Americans (9th Annual Report).* Washington, DC: National Asian Pacific American Legal Consortium.

O'Brien, Tim. 2000. "Novel Legal Service: Racial Profiling Insurance." *The Recorder,* December 8, 3.

Parker, Theresa. 1994. "The California Story: Immigrants Come to California as a Result of Federal—Not State—Policies." *Public Welfare* 52: 16–20.

Parloff, Roger. 2002. *"Bakke* Is as Good a Fudge as Any in Achieving Racial Diversity in Colleges." *Fulton County Daily Report,* February 8, 1.

Perea, Juan. 1992. "Demography and Distrust: An Essay on American Languages, Cultural Pluralism, and Official English." *Minnesota Law Review* 77: 269–373.

Perea, Juan, Richard Delgado, Angela Harris, and Stephanie Wildman. 2000. *Race and Races: Cases and Resources for a Diverse America.* St. Paul, MN: West Group.

Philip, Einat. 2002. "Diversity in the Halls of Academia: Bye-bye Bakke?" *Journal of Law and Education* 31: 149–166.

Platt, Anthony. 1997. "End Game: The Rise and Fall of Affirmative Action in Higher Education." *Social Justice* 24(2): 103–118.

Ramirez, Deborah, and Jana Rumminger. 2000–2001. "Civil Rights in the New Decade: Race, Culture, and the New Diversity in the New Millennium." *Cumberland Law Review* 31: 481–522.

Roberts, Dorothy. 1999. "Race, Vagueness, and the Social Meaning of Order-Maintenance Policing." *Journal of Criminal Law and Criminology* 89: 775–836.

Romero, Mary. 2001. "State Violence and the Social and Legal Construction of Latino Criminality: From El Bandido to Gang Member." *Denver University Law Review* 78: 1081–1118.

Romero, Victor. 2000. "Racial Profiling: 'Driving While Mexican' and Affirmative Action." *Michigan Journal of Race and Law* 6: 195–207.

Rosen, James. 2001. "Reality Meets Rhetoric over Race Profiling." *Sacramento Bee,* December 30, A9.

Ross, William. 1994. *Forging New Freedoms: Nativism, Education, and the Constitution, 1917–1927.* Lincoln: University of Nebraska Press.

Rudovsky, David. 2002. "Breaking the Pattern of Racial Profiling." *Trial* 38: 29–36.

Saito, Natsu. 1997. "Alien and Non-Alien Alike: Citizenship, 'Foreignness,' and Racial Hierarchy in American Law." *Oregon Law Review* 76: 261–345.

Scafidi, Susan. 1999. "Native Americans and Civic Identity in Alta California." *North Dakota Law Review* 75: 423–448.

Schevitz, Tanya. 2002. "FBI Sees Leap in Anti-Muslim Hate Crimes." *San Francisco Chronicle,* November 26, A1.

Schmidley, Dianne, and Herman Alvarado. 1998. *The Foreign Born Population: March 1997 (Update).* U.S. Census Bureau, Current Population Reports, P20-507. Washington, DC.

Schuler, Kristen. 1996. "Equal Protection and the Undocumented Immigrant: California's Proposition 187." *Boston College Third World Law Journal* 16: 275–312.

Selingo, Jeffrey. 2002. "Critics Blast Plan to Expand Class-Rank Policy in Texas as Affirmative-Action Ploy." *Chronicle of Higher Education,* January 11, 29.

———. 2003. "The Broad Reach of the Michigan Cases." *Chronicle of Higher Education,* January 31, A21–A22.

Simms Parris, Michele. 1998. "What Does It Mean to See a Black Church Burning? Understanding the Significance of Constitutionalizing Hate Speech." *University of Pennsylvania Journal of Constitutional Law* 1: 127–153.

Springer, Ann. 2003. *Update on Affirmative Action in Higher Education: A Current Legal Overview.* Washington, DC: American Association of University Professors.

Sterngold, James. 2000. "Appeals Court Voids Ethnic Profiling in Searches." *New York Times,* April 13, A20.

Strauss, David. 1995. "Affirmative Action and the Public Interest." *Supreme Court Review* 1995: 1–43.

Thornton, Kelly. 2000. "Officials Call Attack on Migrant Workers Shocking." *San Diego Union-Tribune,* July 12, B1.

Trounson, Rebecca. 2003. "Admission Studies Find Flaws." *Los Angeles Times,* February 11, A1.

"U. of Florida to Open Its Doors to Top 5 Percent of Each High-School Graduating Class." 2002. *Chronicle of Higher Education,* March 22, 22.

U.S. Commission on Civil Rights. 2002. *Toward an Understanding of Percentage Plans in Higher Education: Are They Effective Substitutes for Affirmative Action?* On-line; available: http://www.usccr.gov/pubs/percent/stmnt.htm.

U.S. Department of Justice. 2001. *Contacts between Police and the Public: Findings from the 1999 National Survey.* Bureau of Justice Statistics. Washington, DC.

Vernez, Georges. 1994. *Undocumented Immigration: An Irritant or Significant Problem in U.S.-Mexico Relations?* Santa Monica, CA: RAND.

Vu, Huong. 2002. "Us against Them: The Path to National Security Is Paved by Racism." *Drake Law Review* 50: 639–693.

Walker, Richard. 1993. "Bashing Newcomers: It's Just a Diversion." *San Francisco Examiner,* November 10, A23.

Weiss, Joanna. 1998. "Jasper Gripped by Shame, Fear." *New Orleans Times-Picayune,* June 14, A1.

Wellman, David. 1997. "Minstrel Shows, Affirmative Action Talk, and Angry White Men: Marking Racial Otherness in the 1990s." In *Displacing Whiteness: Essays in Social and Cultural Criticism,* ed. R. Frankenberg, 311–331. Durham, NC: Duke University Press.

Winborne, Wayne, and Renae Cohen. 1999. "Hating Those Different from Ourselves: The Origins of Racial, Ethnic, and Religious Hatred." In *Violence in Homes and Communities: Prevention, Intervention, and Treatment,* ed. Thomas Gullotta and Sandra McElhaney, 157–179. Thousand Oaks, CA: Sage.

Woodhouse, Shawn. 2002. "The Historical Development of Affirmative Action: An Aggregated Analysis." *Western Journal of Black Studies* 26: 155–158.

4

Chronology

The persons, places, and events listed in the chronology are associated with the portrait of a diverse and multicultural society. The starting point of the chronology is arbitrary; it serves a heuristic purpose to document the start of events that have defined the social relations for race and ethnicity in American society. The chronology also serves as a framework for linking diversity and multiculturalism in American society. As such, the chronology is a guidepost rather than an exhaustive inventory of the persons, places, and events that have contributed to the building of a diverse and multicultural American society. Readers are encouraged to use the internet, especially on-line encyclopedias, as a tool for pursuing further inquiry regarding the persons and events listed in the chronology.

1513   Ponce de Leon discovers Florida.

1540   Francisco Coronado explores the Colorado River.

1541   Hernando de Soto explores the Mississippi River.

1600   Spain has explored and claimed Florida, California, and the southwestern region of the United States.

1607   The slave trade brings Africans to America. By the time of the American Revolution there were about 500,000 African slaves and their descendents in the colonies.

        James I gives a charter to a group of merchants to establishment a settlement in America, Jamestown, Virginia.

1609   The first wave of Dutch immigrants arrives in America.

1620   Mayflower arrived at Plymouth to found first colony in New England.

87

1622   First Indian uprising in an English colony (Virginia).

1624   William Tucker, first black child born in America, baptized in Jamestown.

A permanent settlement, New Netherland, is established in America by Dutch immigrants.

1626   Peter Minuit purchases Manhattan Island from American Indians for $24 worth of glass beads and trinkets.

1662   Virginia passes laws that defined Africans as property for life.

1680   The Pueblo Revolt begins at Taos Pueblo.

1700   Spanish settlement of Arizona begins.

1716   Spanish settlement of Texas begins.

1763   First recorded settlement of Filipinos in America.

1769   Spanish settlement of California begins with the building of the first California mission.

1778   Continental Congress made first treaty with Indians (Delawares).

1789   United States Constitution ratified by the states; Indian rights reaffirmed.

1790   Congress enacted first law regulating trade and land sales with Indians.

First recorded arrival of an Asian Indian in America.

1793   The first Fugitive Slave Law is passed by Congress to help Southern slaveholders to retrieve fugitive slaves. The statute allowed Southern slave owners to recapture runaway slaves, but did not require federal marshals to assist owners, and did not empower judges to issue warrants of arrest.

1799   New York State abolished slavery.

1804   The first documented "underground railroad" activity begins in Lancaster County, Pennsylvania, as William Wright begins transporting fugitive slaves across the Susquehanna River and through Lancaster County using various disguises and ruses.

1820   First organized emigration of U.S. blacks back to Africa, from New York to Sierra Leone.

1822   Denmark Vesey's slave rebellion in South Carolina is aborted when his plans are revealed to authorities by slave George Wilson.

        Public schools for black students open in Philadelphia.

1824   Freed American slaves establish country of Liberia on the west coast of Africa.

        Bureau of Indian Affairs established in War Department.

1825   Free blacks allowed to legally marry each other, but not allowed to marry slaves.

1827   Cherokee Republic formed in an attempt to avoid forced removal.

        First black newspaper, *Freedom's Journal,* published by John Russwurm and Samuel Cornish.

1830   Kentucky slave, Tice Davids, successfully flees slavery and escapes to Ripley, Ohio. Based on his escape and disappearance, the term "underground railroad" is said to have been adopted.

        Indian Removal Act passed by Congress that legalized removal of all Indians east of Mississippi to lands west of the river.

1831   William Lloyd Garrison began publishing an abolitionist newspaper, *The Liberator,* in Boston.

1831,   Hanging of Nat Turner, leader of the slave revolt in
cont.   Southampton, Virginia.

1832   Chief Justice John Marshall issues opinion that state law
does not apply to Indians on tribal lands.

The position of Commissioner of Indian Affairs established in War Department.

1834   Trade and Intercourse Act prohibits sale of intoxicants to
Indians and requires license to travel in Indian land.

1845   Frederick Douglass publishes autobiography.

1847   Three Chinese students arrive in New York City for
schooling. One of them, Yung Wing, graduated from Yale
in 1854 becoming the first Chinese to graduate in the
United States.

Refugees from the Irish potato famine arrive in large
numbers in America.

1848   The discovery of gold at Sutter's Mill draws Chinese
immigrants to California to mine gold.

The Treaty of Guadalupe Hidalgo settles the Mexican-
American War.

1849   Bureau of Indian Affairs shifted to Interior Department.

1851   Sojourner Truth addressed the first Black Women's
Rights Convention in Akron, Ohio.

1852   California imposes a Foreign Miner's License Tax to dis-
courage Chinese immigrants from mining for gold.

Uncle Tom's Cabin published by Harriet Beecher Stowe.

1853   Harriet Tubman is believed to have conducted approximately 300 slaves to freedom in the North on the "underground railroad."

1854   *People v. Hall* rules that Chinese cannot give testimony in California courts against whites.

1856   Pottawatomie massacre occurs.

1857   *Dred Scott v. Sanford.* On April 6, 1846, Dred Scott and his wife Harriet filed suit against Irene Emerson for their freedom. On March 6, 1857, the U.S. Supreme Court ruled that Dred Scott should remain a slave, and that as a slave, Dred Scott was not a citizen of the United States and therefore had no right to bring suit in the federal courts on any matter.

1858   Lincoln-Douglas Debates. Senate candidate Abraham Lincoln says the slavery issue has to be resolved, stating that "A house divided against itself cannot stand."

John Brown organized raid at Harper's Ferry.

William Wells Brown publishes first black drama, *Leap to Freedom.*

1859   The Chinese are excluded from public schools in San Francisco.

1862   Minnesota Uprising of Sioux; 38 hanged at Mankato.

Emancipation Proclamation announced.

California imposes a "police tax" of $2.50 a month on every Chinese person.

Congress passes bill ending slavery in Washington, D.C.

1863   Harriet Tubman led Union Army guerillas into Maryland, freeing more than 700 slaves.

President Abraham Lincoln signs the Emancipation Proclamation, freeing slaves in states that seceded from the Union. The Proclamation actually freed no slaves; in fact, it went no further than Congress had already gone in legislation on the subject, for it applied only to areas

1863, over which the federal government exercised no control,
cont. specifically exempting all regions under federal military
occupation.

1864 Congress rules that black soldiers must receive equal pay.

1865 13th Amendment ratified outlawing slavery.

Central Pacific Railroad Co. recruits Chinese workers for
the transcontinental railroad.

1868 The 14th Amendment confers U.S. citizenship on black
persons.

1869 The first black labor convention is organized, Convention
of the Colored National Labor Union.

1870 California passes law against importation of Chinese,
Japanese, and "Mongolian" women for prostitution.

1871 U.S. Congress passes law putting an end to further
treaties with Indians.

Segregated street cars are integrated in Louisville,
Kentucky, following a sit-in staged by a black teenager.

1872 California's Civil Procedure Code removes law barring
Chinese from testifying in court.

Maria Amparo Ruiz de Burton publishes *Who Would Have
Thought It*, the first known English-language novel written and published by a Mexican-American author. It is a
satire of Yankee racism pre- and post–Civil War.

1875 Page Law in Congress bars entry of Chinese, Japanese, and "Mongolian" prostitutes, felons, and contract
laborers.

1876 Battle of Little Big Horn. Sioux and Cheyenne Indians
defeat U.S. cavalry forces led by Lieutenant Colonel
George Custer.

1877   Japanese Christians set up the Gospel Society in San Francisco, the first immigrant association formed by the Japanese.

1879   California's second constitution prevents municipalities and corporations from employing Chinese workers. The California state legislature also passes a law requiring the removal of persons of Chinese ancestry to the outskirts of all incorporated towns and cities. The U.S. circuit court, however, declares the law unconstitutional.

1880   Section 69 of California's Civil Code prohibits the issuing of marriage licenses for unions between whites and "Mongolians, Negroes, mulattoes and persons of mixed blood."

1881   Booker T. Washington opens Tuskegee Institute in Alabama.

1882   Chinese community leaders form Chinese Consolidated Benevolent Association (CCBA) in San Francisco.

1883   Sojourner Truth dies.

        Chinese in New York establish CCBA.

1884   Helen Hunt Jackson publishes *Ramona.*

        Chinese Six Companies sets up Chinese language school in San Francisco.

        Joseph and Mary Tape sue San Francisco school board to enroll their Chinese daughter Mamie in a public school.

1885   San Francisco builds segregated "Oriental School" as a result of Mamie Tape case.

1886   Residents of Tacoma, Seattle, and other cities in the American West forcibly expel the Chinese.

        Chinese laundrymen win case in *Yick Wo v. Hopkins,* declaring that a law with unequal impact on different groups is discriminatory.

1887   Dawes General Allotment Act passed by Congress. An act to provide for the allotment of lands in severally to Indians on the various reservations, and to extend the protection of the laws of the United States and the Territories over the Indians.

1888   Scott Act renders 20,000 Chinese reentry certificates null and void.

1889   *Chae Chan Ping v. U.S.* upholds constitutionality of Chinese exclusion laws.

1890   On December 29 almost 400 Sioux Indians are massacred by U.S. troops at Wounded Knee.

1891   Ellis Island opens.

1892   The Geary Act prohibits Chinese immigration to the United States for another 10 years. *Fong Yue Ting v. U.S.* upholds constitutionality of Geary Law.

1893   Japanese in San Francisco form first trade association, the Japanese Shoemakers' League.

1894   Saito, a Japanese man, applies for U.S. citizenship, but U.S. circuit courts refuse because he is neither white nor black.

The Alianza Hispano-Americana is founded in Arizona.

1895   Booker T. Washington's Atlanta Compromise speech.

1896   National Association of Colored Women founded by Mary Church Terrell in Washington, D.C.

Plessy v. Ferguson upholds separate but equal.

1898   The Philippine Islands become a protectorate of the United States under the Treaty of Paris ending the Spanish-American War. Hawaii is also annexed to the United States.

Wong Kim Ark v. U.S. decides that Chinese persons born in the U.S. cannot be stripped of their citizenship.

Japanese in San Francisco set up Young Men's Buddhist Association.

1900   Bubonic plague scare in San Francisco, Chinatown cordoned and quarantined.

1902   Congress indefinitely extends the prohibition against Chinese immigration.

1903   Japanese and Mexican sugar beet workers strike in Oxnard, California.

1906   Japanese nurserymen form California Flower Growers Association.

Japanese scientists studying the aftermath of the San Francisco earthquake are stoned.

The San Francisco school board declares that all persons of Asian ancestry must attend segregated schools in Chinatown.

California amends an antimiscegenation law to prohibit marriage between white and "Mongolian" persons.

Basic Naturalization Act passed that requires knowledge of English for naturalization.

1907   Immigration Act of 1907 establishes the Dillingham Commission that increases the list of undesirables, for example, unaccompanied children under the age of 16, persons with tuberculosis, and persons with physical or mental defects.

Gentlemen's Agreement restricts Japanese immigration to the United States by denying passports to laborers wanting to emigrate to the United States.

President Theodore Roosevelt signs Executive Order 589 prohibiting Japanese persons with passports for Hawaii, Mexico, or Canada to re-emigrate to the United States.

1907, Asian Indians are driven out of Bellingham, Washington.
cont.

1908 Japanese form Japanese Association of America.

Asian Indians are driven out of Live Oak, California.

1909 NAACP (National Association for the Advancement of Colored People) founded in Springfield, Illinois.

1910 Angel Island Immigration Station opens to process and deport Asian immigrants.

Founded in 1910, the National Urban League is the premier social service and civil rights organization in America. The League is a nonprofit, community-based organization headquartered in New York City, with 115 affiliates in 34 states and the District of Columbia.

Administrative measures used to restrict influx of Asian Indians into California.

1911 The Mexican Protective Association, a Mexican American agricultural union, is founded in Texas.

Japanese form Japanese Association of Oregon in Portland.

1912 Japanese in California hold statewide conference on Nisei education.

1913 California passes alien land law prohibiting "aliens ineligible to citizenship" from buying land or leasing it for longer than three years.

Timothy Drew, known as Prophet Noble Drew Ali, founds the Moorish Science Temple of America in Newark, New Jersey. His central teaching is that blacks are of Muslim origin.

Fannie M. Jackson, first black woman college graduate in the United States, dies.

Harriet Tubman, "engineer of the underground railroad," dies.

1915   Booker T. Washington, educator and founder of Tuskegee Institute, dies.

Xavier University, first black Catholic College in United States, opened in New Orleans, Louisiana.

1917   Arizona passes an Alien Land Law.

1918   Servicemen of Asian ancestry who served in World War I receive right of naturalization.

Asian Indians form the Hindustani Welfare Reform Association in the Imperial and Coachella Valleys in southern California.

1919   First Pan-African Congress organized in Paris by W. E. B. DuBois.

1920   Marcus Garvey presents his "Back To Africa" program in New York City.

National Negro Baseball League is organized.

1921   The Sons of America is organized in San Antonio, Texas, to fight for equality and raise awareness of Mexican Americans' rights as U.S. citizens.

Japanese farm workers driven out of Turlock, California.

Filipinos establish a branch of the Caballeros Dimas Alang in San Francisco and a branch of the Legionarios del Trabajo in Honolulu.

Washington and Louisiana pass alien land laws.

First Quota Law limits immigration to 3 percent of national origin of 1910 foreign born, for a total of 357,000 per year.

1921,
cont.
Takao Ozawa v. U.S. declares Japanese ineligible for naturalized citizenship.

New Mexico passes an alien land law.

Cable Act declares that any American female citizen who marries "an alien ineligible to citizenship" would lose her citizenship.

1923 *U.S. v. Bhagat Singh Thind* declares Asian Indians ineligible for naturalized citizenship.

Idaho, Montana, and Oregon pass alien land laws.

Terrace v. Thompson upholds constitutionality of Washington's alien land law.

Porterfield v. Webb upholds constitutionality of California's alien land law.

Webb v. O'Brien rules that sharecropping is illegal because it is a ruse that allows Japanese to possess and use land.

Frick v. Webb forbids aliens "ineligible to citizenship" from owning stocks in corporations formed for farming.

1924 All Indians declared citizens of the United States.

National Origins Act of 1924 (Johnson Reed Act) imposes permanent numerical limit on immigration by limiting immigration to 2 percent of national origin of 1890 foreign born for a total of 164,000 per year.

1925 Hilario Moncado founds Filipino Federation of America.

1926 The Spanish-language newspaper *La Opinion* begins publication in Los Angeles.

1928 Filipino farm workers are driven out of Yakima Valley, Washington.

The *Confederacion de Uniones Obreras Mexicanas* (CUOM)

is formed to organize all Mexican workers in the U.S., achieve wage parity, and end discrimination.

Octaviano Larrazola of New Mexico is the first Mexican American elected to the U.S. Senate.

1929   Martin Luther King, Jr., civil rights leader, born.

LULAC (League of United Latin American Citizens) is founded in Corpus Christi, Texas.

U.S. government requires Mexicans to obtain visas in order to enter the United States.

1930   The repatriation of thousands of Mexicans and Mexican Americans begins during the Great Depression.

Anti-Filipino riot in Watsonville, California.

1931   Female Mexican-American garment workers in Los Angeles are unionized by labor organizer Rose Pesotta.

Roberto Alvarez v. Lemon Grove School Board decides that Mexican children are considered Caucasian according to the law of segregation that legally segregated Native American, black, and Asian students, and that as a result, school segregation denies Mexican children socialization and interaction with American children, as well as their rights as U.S. citizens.

Amendment to Cable Act declares that no American-born woman who loses her citizenship (by marrying an alien ineligible to citizenship) can be denied the right of naturalization at a later date.

1934   Wheeler-Howard Act passed by Congress. An Act to conserve and develop Indian lands and resources, to extend to Indians the right to form business and other organizations, to establish a credit system for Indians, to grant certain rights of home rule to Indians, and to provide for vocational education for Indians.

1936   American Federation of Labor (AFL) grants charter to a Filipino Mexican union of fieldworkers.

1940   AFL charters the Filipino Federated Agricultural Laborers Association.

1942   The Bracero Program begins allowing Mexican laborers to enter the United States as short-term agricultural contract workers.

Sleepy Lagoon incident in Los Angeles. Sleepy Lagoon was a water reservoir in rural Los Angeles that was used as a swimming hole by Mexican American kids who were denied access to city owned recreation facilities. The murder of a young man on August 1 resulted in a violent clampdown by Los Angeles police on Mexican American youth.

President Franklin D. Roosevelt signs Executive Order 9066 that results in the internment of over 100,000 Japanese persons, a large number of whom were second and third generation American citizens, in 10 relocation camps in the United States. Congress passes Public Law 503 to impose penal sanctions on anyone disobeying orders to carry out Executive Order 9066.

Protests at Poston and Manzanar relocation centers.

1943   Congress of Racial Equality (CORE) is formed.

Zoot-suit riots in Los Angeles. U.S. servicemen attack Mexican American youth wearing zoot-suits, ballooned pants and long coats. The zoot-suited youth were labeled as unpatriotic and un-American by the servicemen.

Protest at Topaz Relocation Center.

The Chinese Exclusion Act of 1882 is repealed (grants right of naturalization and a small immigration quota to Chinese).

George Washington Carver, African American scientist

renowned for developing innovative uses for a variety of agricultural crops such as peanuts, soybeans, and sweet potatoes dies.

1944   United Negro College Fund established.

Tule Lake Relocation Center placed under martial law.

Military draft reinstated for Nisei.

Draft resistance at Heart Mountain Relocation Center.

Smith v Allwright rules that excluding Blacks from primary voting is illegal.

1945   The relocation camps for Japanese internees are closed.

1946   U.S. citizenship is offered to all Filipinos living in the United States.

Luce-Celler bill grants right of naturalization and small immigration quotas to Asian Indians and Filipinos.

Wing F. Ong becomes first Asian American to be elected to state office in the Arizona House of Representatives.

1947   The Community Service Organization (CSO) is established in Los Angeles to encourage voter registration and provide grass-roots political support for Mexican Americans.

Mendez v. Westminster decision prohibits school segregation on the basis of Mexican descent in California.

Jackie Robinson breaks color line in baseball.

1948   President Harry Truman signs Executive Order 9981 ending segregation in the U.S. Armed Forces.

Hector Perez Garcia forms the American GI Forum on March 26 in order to provide health care for veterans who were refused care because they were "Mexicans."

1948,
cont.
The U.S. Congress passes the Displaced Persons Act that results in the conferral of permanent resident status to over 3,000 Chinese visitors, seamen, and students who relocated to the U.S. because of the Chinese civil war.

California repeals law banning interracial marriage.

The U.S. Congress passes the Evacuation Claims Act that authorizes payment of settlements, 10 cents returned for every $1, to people of Japanese ancestry who suffered economic losses from their internment in relocation camps.

1950
Gwendolyn Brooks, first black awarded a Pulitzer Prize, for poetry.

Operation Wetback begins to deport undocumented Mexican workers from the United States.

1952
Immigration and Naturalization Act of 1952 (McCarren Walter Act) continues national origin quotas, establishes preference category system, eliminates racial and gender barriers to naturalization, and sets quota for skilled aliens whose services are urgently needed.

1953
Refugee Relief Act admits over 200,000 refugees outside of existing quotas.

1954
Ellis Island is closed.

Brown v. Board of Education of Topeka, Kansas rules that separate but equal is unconstitutional.

1955
Rosa Parks initiates black boycott of buses in Montgomery, Alabama.

Interstate Commerce Commission bans segregation in buses and terminals.

1956
California repeals its alien land laws.

Dalip Singh from the Imperial Valley (California) is elected to Congress.

1957   Langston Hughes, poet laureate, dies.

Southern Christian Leadership Conference founded.

Refugee Escape Act defines escapees as any alien who fled from any Communist country or from the Middle East because of persecution or the fear of persecution on account of race, religion, or political opinion.

1960   Greensboro, N.C., lunch counter sit-ins.

Cuban Refugee Program established.

1961   CORE (Congress of Racial Equality) begins freedom rides from Washington, D.C. to force desegregation of bus terminals in the South.

1962   President John F. Kennedy authorizes use of federal troops to integrate the University of Mississippi. James Meredith becomes first black student at the University of Mississippi.

James Baldwin publishes a ground-breaking article in the *New Yorker* regarding civil rights struggles in the United States.

Jackie Robinson, first black elected to the Baseball Hall of Fame.

1963   The *Alianza Federal de Mercedes* (Federal Alliance of Land Grants) is incorporated by Reies Lopez Tijerina.

NAACP Youth Council begins sit-ins at lunch counters in Oklahoma City.

Martin Luther King, Jr. begins Birmingham desegregation crusade.

Civil Rights March on Washington, D.C. where Martin Luther King Jr. makes "I Have A Dream" speech at Lincoln Memorial.

Medgar Evers, civil rights activist, assassinated.

1963, W. E. B. DuBois, sociologist and civil rights leader, dies in
cont. Ghana.

John Fitzgerald Kennedy is assassinated.

1964   President Lyndon B. Johnson announces War on Poverty
programs.

Freedom Summer voter registration campaign in Mississippi.

Civil Rights Act passed.

U.S. ends the Bracero Program.

Martin Luther King Jr. wins the Nobel Peace Prize.

1965   El Teatro Campesino is founded in Delano, California. El
Teatro Campesino was a traveling theatre group that satirized the Anglo controlled agribusiness in California and
its treatment of Mexican and Chicano farmworkers.

Race riots in Watts (Los Angeles) against poverty and
police brutality.

Malcolm X assassinated, February 21, in New York City.

Immigration and Nationality Amendments of 1965 repeal
national origin quotas, establish uniform per country limits of 20,000 and preference category system with overall
ceiling of 170,000 for the Eastern Hemisphere, and place
overall ceiling at 120,000 starting in 1968 for immigration
from the Western Hemisphere for first time.

1966   Reies Lopez Tijerina and 350 supporters occupy part of
the Kit Carson National Forest on behalf of the *Pueblo de
San Joaquin de Chama* and arrest two park rangers for trespassing.

César Chavez forms the United Farm Worker Organizing
Committee.

Black Panther Party established in Oakland, California.

1967   Thurgood Marshall appointed to the U.S. Supreme Court.

The Brown Berets, a Chicano activist community-based group, is started in Los Angeles.

1968   Shirley Chisholm becomes first black woman elected to Congress.

Race riots in Newark and Detroit.

Martin Luther King, Jr. assassinated in Memphis, Tennessee.

1969   The U.S. Supreme Court rules that the suspension of Adam Clayton Powell Jr. from the House of Representatives is unconstitutional.

American Indian Movement (AIM) begins to form.

1970   National Chicano Moratorium to protest the Vietnam War.

1971   Congressional Black Caucus organized.

1974   *Lau v. Nichols* rules that school districts with children who speak little English must provide them with bilingual education.

1975   Indochinese Refugee Resettlement Program begins.

1976   Kenneth A. Gibson elected as the first African American president of the U.S. Conference of Mayors.

Immigration and Nationality Act Amendments of 1976 extends 20,000 per country limits to Western Hemisphere.

President Gerald Ford rescinds Executive Order 9066 (regarding the internment of Japanese in relocation camps).

1978   Massive exodus of "boat people" from Vietnam.

Supreme Court issues *Bakke* decision.

American Indian Religious Freedom Act. Act makes it the policy of the United States to protect and preserve for American Indians their inherent right of freedom to believe, express, and exercise the traditional religions of the American Indian, Eskimo, Aleut, and Native Hawaiians, including but not limited to access to sites, use and possession of sacred objects, and the freedom to worship through ceremonials and traditional rites.

1980   Refugee Act of 1980 sets up permanent and systematic procedure for admitting refugees, removes refugees as a category from preference system, defines refugees according to international versus ideological standards, establishes process of domestic resettlement, and codifies asylum status.

1982   Vincent Chin, a Chinese American, is beaten to death in Detroit by two jobless white automobile workers that reportedly mistake him for a Japanese and blame him for problems in the U.S. automobile industry. Chin's attackers were acquitted of murder charges in a jury trial.

1983   Fred Korematsu, Min Yasui, and Gordon Hirabayashi file petitions to overturn their World War II convictions for violating the curfew and evacuation orders.

1984   Filipino World War II veterans are denied U.S. citizenship.

1985   The Immigration Reform and Control Act (IRCA) is passed by the House of Representatives on October 17, 1987, and signed by President Reagan on November 6, 1987. IRCA raises the quota for immigrants from Hong Kong from 600 to 5,000 a year and allows aliens who can prove that they were in the U.S. prior to January 1, 1982, to apply for temporary status and become U.S. citizens after seven years from the time of application.

1987   The White House signs the first Proclamation of Asian Pacific American Heritage Week.

1988   American Homecoming Act allows children in Vietnam born of American fathers to immigrate to the United States.

        The Civil Liberties Act of 1988, which implements the recommendations of the Commission on Wartime Relocation and Internment of Civilians, is signed into law by the president. The Act apologizes and offers reparations to Japanese Americans who were denied their civil and constitutional rights by the U.S. government during World War II.

1989   President George H. W. Bush signs into law an entitlement program to pay each surviving Japanese American internee $20,000.

1990   Immigration Act of 1990 increases legal immigration ceilings by 40 percent, triples employment-based immigration, emphasizing skills, creates diversity admissions category, and establishes temporary protected stays for those in the U.S. jeopardized by armed conflict or natural disasters in their native countries.

        Native American Grave Protection and Repatriation Act. Congressional Act that provides for the protection of Native American graves.

1992   Korean businesses looted and burned as a result of riots in Los Angeles due to outrage over Rodney King verdict.

1993   César Chavez, founder of the United Farm Workers (UFW), dies.

1994   Proposition 187 is approved by voters in California to prohibit undocumented immigrants from using public services.

1995   The Million Man March is held in Washington D.C. The march was the idea of Nation of Islam leader Louis

1995, Farrakhan, who called the event, "A Day of Atonement
cont. and Reconciliation." The march was described as a call to
black men to take charge in rebuilding their communities
and show more respect for themselves and devotion to
their families.

1996 Illegal Immigration Act of 1996 increases border enforcement, expands restrictions on access of legal immigrants
to welfare benefits, and pilot–tests procedure that allows
employers to verify legal status of applicant by phone.

Anti-Terrorism Act excludes foreign-born persons who
are members of terrorist organizations, provides for automatic deportation of foreign-born legal immigrants con-
victed of felony crimes, and authorizes state and local
police to arrest legal immigrants.

Personal Responsibility and Work Opportunity Reconciliation Act restricts access to public assistance programs
for legal immigrants during their first five years in the
United States.

California voters approve Proposition 209 to ban affirmative action programs in California.

1997 Black American women participate in the Million Woman
March in Philadelphia, focusing on health care, education, and self-help.

1998 California voters approve Proposition 227 to end bilingual education in California public schools.

James Byrd, Jr., a black man, is chained to the back of a
pickup truck by white supremacists in Jasper, Texas, and
dragged to his death.

2000 More than 46,000 protesters rally in a march on the state
capitol at Columbia, South Carolina, to protest the
Confederate battle flag flying atop the statehouse dome.

California makes Cesar Chavez Day a full, paid holiday
for state employees. Texas currently has the holiday on a

"volunteer" status, and Arizona is working on adding the holiday.

2003   In cases involving the University of Michigan's under-graduate (*Gratz v. Bollinger*) and law school (*Grutter v. Bollinger*) admissions policies, the court said colleges may consider race in deciding whom to admit, so long as it is not the only or controlling factor. It rejected a more rigid system in which minority applicants were awarded points for their race.

5

Biographical Sketches

I wish to make a caveat regarding the biographical sketches in this chapter. The people presented in these biographical sketches are *representative* of scholars writing and conducting research in the areas of diversity, race, and ethnic relations in the United States. This compilation of biographical sketches is not intended to be an exhaustive inventory of scholars. Imagine a very large fish net thrown out into the water. When the net is reeled in, fish, and perhaps other water creatures, will be trapped in the net. The fish trapped in the net will neither exhaust the supply of fish in the water nor reflect the range of the types of fish found in the water. The fish trapped in the net *will* show that there are fish in the water, and they will be representative of the types of fish living in the water. Similarly, this compilation of biographical sketches is designed to show that there are scholars working in the areas of diversity, race, and ethnic relations, and these are the types of scholars one is likely to encounter in the study of diversity, race, and ethnic relations in the United States.

The biographical sketches I have included in this chapter show the range of discourse regarding the study of diversity, race, and ethnic relations. For example, Derrick A. Bell Jr. and Richard Delgado have revolutionized the field of legal studies by constructing critical race theory, an area of study that examines the role of the master narrative and white hegemony in constructing the lived experiences of persons of color in the United States. Other scholars who have helped shape the area of critical race theory include Mari Matsuda, Kevin Johnson, Jean Stefancic, Charles R. Lawrence III, Cornel West, Kimberle Crenshaw, Neil Gotanda, Gary Peller, and Patricia Williams. One can readily see that it would be overwhelming to construct a biographical profile for all critical race theory scholars. However, by starting with Bell and Delgado, students of diversity, race, and ethnic relations will find their way to other critical race theory scholars.

Accordingly, the following biographical sketches can serve as a starting point for persons interested in pursuing further study on a particular topic or issue regarding diversity, race, and ethnic relations in the United States. Ernesto Galarza, Carey McWilliams, and Julian Samora were outspoken critics of immigration and the exploitation of Mexican farmworkers in California. Their research and commentary served as a model for using research as a vehicle for public advocacy and for educating the public about the abuses faced by the less fortunate in society. Similarly, Vine Deloria Jr. and Winona LaDuke are vocal critics of the way the federal government has ignored the American Indian population in the United States and of the way it has historically deprived that population of its land and resources.

Joe R. Feagin, Mary Romero, Ronald Takaki, and Frank H. Wu use their research to construct real-life identities for racial and ethnic minority persons who are victims of racism, discrimination, and commercial exploitation in U.S. society. In contrast, bell hooks and Richard Rodriguez raise questions from competing perspectives regarding the value and meaning of racial and ethnic diversity and personal identity in U.S. society. Finally, George I. Sanchez, regarded by many as often overlooked in the study of race and ethnic relations, was a pioneer in challenging U.S. schools to address the educational needs of Mexican American students; in particular, he argued that standardized tests, such as intelligence tests, harmed Mexican American students in the educational process.

Finally, each of the biographical sketches in this chapter reflects an area, a concern, an idea, or a stream of thinking regarding diversity, race, and ethnic relations in the United States. However, if one were to ask the persons sketched in this chapter to identify those who had helped them find their way in their studies, they might mention such names as Robert Park, Milton Gordon, Tamotsu Shibutani, Troy Duster, W. E. B. DuBois, Jacqueline Jackson, and Clark Knowlton. In short, one would readily see the richness and depth of ideas that race, ethnicity, and diversity have generated in studying the social fabric of U.S. society. It is my expectation that the reader will find these biographical sketches serving as windows to the study of race, ethnicity, and diversity.

Derrick A. Bell Jr. (1930–)

Derrick Bell is a compelling voice on issues of race and class in U.S. society. Throughout his forty-year career as a lawyer, activist, teacher, and writer, he has provoked his critics and challenged his readers with his uncompromising candor and original, progressive views. In 1971, Bell became the first tenured black professor at the Harvard Law School. He relinquished his position in 1992, when he refused to return from a two-year unpaid leave of absence that he had taken to protest the lack of women of color on the Harvard faculty.

Bell is not a newcomer to personal protests. In 1980, he left Harvard for five years to accept the deanship of the Oregon Law School. He left the post in Oregon when the faculty directed that he not extend an offer to an Asian American woman faculty candidate who, after an extended search, had been listed third on the list of candidates. When the top two candidates, both white males, declined the position, the faculty decided to reopen the search rather than extending an offer to the Asian American woman. Harvard offered him his old position back, and he returned. But in 1990, he resigned a second time when Harvard failed to grant tenure to any black women in the law school. He moved to New York University, where he has been teaching constitutional law.

The son of working-class parents who did not finish high school, Bell served in the Korean War and returned home to earn a law degree from the University of Pittsburgh School of Law in 1957. During Dwight D. Eisenhower's administration, he became one of only three black attorneys in the Civil Rights Division of the U.S. Justice Department. He left that post in 1959 after he was ordered to cancel his membership in the National Association for the Advancement of Colored People (NAACP), and he went on to oversee litigation in the South for the NAACP Legal Defense Fund during the early 1960s, a dangerous and eventful time for the civil rights movement. Prior to assuming the faculty positions at Harvard and the University of Oregon, he had served as executive director of the Western Center on Law and Poverty at the University of Southern California Law School, counsel for the NAACP Legal Defense Fund, and deputy director of the Office for Civil Rights in the U.S. Department of Health, Education, and Welfare.

Bell has written numerous articles in legal journals published by Harvard, Yale, Columbia, the University of Michigan, the University of California–Berkeley, the University of Pennsylvania, the University of California–Los Angeles, and the University of Wisconsin. His essays have appeared in such national magazines as *Essence, Mother Jones,* and the *New York Times Sunday Magazine* and in such newspapers as the *Boston Globe,* the *Los Angeles Times,* and the *Christian Science Monitor.* His book *Race, Racism, and American Law* (2000), published initially in 1973, is now in its fourth edition. His autobiographical work, *Confronting Authority: Reflections of an Ardent Protester* (1994) offers an honest appraisal of his struggles as an educator, writer, and nonconformist in a society plagued by racism.

Bell is also known for the series of allegorical stories featuring his fictional heroine, Geneva Crenshaw. These stories are found in his books *Afrolantica Legacies* (1998), *Faces at the Bottom of the Well: The Permanence of Racism* (1992), *Gospel Choirs: Psalms of Survival in an Alien Land Called Home* (1996), and *And We Are Not Saved: The Elusive Quest for Racial Justice* (1987). Bell's story "Space Traders" from his book *Faces at the Bottom of the Well* was produced as an HBO movie featuring Robert Guillaume in 1994.

Richard Delgado

Richard Delgado earned his B.A. degree in mathematics and philosophy from the University of Washington and his J.D. degree in 1974 from the University of California–Berkeley. He is currently the Jean Lindsley Professor of Law at the University of Colorado–Boulder School of Law. In May 2003, he assumed the position of Derrick A. Bell Fellow and Professor of Law at the University of Pittsburgh Law School. Delgado is one of the leading commentators on race, civil rights, law reform, and legal scholarship in the United States.

Delgado is a founding member of the Conference on Critical Race Theory and has written more than one hundred journal articles and fifteen books. His books have received numerous national book prizes, including six Gustavus Myers Awards. *The Coming Race War* (1996) was the American Library Association Choice Outstanding Academic Book, and *The Rodrigo Chronicles* (1995) was nominated for a Pulitzer Prize in 1995. Both books also won the Gustavus Myers Award. His work has been praised or reviewed in *The Nation, The New Republic,* the *New York Times,* the *Washington Post,* and the *Wall Street Journal.* The legal citation index *The Most Prolific Law Professors in the Most-Cited Law Reviews* has ranked Delgado first among the nation's approximately 5,500 law professors.

Vine Deloria Jr. (1933–)

Vine Deloria Jr. is a leading Native American scholar whose research, writings, and teaching have encompassed history, law, religious studies, and political science. Deloria, Standing Rock Sioux, was born in Martin, South Dakota. He obtained his B.S. degree from Iowa State University in 1958, a master's degree in theology from the Lutheran School of Theology in Chicago in 1963, and his law degree from the University of Colorado in 1970. Deloria is respected as a lawyer and advocate for indigenous peoples' rights, and he is one of the most prolific and influential scholars of the twentieth century on American Indian law and policy, history, and philosophy.

He is the former executive director of the National Congress of American Indians, a retired professor of political science at the University of Arizona, and a retired professor emeritus of history at the University of Colorado. In 1996, he received the Lifetime Achievement Award from the Native Writers Circle of the Americas; in 2002, he received the Wallace Stegner Award from the Center of the American West at the University of Colorado–Boulder; and in 2003, he won the American Indian Festival of Words Author Award from the Tulsa Library Trust. Among his many published works are *American Indian Policy in the Twentieth Century* (1985), *American Indians, American Justice* (with Clifford M. Lytle; 1983), *Behind the Trail of Broken Treaties: An Indian Declaration of Independence* (1974), *Custer Died for Your Sins* (1969), *God Is Red: A Native View of Religion* (1994), *The Metaphysics of Modern Existence* (1979), *The Nations Within: The Past and Future of American Indian Sovereignty* (with Clifford M. Lytle; 1984), *Red Earth, White Lies: Native Americans and the Myth of Scientific Fact* (1995), and *We Talk, You Listen: New Tribes, New Turf* (1970).

Joe R. Feagin

Joe R. Feagin is one of the most prolific sociologists of race and ethnic relations in the United States. He was born in San Angelo, Texas, at the end of the Great Depression. He spent most of his life growing up in Houston, Texas, where he completed high school. He graduated from Baylor University in 1960. After completing his studies at Baylor, he moved to Boston, Massachusetts, to begin graduate work at Harvard University in social relations (sociology). After completing his Ph.D. degree in 1966, Feagin became an assistant professor of sociology at the University of California–Riverside. Four years later, he accepted a position as an associate professor of sociology at the University of Texas–Austin, where he taught for twenty years. In 1990, Feagin moved to the University of Florida, where he became the graduate research professor in sociology. From 1974 to 1975, Feagin served as scholar-in-residence at the U.S. Commission on Civil Rights.

Feagin's major books on race and ethnic relations include *The Agony of Education: Black Students at White Colleges and Universities* (with Hernan Vera and Nikitah Imani; 1996), *Double Burden: Black Women and Everyday Racism* (with Yanick St. Jean; 1998), *Living with Racism: The Black Middle Class Experience* (with Mel Sikes; 1994), *The New Urban Paradigm* (1998), *Racial and Ethnic Relations* (with Clairece Booher Feagin; 1999), and *White Racism: The Basics* (with Hernan Vera; 1995). Feagin's book with Harlan Hahn, *Ghetto Revolts* (1973), was nominated for a Pulitzer Prize, and *Living with Racism* and *White Racism* have won the Gustavus Myers Center's Outstanding Human Rights Book Award.

Ernesto Galarza (1905–1984)

Ernesto Galarza has been described as a humble man of letters, but his reputation in the international academic community resulted in his being nominated for the Nobel Peace Prize. He was born in Jolocotan, Nayarit, Mexico on August 15, 1905. He and his family moved to the United States during the early period of the Mexican Revolution. His family settled in Sacramento, California, where Galarza assisted his family during the harvest season as a farmworker while he attended Lincoln Elementary and Sacramento High School. As a youth, he became involved with the farm labor movement, becoming an advocate for pesticide-free working conditions and clean drinking water for farmworkers.

Unsure about his educational plans, Galarza was encouraged by a teacher to attend Occidental College. He received a scholarship to attend college but returned to Sacramento during the summer to work as a farm laborer and cannery worker. During his senior year at Occidental, he traveled to Mexico on a study-abroad program. While in Mexico, he gathered information for a senior thesis on the Roman Catholic church as a factor in the political and social history of Mexico. After graduating from Occidental, he attended Stanford University, where he received his master's degree in history and political science. After Stanford, Galarza received a fellowship to attend Columbia University to complete his graduate studies.

For his doctoral dissertation topic, Galarza decided to focus on the development of electricity in Mexico. In 1942, the Fondo de Cultural Economica published what would be his dissertation, "La Industria Electrica en Mexico" ("The Electric Industry in Mexico"). Columbia University awarded him a Ph.D. in economics in 1947. In the interim period between completing his graduate course work and finishing his doctoral dissertation, Galarza was hired by the Pan American Union as a research associate in education. In 1940, he was appointed to head a new division, the Division of Labor and Social Information, within the Pan American Union. During his work with the Pan American Union, he focused much of his interest on tin workers in Bolivia and Mexican farmworkers in the United States.

Galarza's focus on Bolivian tin workers and Mexican farmworkers shaped his political views on workers' rights. When the Bolivian government passed fair labor legislation in 1942 that would require higher wages and better working conditions, he saw an opportunity to improve the Bolivian tin workers' quality of life. However, he resigned from his position in the Pan American Union when the U.S. State Department tried to influence Bolivia not to sign these laws. Galarza argued that the State Department opposed the laws in order to maintain a high profit margin for U.S. companies. He was asked to return to the Pan American Union by Franklin D. Roosevelt's administration, but he resigned for a second time from the Pan American Union when the president of Bolivia was assassinated. Galarza again charged State Department involvement. This time, he did not return to the Pan American Union.

Galarza's other major area of interest while at the Pan American Union was Mexican workers in the United States. The United States had established a worker-exchange program with Mexico, known as the Bracero Program, that allowed Mexican workers to work in the U.S. agricultural industry. Galarza regarded the Bracero Program as a means of exploiting Mexicans working in the United States for the benefit of an expanding agribusiness industry. He lobbied against it but lost. By the end of his stay with the Pan

American Union, he had lost faith that the union could produce the kind of changes he felt were necessary for workers.

After leaving Washington, he was recruited as the regional director of research and education for the National Farm Labor Union (NFLU) for Florida, Louisiana, Texas, Arizona, and California. Galarza established his home in San Jose, California. His first assignment with the NFLU was to assist in the strike against the Di Giorgio Fruit Corporation in Arvin, California. Galarza participated in numerous worker strikes with the NFLU: In 1950, he led the tomato strikers in Tracy, California; in 1951, he led the cantaloupe strikers in California's Imperial Valley; and from 1953 to 1954, he assisted in organizing sugarcane workers and strawberry pickers in Louisiana.

The 1950s were an important decade for Galarza because during those years he sharpened his criticism of the abuses faced by Mexican workers in the agricultural industry. He became a familiar face in congressional hearings, where he exposed the abuses of the Bracero Program and the socioeconomic status of Mexican Americans. He argued that the unionization of Mexican farmworkers was not possible as long as the Bracero Program existed. By the time the National Farm Labor Union was renamed the National Agricultural Workers Union (NAWU) in 1956, Galarza had become disillusioned by the corporate relationship between agribusiness, government bureaucrats, and organized labor. He resolved to challenge the corporate relationship by documenting and publicizing the abuses, corruption, and scandals inherent in the Bracero Program. In 1955, he received money from the Fund for the Republic to write a report on the Bracero Program. The report he wrote, *Strangers in the Field,* was given national press and quickly became regarded as a serious indictment of the Bracero Program.

Strangers in the Field served as a signal for the shaping of his literary and academic career. It was followed by *Merchants of Labor,* an analysis of the Bracero Program. While working on *Merchants of Labor,* Galarza moved to Los Angeles where he found a new area of interest: Mexican American urban populations. It was during this period, the 1960s, that Galarza began his career as an academic, assuming faculty positions at the University of Notre Dame, San Jose State University, the University of California–San Diego, and the University of California–Santa Cruz. The academic atmosphere facilitated Galarza's completion of several books on farm labor: *Barrio Boy* (1971), *Farmworkers and Agribusi-*

ness (1977), *Mexican Americans in the Southwest* (1969), and *Spiders in the House and Workers in the Field* (1970).

Galarza was a prolific writer. His publications number well over one hundred items and include more than a dozen books and scores of articles, reports, government hearings, and literary works. His published works cover the areas of Latin America, farm labor, bilingual education, urban sociology, education, and Chicano Studies. His works are cited in virtually all major works on Chicanos and are represented in all major Chicano bibliographies.

bell hooks (1952–)

Née Gloria Watkins, bell hooks was born in Hopkinsville, Kentucky. She received her B.A. from Stanford University in 1973, her M.A. in 1976 from the University of Wisconsin, and her Ph.D. in 1983 from the University of California–Santa Cruz. She is Distinguished Professor of English at City College in New York. She is regarded primarily as a feminist thinker, but her writings cover a broad range of topics on gender, race, teaching, and the significance of media for contemporary culture. She argues that race, gender, and class must be treated as interconnected phenomena in order to understand their cumulative effect in society. She has published numerous books and essays, among them *Ain't I a Woman: Black Women and Feminism* (1981), *Be Boy Buzz* (2002), *Black Looks: Race and Representation* (1992), *Feminist Theory from Margin to Center* (1984), *Reel to Real: Race, Sex, and Class at the Movies* (1996), *Remembered Rapture: The Writer at Work* (1999), and *Yearning: Race, Gender, and Cultural Politics* (1990).

Winona LaDuke (1959–)

Winona LaDuke grew up in Los Angeles, California. She is Anishinabe from the Makwa Dodaem (Bear Clan) of the Mississippi Band of the White Earth Reservation in northern Minnesota. Her father was a supporting actor in westerns as well as an American Indian activist, and her mother was a Jewish art professor; LaDuke credits her parents with instilling a passion for activism in her. She lives on the White Earth Reservation in Minnesota, where she works on restoring the local land base and culture. She was Ralph Nader's vice presidential running mate in the 1996 presidential election.

LaDuke graduated from Harvard in 1982. While there, she

became involved in American Indian environmental issues. At the age of eighteen she became one of the youngest persons in history to speak in front of the United Nations. Her address before the United Nations regarding American Indian issues transformed her into a vocal and authoritative voice for American Indian economic and environmental concerns throughout the United States. After graduating from Harvard, she moved to the White Earth Reservation in Minnesota, where she became involved in a lawsuit to recover lands originally held by the Anishinabe people and taken illegally by the federal government. Disappointed with the court's inability to resolve the lawsuit, she founded the White Earth Land Recovery Project in order to raise funds to purchase original White Earth land holdings.

LaDuke has been the recipient of numerous awards and honors. In 1989, she received the International Reebok Human Rights Award, and in 1994, she was named by *Time* magazine as one of America's fifty most promising leaders under forty years of age. She serves as the board cochair for the Indigenous Women's Network and works in a national capacity as program director for Honor the Earth Fund, providing vision and leadership for the organization's Regranting Program and its strategic initiatives. She is the author of several books, including *All Our Relations: Native Struggles for Land and Life* (1999) and *Last Standing Woman* (1997). She teaches courses on native environmentalism at the University of Minnesota.

Carey McWilliams (1905–1980)

Carey McWilliams, a self-styled American radical, was a prolific writer on such issues as farm labor, water rights, immigration, and racial prejudice. He was an advocate for workers' rights and a critic of interests that sought to curtail workers' quality of life. For example, as a lawyer in the 1930s, he defended Hollywood studio workers who were struggling to save their union from the mob. He was editor of *The Nation* for more than twenty years. He was selected as one of the "30 at 30" in the November 1999 *California Journal*, which profiled thirty people who influenced California politics and government, selected to commemorate the *California Journal*'s thirtieth anniversary.

McWilliams is regarded as a pioneer in the study of minority-group relations, particularly in California. His book *Factories in the Field* (1939) is regarded as a pathbreaking work on the oppressive working conditions experienced by agricultural field-workers in California. McWilliams starts with the scandals of the Spanish land-grant purchases and continues on to examine the experience of the various ethnic groups that have provided labor for California's agricultural industry—Chinese, Japanese, Mexicans, Filipinos, Armenians—the strikes, and the efforts to organize labor unions. In *Prejudice* (1944), he examined the roots of intolerance toward Japanese Americans, and in *North from Mexico* (1949), he examined the role of Mexican immigration in shaping Californian society.

Richard Rodriguez

Richard Rodriguez was born in San Francisco, California, the third of four children. When his older brother developed asthma, the family decided to follow their doctor's advice to move to a drier climate and moved to Sacramento, California. Rodriguez has captured the experiences that shaped his literary interests and perspectives on social issues in two autobiographical books, *Hunger of Memory* (1982) and *Days of Obligation* (1992). He is regarded as a controversial critic of affirmative action, often arguing that affirmative action requires that a person regard him- or herself as disadvantaged.

Mary Romero

Mary Romero is professor of justice studies at Arizona State University. She earned a B.A. degree in sociology (with a Spanish minor) at Regis College (Denver, Colorado) in 1974 and a Ph.D. in sociology from the University of Colorado in 1980. Her research and publication interests are in the areas of social inequality, race and ethnic relations, Latino/Latina critical theory, and Chicanas in U.S. society. She has published numerous articles in professional journals and has written or edited several books, including *Challenging Fronteras: Structuring Latina and Latino Lives in the U.S.* (coedited with Pierrette Hondagneu-Sotelo and Vilma Ortiz; 1997), *Community Empowerment and Chicano Scholarship* (coedited with Cordelia Candelaria; 1992), *Latino/a Popular Culture* (coedited with Michelle Habell-Pallan; 2002), *Maid in the U.S.A.* (1992), *Women and Work: Exploring Race, Ethnicity, and Class* (coedited with Elizabeth Higginbotham; 1997), and *Women's Untold Stories: Breaking Silence, Talking Back, Voicing Complexity* (coedited with Abigail J. Stewart; 1999).

Julian Samora (1920–1996)

Julian Samora was born in Pagosa Springs, Colorado. He received his undergraduate degree in 1942 from Adams State College in Colorado and a master's degree from Colorado State University in 1947. In 1953, he became the first Mexican American to earn a Ph.D. in sociology and anthropology from Washington University in Saint Louis, Missouri. The title of his doctoral dissertation was "Minority Leadership in a Bi-Cultural Community." The discrimination Samora encountered throughout much of his early life played a crucial role in his determination to advance the cause of Hispanics and all minorities in U.S. society, especially in his scholarly pursuits.

Samora had a long and distinguished academic career. He began his academic career at the University of Colorado School of Medicine. From there, he moved to Michigan State University, arriving on the campus of Notre Dame University in 1959. Samora spent twenty-five years at Notre Dame. During his tenure at Notre Dame, he served as head of the Sociology and Anthropology Department, he founded and directed the Mexican American Graduate Studies Program, and he served as director of graduate studies. He also served as visiting professor at the University of New Mexico (1954), Michigan State University (1955), Universidad Nacional de Colombia in Bogota (1963), University of California–Los Angeles (1964), and the University of Texas–Austin (1971).

Samora's most significant publications—which carved a niche for him in the study of minorities in U.S. society—were *Gunpowder Justice: A Reassessment of the Texas Rangers* (with Joe Bernal and Albert Pena; 1979), *A History of the Mexican American People* (with Patricia Vande Simon; 1977; revised in 1993 with Cordelia Chavez Candelaria and Alberto Pulido), *La Raza: Forgotten Americans* (1966), *Los Mojados: The Wetback Story* (1971), *Mexican Americans in a Midwest Metropolis: A Study of East Chicago* (with Richard A. Lamanna; 1967), and *Mexican Americans in the Southwest* (with Ernesto Galarza and Herman Gallegos; 1969).

In addition to his scholarly work, Samora was a member of numerous commissions and agencies dealing with public policy: the President's Commission on Rural Poverty; the President's Commission on Income Maintenance Programs, National Upward Bound, the Indiana Civil Rights Commission, the Mexican American Legal Defense and Educational Fund, and the National

Assessment of Education Progress. He served as a consultant to government agencies and foundations, such as the U.S. Commission on Civil Rights, the U.S. Public Health Service, the Rosenburg Foundations, the Ford Foundation, the John Hay Whitney Foundation, the National Endowment for the Humanities, the National Institutes for Mental Health, the U.S. Bureau of the Census, the National Science Foundation, the W. K. Kellogg Foundation, and the Smithsonian Institution.

Samora's prominence as a scholar is evidenced by the numerous awards and honors he received. Among them were a John Hay Whitney Foundation Fellowship, a Sydney Spivack Fellowship, the La Raza Award from the National Council of La Raza, and an honorary doctor of laws degree from Incarnate Word College in San Antonio, Texas. Upon his retirement from Notre Dame in 1985, he received a Special Presidential Award from the university and the White House Hispanic Heritage Award. In 1987, he was appointed Martin Luther King–Rosa Parks Visiting Professor at the University of Michigan. In 1988, Michigan State University created the Julian Samora Research Institute in his honor to continue and expand research into the Chicano experience in the Midwest. In a ceremony in Mexico City in 1990, the Mexican government awarded him its highest civilian award for nonresidents, the Aguila Azteca Medal.

Julian Samora is regarded by many scholars as a pioneer in studies of folk medicine and the role of ethnicity in the understanding of sickness and health. Samora's work for the Ford Foundation on population and fertility in the Third World is regarded as being on the cutting edge of scholarship. His studies of immigration and the U.S.-Mexican border are considered blueprints for conducting research on the Mexican-origin population in the United States. Throughout his work, Samora stressed the importance of social science research in changing policies and conditions that affected the disadvantaged in society.

George I. Sanchez (1906–1972)

George Isidore Sanchez was an educator, historian, and author in the United States, Mexico, Peru, and Venezuela. He devoted fifty years of his life to the education of Mexican, Navajo, and black children and is known as the father of the movement for quality education for Mexican-Americans. He was born in Albuquerque, New Mexico. He earned a bachelor's degree in education and

Spanish from the University of New Mexico, an M.S. in educational psychology and Spanish in 1931 from the University of Texas, and an Ed.D. degree in 1934 from the University of California–Berkeley. His master's thesis at the University of Texas was one of the earliest studies to question the use of standardized tests for Spanish-speaking children.

From 1931 to 1935, he directed the Division of Information and Statistics for the New Mexico State Department of Education. In 1935–1936, he conducted a field study of rural education in Mexico that resulted in a book, *Mexico: A Revolution by Education* (1936). In 1937–1938, he was in the Venezuelan Ministry of Education and served as the director of the Instituto Pedagógica Nacional, a normal school. From 1938 to 1940, he taught at the University of New Mexico and directed a Carnegie Foundation survey of Taos County that resulted in his book *Forgotten People: A Study of New Mexicans* (1940). In 1940, he accepted a position as professor of Latin American Studies at the University of Texas. In the same year, he accepted the office of president-elect of the League of United Latin American Citizens.

Sanchez served in numerous organizations. He was a member of the editorial board of *The Nation's Schools;* he served as a consultant to the U.S. Bureau of Indian Affairs, the National Manpower Council, the U.S. Office of Education, the Navajo Tribal Council, and the U.S. Department of the Interior; he was a member of John F. Kennedy's Committee of Fifty on New Frontier Policy in the Americas and of the National Advisory Committee for the Peace Corps; he served on the boards of the Migrant Children's Fund and the National Council on Agricultural Life and Labor; and he belonged to numerous civic organizations, including the American Civil Liberties Union, League of United Latin American Citizens, the American G.I. Forum, and the Mexican American Legal Defense and Educational Fund. He also founded the American Council of Spanish Speaking People as a means of funding civil rights lawsuits involving Mexican Americans.

Sanchez was the recipient of numerous awards and honors. The U.S. Office of Education named a work section for him in 1978. In recognition of his efforts in challenging laws that victimized Mexican Americans, he was honored with a retrospective in 1984 at the University of California–Berkeley School of Law. The Foundation Advisory Council of the College of Education at the University of Texas–Austin endowed the George I. Sanchez Centennial Professorship in Liberal Arts through the College of Education in 1984. The endowed chair was the first such honor accorded a Mexican American professor in the United States. In 1985, a room in the U.S. Office of Education Building was named after Sanchez.

Ronald Takaki (1939–)

Ronald Takaki is a pioneer in the study of multiculturalism in U.S. society. During the 1960s, there was a growing demand for the development of ethnic-studies programs at universities across the United States. Takaki describes his involvement with ethnic studies thus:

> I was a student . . . at Berkeley in the 1960s and I was inspired by the moral vision of Martin Luther King and I participated in the free speech movement of 1964, which essentially was a movement for civil rights. I graduated from Berkeley in 1967 with a Ph.D. in history and I went to UCLA to teach the first black history course. While I was teaching there, I looked at the faces of the students in my class and I saw not only the faces of American students, whose ancestry went back to Europe and Africa, but also Asian American and Mexican American students. I thought it would be important to rethink race in our history and to offer a comparative course on racial inequality that includes the histories of Asian Americans and Mexican Americans. That was in the late '60s. I joined the Berkeley faculty in 1972, almost 28 years now, and I brought that course with me to Berkeley. It was called "Racial Inequality in America: A Comparative Perspective." That course has become, at Berkeley, Ethnic Studies 130, which forms a basis for the ethnic studies undergraduate major and also the ethnic studies Ph.D. program. (*AsianWeek* 2000)

Ron Takaki was one of the first scholars to put together a curriculum focused on race, ethnicity, multiculturalism, and diversity. In the fall of 1967, Takaki offered the first African American history course at UCLA. He became very involved in the organization of the Black Students Union on the UCLA campus and acted as the group's faculty adviser. He was also involved with Chicano and Asian American student affairs on campus. After two years at UCLA, he developed a groundbreaking course entitled "The History of Racial Inequality." His involvement in creating a multicultural curriculum and promoting minority student organizations may have contributed to his not being granted tenure on the UCLA campus. According to Takaki, "I became involved in an intense, bitter controversy with the senior faculty and to this day, I believe I was not granted tenure due to political reasons" (*AsianWeek* 2000).

Takaki left UCLA to return to his alma mater, the University of California–Berkeley, where he remains today as a professor of ethnic studies. Over the years, he has traveled extensively to share his work and views. He has appeared on numerous television shows, such as NBC's *Today Show*, ABC's *Good Morning America*, and PBS's *News Hour with Jim Lehrer*. He has written twenty books on such topics as the immigration and adaptation of Asian peoples into American culture and the multicultural history of the United States. His books addressing the study of diversity in the United States include *A Different Mirror: A History of Multicultural America* (1993), *Double Victory: A Multicultural History of America in World War II* (2000), and *Iron Cages: Race and Culture in Nineteenth-Century America* (1979).

Frank H. Wu (1967–)

Frank Wu is a leading legal scholar and advocate for affirmative action, the rights of immigrants in the United States, and Asian American civil rights. He received his undergraduate degree in writing from Johns Hopkins University in 1988 and his law degree from the University of Michigan in 1991. After law school, Wu held a clerkship with the late U.S. district court judge Frank J. Battisti in Cleveland, Ohio. Wu then joined a civil litigation practice group in San Francisco, where he worked on class actions and commercial disputes, and he devoted a quarter of his time to representing indigent individuals. He also worked as a campaign organizer with Californians United against Prop. 187, a coalition movement that responded to an anti-immigrant ballot referendum in the 1994 California election. He served as a teaching fellow at Stanford University's Law School during the 1994–1995 academic year. Wu joined the faculty of the Howard University School of Law, in Washington, D.C., in 1995. He teaches in the clinical program—courses such as civil procedure and federal courts—and he supervises students who appear in the D.C. Superior Court.

Wu has testified before the U.S. House of Representatives Judiciary Committee against legislation that would abolish affirmative action. He has appeared as a witness before the U.S. Commission on Civil Rights. In 1997, he was counsel of record on an amicus brief ("friend of the court" brief) on behalf of Asian American community groups in the Proposition 209 (California) litigation before the U.S. Court of Appeals. He delivered the 1998 James A. Thomas Lecture at Yale University Law School. Professor Wu has appeared on the *Oprah Winfrey Show,* MS-NBC, Fox Cable, BBC Radio, and NPR. His televised debate against Dinesh D'Souza on affirmative action, held at Brown University in October 1997, attracted attention nationwide (C-SPAN, *American Perspectives*). He has been a guest host of the PBS-syndicated television show *Asian America.* He was named one of fifteen "Up and Coming" scholars by *Black Issues in Higher Education* in 1999.

Wu's commentaries on such topics as affirmative action, Asian American issues, and immigrant rights have appeared in the *Washington Post*, the *Los Angeles Times*, the *Chicago Tribune*, the *Toronto Star*, the *Atlanta Journal and Constitution*, the *Chronicle of Higher Education*, *The National Law Journal*, *Legal Times*, *The Nation* and *Progressive Magazine*. He writes a column in *A. Magazine,* the largest Asian American interest periodical in the United States. In addition to his articles in the law reviews, he is author of the books *Race, Rights, and Reparation: Law and the Japanese American Internment* (with Eric Yamamoto, Margaret Chon, Carol Izumi, and Jerry Kang; 2001) and *Yellow: Race in America beyond Black and White* (2002).

References

AsianWeek. 2000. "Interview." Available at http://www.asianweek.com/2000 10-12/feature.html.

Bell, Derrick A., Jr. 1987. *And We Are Not Saved: The Elusive Quest for Racial Justice.* New York: Basic Books.

———. 1992. *Faces at the Bottom of the Well: The Permanence of Racism.* New York: Basic Books.

———. 1994. *Confronting Authority: Reflections of an Ardent Protester.* Boston: Beacon Press.

———. 1996. *Gospel Choirs: Psalms of Survival in an Alien Land Called Home.* New York: Basic Books.

————. 1998. *Afrolantica Legacies*. Chicago: Third World Press.

————. 2000. *Race, Racism, and American Law*. 4th ed. New York: Aspen.

Delgado, Richard. 1995. *The Rodrigo Chronicles*. New York: New York University Press.

————. 1996. *The Coming Race War*. New York: New York University Press.

Deloria, Vine, Jr. 1969. *Custer Died for Your Sins*. New York: Macmillan.

————. 1970. *We Talk, You Listen: New Tribes, New Turf*. New York: Macmillan.

————. 1974. *Behind the Trail of Broken Treaties: An Indian Declaration of Independence*. New York: Dell.

————. 1979. *The Metaphysics of Modern Existence*. New York: Harper and Row.

————. 1985. *American Indian Policy in the Twentieth Century*. Norman: University of Oklahoma Press.

————. 1994. *God Is Red: A Native View of Religion*. Golden, CO: North American Press.

————. 1995. *Red Earth, White Lies: Native Americans and the Myth of Scientific Fact*. New York: Scribner.

Deloria, Vine, Jr., and Clifford M. Lytle. 1983. *American Indians, American Justice*. Austin: University of Texas Press.

————. 1984. *The Nations Within: The Past and Future of American Indian Sovereignty*. New York: Pantheon Books, 1984.

Feagin, Joe R. 1998. *The New Urban Paradigm*. Lanham, MD: Rowman and Littlefield.

Feagin, Joe R., and Clairece Booher Feagin. 1999. *Racial and Ethnic Relations*. 6th ed. Upper Saddle River, NJ: Prentice-Hall.

Feagin, Joe R., and Harlan Hahn. 1973. *Ghetto Revolts*. New York: Macmillan.

Feagin, Joe R., and Mel Sikes. 1994. *Living with Racism: The Black Middle Class Experience*. Boston: Beacon.

Feagin, Joe R., and Yanick St. Jean. 1998. *Double Burden: Black Women and Everyday Racism*. New York: M. E. Sharpe.

Feagin, Joe R., and Hernan Vera. 1995. *White Racism: The Basics*. New York: Routledge.

Feagin, Joe R., Hernan Vera, and Nikitah Imani. 1996. *The Agony of Education: Black Students at White Colleges and Universities.* New York: Routledge.

Galarza, Ernesto. 1970. *Spiders in the House and Workers in the Field.* South Bend, IN: Notre Dame University Press.

———. 1971. *Barrio Boy.* Notre Dame, IN: Notre Dame University Press.

———. 1977. *Farmworkers and Agribusiness in California, 1947–1960.* Notre Dame, IN: Notre Dame University Press.

Galarza, Ernesto, Herman Gallegos, and Julian Samora. 1969. *Mexican Americans in the Southwest.* Santa Barbara, CA: McNally and Lofton.

hooks, bell. 1981. *Ain't I a Woman: Black Women and Feminism.* Boston, MA: South End Press.

———. 1984. *Feminist Theory from Margin to Center.* Boston, MA: South End Press.

———. 1990. *Yearning: Race, Gender, and Cultural Politics.* Boston, MA: South End Press.

———. 1992. *Black Looks: Race and Representation.* Boston, MA: South End Press.

———. 1996. *Reel to Real: Race, Sex, and Class at the Movies.* New York: Routledge.

———. 1999. *Remembered Rapture: The Writer at Work.* New York: Henry Holt.

LaDuke, Winona. 1997. *Last Standing Woman.* Stillwater, MN: Voyager Press.

———. 1999. *All Our Relations: Native Struggles for Land and Life.* Minneapolis, MN: Honor the Earth.

McWilliams, Carey. 1939. *Factories in the Field.* New York: Little, Brown.

———. 1944. *Prejudice.* New York: Little, Brown.

———. 1949. *North from Mexico: The Spanish-Speaking People of the United States.* Philadelphia, PA: Lippincott.

Rodriguez, Richard. 1982. *Hunger of Memory.* Boston, MA: Godine.

———. 1992. *Days of Obligation.* New York: Viking.

Romero, Mary. 1992. *Maid in the U.S.A.* New York: Routledge.

Romero, Mary, and Cordelia Candelaria, eds. 1992. *Community Empowerment and Chicano Scholarship.* Houston, TX: National Association for Chicano Studies.

Romero, Mary, and Michelle Habell-Pallan, eds. 2002. *Latino/a Popular Culture.* New York: New York University Press.

Romero, Mary, and Elizabeth Higginbotham, eds. 1997. *Women and Work: Exploring Race, Ethnicity, and Class.* Thousand Oaks, CA: Sage.

Romero, Mary, Pierrette Hondagneu-Sotelo, and Vilma Ortiz, eds. 1997. *Challenging Fronteras: Structuring Latina and Latino Lives in the U.S.* New York: Routledge.

Romero, Mary, and Abigail J. Stewart, eds. 1999. *Women's Untold Stories: Breaking Silence, Talking Back, Voicing Complexity.* New York: Routledge.

Samora, Julian. 1966. *La Raza: Forgotten Americans.* Notre Dame, IN: Notre Dame University Press.

———. 1971. *Los Mojados: The Wetback Story.* South Bend, IN: Notre Dame University Press.

Samora, Julian, and Patricia Vandel Simon, with Cordelia Chavez Candelaria and Alberto Pulido. 1993. Rev. ed. *A History of the Mexican American People.* South Bend, IN: Notre Dame University Press.

Samora, Julian, and Richard A. Lamanna. 1967. *Mexican Americans in a Midwest Metropolis: A Study of East Chicago.* Advance Report 8. Los Angeles: University of California–Los Angeles Mexican American Study Project.

Samora, Julian, Joe Bernal, and Albert Pena. 1979. *Gunpowder Justice: A Reassessment of the Texas Rangers.* South Bend, IN: Notre Dame University Press.

Sanchez, George I. 1936. *Mexico: A Revolution by Education.* New York: Viking.

———. 1940. *Forgotten People: A Study of New Mexicans.* Albuquerque: University of New Mexico Press.

Takaki, Ronald. 1979. *Iron Cages: Race and Culture in Nineteenth-Century America.* New York: Knopf.

———. 1993. *A Different Mirror: A History of Multicultural America.* Boston: Little, Brown.

———. 2000. *Double Victory: A Multicultural History of America in World War II.* Boston: Little, Brown.

Wu, Frank H. 2002. *Yellow: Race in America beyond Black and White.* New York: BasicBooks.

Wu, Frank H., Eric Yamamoto, Margaret Chon, Carol Izumi, and Jerry Kang. 2001. *Race, Rights, and Reparation: Law and the Japanese American Internment.* New York: Aspen.

6

Statistics, Laws, and Quotations

The statistical data in this chapter on racial and ethnic populations in the United States supplements the data discussed in Chapters 1–3. This chapter also contains a section of quotations focused on the topics of diversity and pluralism. The quotations illustrate the centrality of diversity in the viewpoints of historical and contemporary writers, thinkers, and activists.

Statistics

Diverse U.S. Populations by State

According to the 2000 Census, approximately 30 percent of the United States population is nonwhite (see Chapter 2 for census figures). Between 1990 and 2000, racial and ethnic minority populations increased their numbers in almost all of the 50 states. To illustrate the spread of diversity in the United States between 1990 and 2000 I have summarized census data for states experiencing an increase in their racial and ethnic minority populations during the 1990s. The interested reader may review the state-by-state census data by accessing the U.S. Bureau of the Census Web site on the Internet.

Highlights of details from the 2000 U.S. Census for states, including the District of Columbia, that experienced changes in their racial and ethnic populations are summarized here:

Alabama: The state's population grew 10 percent during the 1990s to 4,447,100. The Hispanic population grew by 208 percent to 75,830 and the Asian/Pacific Islander population increased 49 percent to 31,346.

Arizona: The state's population surged by 40 percent during the 1990s to 5,130,632. The Hispanic population increased 88 percent to 1,280,908 during the 1990s, resulting in Hispanics accounting for one in every four of the state's residents.

Arkansas: The state's population grew 14 percent during the 1990s to 2,673,400. The state's Hispanic population increased 337 percent to 86,866.

California: The state's population grew 14 percent during the 1990s to 33,871,648. The state's Hispanic population increased 43 percent to 10,966,556, resulting in Hispanics comprising one-third of California's population. The American Indian/Alaska Native population increased 38 percent to 333,346; the Asian/Pacific Islander population increased 30 percent to 3,697,513; and the African American population increased 2 percent to 2,263,882.

Colorado: The state's population increased 31 percent to 4,311,882 during the 1990s. The Hispanic population grew 73 percent to 735,601 and the Asian/Pacific Islander population increased 68 percent to 95,213.

Connecticut: The state population grew 4 percent during the 1990s to 3,405,565. The state's Hispanic population increased 50 percent to 320,323.

Delaware: The state's population grew 18 percent to 783,600 during the 1990s. The state's Hispanic population increased 136 percent to 37,277 and the African American population increased 34 percent to 150,666.

District of Columbia: The population decreased 6 percent during the 1990s to 572,059. The African American population decreased 12 percent to 343,312; the Asian/Pacific Islander population increased 66 percent to 15,189; and the Hispanic population increased 37 percent to 44,953.

Florida: The state's population increased 24 percent to 15,982,378 during the 1990s. The Hispanic population increased 70 percent to 2,682,715 or 16.8 percent of the state's population.

Georgia: The state's population increased 26 percent during the 1990s to 8,186,453. The state's Hispanic population increased 300 percent to 435,000.

Idaho: The state's population grew by 29 percent to 1,293,953 during the 1990s. The Hispanic population increased 50 percent to 101,690.

Illinois: The state's population grew 9 percent during the 1990s to 12,419,293. The number of Hispanics increased 70 percent to 1,530,262, making Hispanics 12.3 percent of the state's population.

Indiana: The state's population grew 10 percent during the 1990s to 6,080,485. The state's Hispanic population increased 117 percent to 214,536.

Iowa: The state's population grew 5 percent during the 1990s to 2,926,324. The Hispanic population increased 153 percent to 82,473.

Kansas: The state's population grew 9 percent during the 1990s to 2,688,418. The Hispanic population increased 51 percent to 188,252.

Massachusetts: The state's population grew 6 percent during the 1990s to 6,349,097. The state's Asian/Pacific Islander population increased 68 percent to 238,124 and the number of Hispanics increased 49 percent to 428,729.

Minnesota: The state's population grew 12 percent during the 1990s to 4,919,479. The Hispanic population increased 166 percent to 143,382.

Mississippi: The state's population grew 11 percent during the 1990s to 2,844,658. The Hispanic population increased 148 percent to 39,569.

Missouri: The state's population during the 1990s grew by 9 percent to 5,595,211. The Hispanic population increased 92 percent to 118,592.

Nebraska: The state's population grew 8 percent during the 1990s to 1,711,263. The Hispanic population increased 155 percent to 94,425.

Nevada: The state's population grew by 66 percent during the 1990s to 1,998,257. The state's Hispanic population increased 217 percent to 393,970.

New Hampshire: The state's population grew 11 percent during the 1990s to 1,235,786. The Hispanic population grew by 81 percent to 20,489; the Asian/Pacific Islander population grew by 74 percent to 15,931.

New Jersey: The state's population grew 9 percent during the 1990s to 8,414,350. The state's Asian/Pacific Islander population increased 77 percent to 480,276 and the Hispanic population grew by 51 percent to 1,117,191.

New Mexico: The state's population grew 20 percent during

the 1990s to 1,819,046. The Hispanic population increased from 38 percent (592,224) in 1990 to 42 percent (765,386) in 2000 of the state's population.

New York: The state's population grew 6 percent during the 1990s to 18,976,457. The Asian/Pacific Islander population increased 70 percent to 1,169,200; the Hispanic population grew by 30 percent to 2,867,583; and the African American population grew 13 percent to 3,234,165.

North Carolina: The state's population grew 21 percent during the 1990s to 8,049,313. The Hispanic population grew by 394 percent to 378,963, and the African American population increased 19 percent to 1,737,545.

Ohio: The state's population grew 5 percent during the 1990s to 11,353,140. The Hispanic population grew by 55 percent to 217,123 and the Asian/Pacific Islander population increased 49 percent to 132,633.

Oklahoma: The state's population grew 10 percent during the 1990s to 3,450,654. The state's Hispanic population increased 108 percent to 179,304 and the Asian/Pacific Islander population grew by 46 percent to 46,767.

Oregon: The state's population increased 20 percent during the 1990s to 3,421,399. The Hispanic population increased 144 percent to 275,314 and the Asian/Pacific Islander population grew by 58 percent to 101,350.

Pennsylvania: The state's population grew 3 percent during the 1990s to 12,281,054. The state's Hispanic population grew by 70 percent to 394,088 and the Asian/Pacific Islander population increased 62 percent to 219,813.

Rhode Island: The state's population grew 5 percent during the 1990s to 1,048,319. The state's Hispanic population increased 99 percent to 90,820.

South Carolina: The state's population grew 15 percent during the 1990s to 4,012,012. The state's Hispanic population increased 211 percent to 95,076 and the Asian/Pacific Islander population increased 68 percent to 36,014.

South Dakota: The state's population grew 9 percent during the 1990s to 754,844. The state's Hispanic population grew by 108 percent to 10,903; the Asian/Pacific Islander population increased 49 percent to 4,378; and the African American population increased 44 percent to 4,685.

Tennessee: The state's population grew by 17 percent during the 1990s to 5,689,283. The Hispanic population increased 278 percent to 123,838 and the Asian/Pacific Islander population increased 83 percent to 56,662.

Texas: The state's population increased 23 percent during the 1990s to 20,851,820. The Hispanic population increased 54 percent to 6,669,666 and the Asian/Pacific Islander population increased 80 percent to 562,319.

Utah: The state's population grew by 30 percent during the 1990s to 2,233,169. The Hispanic population increased 138 percent to 201,559; the African American population grew by 53 percent to 17,657; and the Asian/Pacific Islander population increased 44 percent to 37,108.

Vermont: The state's population grew by 8 percent during the 1990s to 608,827. The Asian/Pacific Islander population increased 66 percent to 5,217; the African American population increased 57 percent to 3,063; and the Hispanic population grew by 50 percent to 5,504.

Virginia: The state's population grew 14 percent during the 1990s to 7,078,515. The Hispanic population increased 106 percent to 329,540 and the Asian/Pacific Islander population grew by 67 percent to 261,025.

Washington: The state's population grew 21 percent during the 1990s to 5,894,121. The Hispanic population increased 106 percent to 441,509 and the Asian/Pacific Islander population grew 65 percent to 322,335.

West Virginia: The state's population grew 0.8 percent during the 1990s to 1,808,344. The Hispanic population increased 45 percent to 12,279 and the Asian/Pacific Islander population grew by 30 percent to 9,434.

Wisconsin: The state's population grew 10 percent during the 1990s to 5,363,675. The Hispanic population increased 107 percent to 192,921 and the Asian/Pacific Islander population grew by 68 percent to 88,763.

Table 6.1
Occupational Employment in Private Industry by Race/Ethnic Group/Sex, and by Industry, United States, 2000

ALL INDUSTRIES (197,072 UNITS)

NUMBER EMPLOYED

Race/Ethnic Group/Sex	Total Employment	Officials & Managers	Professionals	Technicians	Sales Workers	Office & Clerical Workers	Craft Workers	Operatives	Laborers	Service Workers
ALL EMPLOYEES	43,995,543	4,721,056	7,011,359	2,670,846	5,357,927	6,271,610	3,492,410	6,030,763	3,449,195	4,990,377
MALE	23,272,569	3,124,974	3,423,726	1,477,351	2,333,475	1,236,197	3,041,845	4,271,365	2,232,870	2,130,766
FEMALE	20,722,974	1,596,082	3,587,633	1,193,495	3,024,452	5,035,413	450,565	1,759,398	1,216,325	2,859,611
WHITE	31,141,848	4,041,205	5,678,392	2,021,657	3,920,011	4,377,333	2,702,541	3,898,351	1,811,664	2,690,694
MALE	16,716,131	2,716,179	2,808,560	1,139,903	1,765,889	812,237	2,387,962	2,844,823	1,170,177	1,070,401
FEMALE	14,425,717	1,325,026	2,869,832	881,754	2,154,122	3,565,096	314,579	1,053,528	641,487	1,620,293
MINORITY	12,853,695	679,851	1,332,967	649,189	1,437,916	1,894,277	789,869	2,132,412	1,637,531	2,299,683
MALE	6,556,438	408,795	615,166	337,448	567,586	423,960	653,883	1,426,542	1,062,693	1,060,365
FEMALE	6,297,257	271,056	717,801	311,741	870,330	1,470,317	135,986	705,870	574,838	1,239,318
BLACK	6,177,400	303,145	477,735	306,826	747,955	1,070,196	344,957	1,046,174	672,535	1,207,877
MALE	2,816,081	163,569	167,485	129,608	271,402	206,748	276,939	682,486	429,368	488,476
FEMALE	3,361,319	139,576	310,250	177,218	476,553	863,448	68,018	363,688	243,167	719,401
HISPANIC	4,547,834	210,861	263,167	174,431	491,408	564,392	338,706	812,366	824,329	868,174
MALE	2,629,151	137,389	130,338	107,483	211,513	143,298	293,637	583,557	553,170	468,766
FEMALE	1,918,683	73,472	132,829	66,948	279,895	421,094	45,069	228,809	271,159	399,408
ASIAN/PACIFIC ISLANDER	1,873,998	147,846	565,665	152,127	163,805	225,186	82,062	232,360	115,013	189,934
MALE	977,226	96,246	304,351	91,517	71,406	66,200	62,343	132,941	63,479	88,743
FEMALE	896,772	51,600	261,314	60,610	92,399	158,986	19,719	99,419	51,534	101,191

AM IND/ALASKAN

NATIVE	254,463	17,999	26,400	15,805	34,748	34,503	24,144	41,512	25,654	33,698
MALE	133,980	11,591	12,992	8,840	13,265	7,714	20,964	27,558	16,676	14,380
FEMALE	120,483	6,408	13,408	6,965	21,483	26,789	3,180	13,954	8,978	19,318

PARTICIPATION RATE

ALL EMPLOYEES	100.0	100.0	100.0	100.0	100.0	100.0	100.0	100.0	100.0	100.0
MALE	52.9	66.2	48.8	55.3	43.6	19.7	87.1	70.8	64.7	42.7
FEMALE	47.1	33.8	51.2	44.7	56.4	80.3	12.9	29.2	35.3	57.3
WHITE	70.8	85.6	81.0	75.7	73.2	69.8	77.4	64.6	52.5	53.9
MALE	38.0	57.5	40.1	42.7	33.0	13.0	68.4	47.2	33.9	21.4
FEMALE	32.8	28.1	40.9	33.0	40.2	56.8	9.0	17.5	18.6	32.5
MINORITY	29.2	14.4	19.0	24.3	26.8	30.2	22.6	35.4	47.5	46.1
MALE	14.9	8.7	8.8	12.6	10.6	6.8	18.7	23.7	30.8	21.2
FEMALE	14.3	5.7	10.2	11.7	16.2	23.4	3.9	11.7	16.7	24.8
BLACK	14.0	6.4	6.8	11.5	14.0	17.1	9.9	17.3	19.5	24.2
MALE	6.4	3.5	2.4	4.9	5.1	3.3	7.9	11.3	12.4	9.8
FEMALE	7.6	3.0	4.4	6.6	8.9	13.8	1.9	6.0	7.0	14.4
HISPANIC	10.3	4.5	3.8	6.5	9.2	9.0	9.7	13.5	23.9	17.4
MALE	6.0	2.9	1.9	4.0	3.9	2.3	8.4	9.7	16.0	9.4
FEMALE	4.4	1.6	1.9	2.5	5.2	6.7	1.3	3.8	7.9	8.0
ASIAN/PACIFIC ISLANDER	4.3	3.1	8.1	5.7	3.1	3.6	2.3	3.9	3.3	3.8
MALE	2.2	2.0	4.3	3.4	1.3	1.1	1.8	2.2	1.8	1.8
FEMALE	2.0	1.1	3.7	2.3	1.7	2.5	0.6	1.6	1.5	2.0
AM IND/ALASKAN NATIVE	0.6	0.4	0.4	0.6	0.6	0.6	0.7	0.7	0.7	0.7
MALE	0.3	0.2	0.2	0.3	0.2	0.1	0.6	0.5	0.5	0.3
FEMALE	0.3	0.1	0.2	0.3	0.4	0.4	0.1	0.2	0.3	0.4

Table 6.1, *continued*

ALL INDUSTRIES (197,072 UNITS)

OCCUPATIONAL DISTRIBUTION

Race/Ethnic Group/Sex	Total Employment	Officials & Managers	Professionals	Technicians	Sales Workers	Office & Clerical Workers	Craft Workers	Operatives	Laborers	Service Workers
ALL EMPLOYEES	100.0	10.7	15.9	6.1	12.2	14.3	7.9	13.7	7.8	11.3
MALE	100.0	13.4	14.7	6.3	10.0	5.3	13.1	18.4	9.6	9.2
FEMALE	100.0	7.7	17.3	5.8	14.6	24.3	2.2	8.5	5.9	13.8
WHITE	100.0	13.0	18.2	6.5	12.6	14.1	8.7	12.5	5.8	8.6
MALE	100.0	16.2	16.8	6.8	10.6	4.9	14.3	17.0	7.0	6.4
FEMALE	100.0	9.2	19.9	6.1	14.9	24.7	2.2	7.3	4.4	11.2
MINORITY	100.0	5.3	10.4	5.1	11.2	14.7	6.1	16.6	12.7	17.9
MALE	100.0	6.2	9.4	5.1	8.7	6.5	10.0	21.8	16.2	16.2
FEMALE	100.0	4.3	11.4	5.0	13.8	23.3	2.2	11.2	9.1	19.7
BLACK	100.0	4.9	7.7	5.0	12.1	17.3	5.6	16.9	10.9	19.6
MALE	100.0	5.8	5.9	4.6	9.6	7.3	9.8	24.2	15.2	17.3
FEMALE	100.0	4.2	9.2	5.3	14.2	25.7	2.0	10.8	7.2	21.4
HISPANIC	100.0	4.6	5.8	3.8	10.8	12.4	7.4	17.9	18.1	19.1
MALE	100.0	5.2	5.0	4.1	8.0	5.5	11.2	22.2	21.0	17.8
FEMALE	100.0	3.8	6.9	3.5	14.6	21.9	2.3	11.9	14.1	20.8
ASIAN/PACIFIC ISLANDER	100.0	7.9	30.2	8.1	8.7	12.0	4.4	12.4	6.1	10.1
MALE	100.0	9.8	31.1	9.4	7.3	6.8	6.4	13.6	6.5	9.1
FEMALE	100.0	5.8	29.1	6.8	10.3	17.7	2.2	11.1	5.7	11.3
AM IND/ALASKAN NATIVE	100.0	7.1	10.4	6.2	13.7	13.6	9.5	16.3	10.1	13.2
MALE	100.0	8.7	9.7	6.6	9.9	5.8	15.6	20.6	12.4	10.7
FEMALE	100.0	5.3	11.1	5.8	17.8	22.2	2.6	11.6	7.5	16.0

[1]Excludes Hawaii

Source: Equal Employment Opportunity Commission (www.eeoc.org)

Table 6.2
Region and Country or Area of Birth of the U.S. Foreign-Born Population: 1850–1900

	1850	1860	1870	1880	1890	1900
Total	2,244,062	4,138,697	5,567,229	6,697,943	9,249,547	10,341,276
Region and/or Country						
England	278,675	431,692	550,924	662,676	908,141	840,513
France	54,069	109,870	116,402	106,971	113,174	104,197
Germany	583,774	1,276,075	1,690,533	1,966,742	2,784,894	2,663,418
Ireland	961,519	1,611,304	1,855,827	1,854,571	1,871,509	1,615,459
Italy	3,679	11,677	17,157	44,230	182,580	484,027
Scandinavia	18,075	72,582	241,685	440,262	933,249	1,134,733
Scotland	70,550	108,518	140,835	170,136	242,231	233,524
Spain	3,113	4,244	3,764	5,121	6,185	7,050
Wales	29,868	45,763	74,533	83,302	100,079	93,586

Source: Campbell J. Gibson and Emily Lennon, *Historical Census Statistics on the Foreign-Born Population of the United States: 1850–1990* (Population Division Working Paper No.29), (Washington, DC: U.S. Bureau of the Census, 1999).

Table 6.3
Race and Ethnicity of the U.S. Population, 1850–1900

	White	Black	American Indian	Asian	Mexican[3]
1850	19,553,068	3,638,808[1]	NA	NA	13,317
1860	26,922,537	4,441,830[2]	44,021	34,933	27,466
1870	33,589,377	4,880,039	25,731	63,254	42,435
1880	43,402,970	6,580,793	66,417	105,613	68,399
1890	54,983,890	7,470,040	58,806	109,514	77,853
1900	66,809,196	8,833,994	237,196	114,189	103,393

[1]Free = 434,495, Slave = 3,204,313
[2]Free = 488,070, Slave = 3,953,760
[3]Reported as foreign-born

Source: Gibson, Campbell J., and Emily Lennon, *Historical Census Statistics on the Foreign-Born Population of the United States, 1850–1990* (Population Division Working Paper No. 29) Washington, DC: U.S. Bureau of the Census, 1999; Gibson, Campbell J., and Kay Jung, *Historical Census Statistics on Population Totals by Race, 1790 to 1990, and By Hispanic Origin, 1970 to 1990, for the United States, Regions, Divisions and States* (Population Division Working Paper No. 56), Washington, DC: U.S. Bureau of the Census, 2002.

Table 6.4
Foreign-Born and Native U.S. Population by Region, 1850–1900

Year		Northeast	Midwest	South	West
1850	Native	7,301,308	4,753,220	8,740,947	151,799
	Foreign-born	1,325,543	650,375	241,665	27,019
1860	Native	8,570,363	7,553,358	10,740,929	439,974
	Foreign-born	2,023,905	1,543,358	392,432	179,002
1870	Native	9,778,124	10,647,826	11,888,045	677,147
	Foreign-born	2,520,606	2,333,285	399,975	313,363
1880	Native	11,692,887	14,447,282	16,068,036	1,267,635
	Foreign-born	2,814,520	2,916,829	448,532	500,062
1890	Native	13,513,368	18,302,165	19,300,467	2,256,703
	Foreign-born	3,888,177	4,060,114	530,346	770,910
1900	Native	16,283,899	22,174,530	23,949,842	3,245,028
	Foreign-born	4,762,796	4,158,474	573,685	846,321

Source: U.S. Bureau of the Census, Internet Release Date: March 9, 1999.

Table 6.5
Black Population, Free and Slave, in the United States, 1790–1860

		Free		Slave	
	Total	Number	Percent	Number	Percent
1790	757,208	59,527	7.9	697,681	92.1
1800	1,002,037	108,435	10.8	893,602	89.2
1810	1,377,808	186,446	13.5	1,191,362	86.5
1820	1,771,656	233,634	13.2	1,538,022	86.8
1830	2,328,642	319,599	13.7	2,009,043	86.3
1840	2,873,648	386,293	13.4	2,487,355	86.6
1850	3,638,808	434,495	11.9	3,204,313	88.1
1860	4,441,830	488,070	11.0	3,953,760	89.0

Source: Gibson, Campbell J., and Kay Jung, *Historical Census Statistics on Population Totals by Race, 1790 to 1990, and by Hispanic Origin, 1970 to 1990, for the United States, Regions, Divisions, and States* (Population Division Working Paper No. 56), Washington, DC: U.S. Bureau of the Census, 2002.

Table 6.6
U.S. Cities with Minorities as More Than Half of the Population in 2000

City	1990 % Minority	2000 % Minority	(1990–2000) % Increase
Albuquerque, NM	41.7	50.1	8.4
Anaheim, CA	43.4	64.1	20.7
Augusta-Richmond, GA	46.0	56.3	10.3
Baton Rouge, LA	47.1	55.3	8.2
Boston, MA	41.0	50.5	9.5
Columbus, GA	42.7	51.4	8.7
Fort Worth, TX	43.5	54.2	10.7
Mobile, AL	41.1	50.2	9.1
Montgomery, AL	43.9	52.9	9.0
Milwaukee, WI	39.2	54.6	15.4
Norfolk, VA	44.4	53.0	8.6
Philadelphia, PA	47.9	57.5	9.6
Riverside, CA	38.7	54.4	15.7
Rochester, NY	41.7	55.7	14.0
Sacramento, CA	46.6	59.5	12.9
San Diego, CA	41.3	50.6	9.3
Shreveport, LA	46.4	54.1	7.7

Source: U.S. Census Bureau (www.census.gov/AmericanFactFinder)

Table 6.7
Number of Persons Claiming Two or More Races: United States 2000

	Number	Percent of Two or More Race Population
Two or More Races	6,826,228	100.0
Two Races	6,368,075	93.3
Three Races	410,285	6.0
Four Races	38,408	0.6
Five Races	8,637	0.1
Six Races	823	–

Source: U.S. Census Bureau, Overview of Race and Hispanic Origin: Census 2000 Brief (March 2001).

Table 6.8
Number of Persons Claiming Two or More Races by Race and Hispanic Origin: United States 2000

	Number
White Population	
White Alone	211,460,626
White; American Indian and Alaska Native	1,082,683
White; Asian	868,395
White; Black or African American	784,764
White; Native Hawaiian or Other Pacific Islander	112,964
Black or African American Population	
Black or African American Alone	34,658,190
Black or African American; White	784,764
Black or African American; American Indian and Alaska Native	82,494
Black or African American; White; American Indian and Alaska Native	112,207
Black or African American; Asian	106,782
American Indian and Alaska Native Population	
American Indian and Alaska Native Alone	2,475,956
American Indian and Alaska Native; White	1,082,683
American Indian and Alaska Native; Black or African American	182,494
American Indian and Alaska Native; White; Black or African American	112,207
American Indian and Alaska Native; Asian	52,429
Asian Population	
Asian Alone	10,242,998
Asian; White	868,395
Asian; Native Hawaiian and Other Pacific Islander	138,802
Asian; Black or African American	106,782
Asian; Native Hawaiian and Other Pacific Islander; White	89,611
Native Hawaiian and Other Pacific Islander	
Native Hawaiian and Other Pacific Islander Alone	398,835
Native Hawaiian and Other Pacific Islander; Asian	138,802
Native Hawaiian and Other Pacific Islander; White	112,964
Native Hawaiian and Other Pacific Islander; Asian; White	89,611
Native Hawaiian and Other Pacific Islander; Black or African American	29,876

Source: U.S. Census Bureau, Overview of Race and Hispanic Origin: Census 2000 Brief (March 2001).

Table 6.9
Linguistic Diversity in the United States, 1980–2000

Chart I
Language Spoken at Home and Self-Reported English-Speaking Ability,
U.S. Residents, Age 5 and Older—1980, 1990, and 2000

	1980	%	1990	%	Change in 1980s	2000	%	Change in 1990s
All speakers, age 5+	210,247,455	100.0	230,445,777	100.0	+9.6%	262,375,152	100.0	+13.9%
English only	187,187,415	89.0	198,600,798	86.2	+6.1%	215,423,557	82.1	+8.5%
Language other than English	23,060,040	11.0	31,844,979	13.8	+38.1%	46,951,595	17.9	+47.4%
Speaks English								
very well	12,879,004	6.1	17,862,477	7.8	+38.7%	25,631,188	9.8	+43.5%
... well	5,957,544	2.8	7,310,301	3.2	+22.7%	10,333,556	3.9	+41.4%
... not well	3,005,503	1.4	4,826,958	2.1	+60.6%	7,620,719	2.9	+57.9%
... not at all	1,217,989	0.6	1,845,243	0.8	+51.5%	3,366,132	1.3	+82.4%
... with some "difficulty"*	10,181,036	4.8	13,982,502	6.1	+37.3%	21,320,407	8.1	+52.5%
Total U.S. population	226,545,805	100.0	248,709,873	100.0	+9.8%	281,421,906	100.0	+13.2%
Foreign-born	14,079,906	6.2	19,767,316	7.9	+40.4%	31,107,889	11.1	+57.4%

*Includes all persons who report speaking English less than "very well," the threshold for full proficiency in English, as determined by the U.S. Department of Education.
Source: UC Linguistic Minority Research Institute (www.lmri.edu)

Laws

USA PATRIOT Act

Official Title: To deter and punish terrorist acts in the United States and around the world, to enhance law enforcement investigatory tools, and for other purposes.

Short Title: USA PATRIOT Act (H.R. 3162)

Legislative Action: Became Public Law No: 107–56 (October 26, 2001)

Sponsor: Rep F. James Sensenbrenner, Jr. (WI)

The USA PATRIOT Act incorporated provisions of two earlier anti-terrorism bills: H.R. 2975, which passed the House on 10/12/2001, and S. 1510, which passed the Senate on 10/11/2001. Provisions of H.R. 3004, the Financial Anti-Terrorism Act, were incorporated as Title III in the USA PATRIOT Act. The key provisions of the USA PATRIOT Act are summarized in the following pages.

Title I: Enhancing Domestic Security Against Terrorism—Establishes in the Treasury the Counterterrorism Fund.

(Sec. 102) Expresses the sense of Congress that: (1) the civil rights and liberties of all Americans, including Arab Americans, must be protected, and that every effort must be taken to preserve their safety; (2) any acts of violence or discrimination against any Americans be condemned; and (3) the Nation is called upon to recognize the patriotism of fellow citizens from all ethnic, racial, and religious backgrounds.

(Sec. 103) Authorizes appropriations for the Federal Bureau of Investigation's (FBI) Technical Support Center.

(Sec. 104) Authorizes the Attorney General to request the Secretary of Defense to provide assistance in support of Department of Justice (DOJ) activities relating to the enforcement of Federal criminal code (code) provisions regarding the use of weapons of mass destruction during an emergency situation involving a weapon (currently, chemical weapon) of mass destruction.

(Sec. 105) Requires the Director of the U.S. Secret Service to take actions to develop a national network of electronic crime task forces throughout the United States to prevent, detect, and investigate various forms of electronic crimes, including potential terrorist attacks against critical infrastructure and financial payment systems.

(Sec. 106) Modifies provisions relating to presidential authority under the International Emergency Powers Act to: (1) authorize the President, when the United States is engaged in armed hostilities or has been attacked by a foreign country or foreign nationals, to confiscate any property subject to U.S. jurisdiction of a foreign person, organization, or country that he determines has planned, authorized, aided, or engaged in such hostilities or attacks (the rights to which shall vest in such agency or person as the President may designate); and (2) provide that, in any judicial review of a determination made under such provisions, if the determination was based on classified information such information may be submitted to the reviewing court ex parte and in camera.

Title II: Enhanced Surveillance Procedures—Amends the Federal criminal code to authorize the interception of wire, oral, and electronic communications for the production of evidence of: (1) specified chemical weapons or terrorism offenses; and (2) computer fraud and abuse.

(Sec. 203) Amends rule 6 of the Federal Rules of Criminal

Procedure (FRCrP) to permit the sharing of grand jury information that involves foreign intelligence or counterintelligence with Federal law enforcement, intelligence, protective, immigration, national defense, or national security officials (such officials), subject to specified requirements. Authorizes an investigative or law enforcement officer, or an attorney for the Government, who, by authorized means, has obtained knowledge of the contents of any wire, oral, or electronic communication or evidence derived therefrom to disclose such contents to such officials to the extent that such contents include foreign intelligence or counterintelligence. Directs the Attorney General to establish procedures for the disclosure of information (pursuant to the code and the FRCrP) that identifies a United States person, as defined in the Foreign Intelligence Surveillance Act of 1978 (FISA). Authorizes the disclosure of foreign intelligence or counterintelligence obtained as part of a criminal investigation to such officials.

(Sec. 204) Clarifies that nothing in code provisions regarding pen registers shall be deemed to affect the acquisition by the Government of specified foreign intelligence information, and that procedures under FISA shall be the exclusive means by which electronic surveillance and the interception of domestic wire and oral (current law) and electronic communications may be conducted.

(Sec. 205) Authorizes the Director of the FBI to expedite the employment of personnel as translators to support counterterrorism investigations and operations without regard to applicable Federal personnel requirements. Requires: (1) the Director to establish such security requirements as necessary for such personnel; and (2) the Attorney General to report to the House and Senate Judiciary Committees regarding translators.

(Sec. 206) Grants roving surveillance authority under FISA after requiring a court order approving an electronic surveillance to direct any person to furnish necessary information, facilities, or technical assistance in circumstances where the Court finds that the actions of the surveillance target may have the effect of thwarting the identification of a specified person.

(Sec. 207) Increases the duration of FISA surveillance permitted for non-U.S. persons who are agents of a foreign power.

(Sec. 208) Increases (from seven to 11) the number of district court judges designated to hear applications for and grant orders approving electronic surveillance. Requires that no fewer than three reside within 20 miles of the District of Columbia.

(Sec. 209) Permits the seizure of voice-mail messages under a warrant.

(Sec. 210) Expands the scope of subpoenas for records of electronic communications to include the length and types of service utilized, temporarily assigned network addresses, and the means and source of payment (including any credit card or bank account number).

(Sec. 211) Amends the Communications Act of 1934 to permit specified disclosures to Government entities, except for records revealing cable subscriber selection of video programming from a cable operator.

(Sec. 212) Permits electronic communication and remote computing service providers to make emergency disclosures to a governmental entity of customer electronic communications to protect life and limb.

(Sec. 213) Authorizes Federal district courts to allow a delay of required notices of the execution of a warrant if immediate notice may have an adverse result and under other specified circumstances.

(Sec. 214) Prohibits use of a pen register or trap and trace devices in any investigation to protect against international terrorism or clandestine intelligence activities that is conducted solely on the basis of activities protected by the first amendment to the U.S. Constitution.

(Sec. 215) Authorizes the Director of the FBI (or designee) to apply for a court order requiring production of certain business records for foreign intelligence and international terrorism investigations. Requires the Attorney General to report to the House and Senate Intelligence and Judiciary Committees semi-annually.

(Sec. 216) Amends the code to: (1) require a trap and trace device to restrict recoding or decoding so as not to include the contents of a wire or electronic communication; (2) apply a court order for a pen register or trap and trace devices to any person or entity providing wire or electronic communication service in the United States whose assistance may facilitate execution of the order; (3) require specified records kept on any pen register or trap and trace device on a packet-switched data network of a provider of electronic communication service to the public; and (4) allow a trap and trace device to identify the source (but not the contents) of a wire or electronic communication.

(Sec. 217) Makes it lawful to intercept the wire or electronic communication of a computer trespasser in certain circumstances.

(Sec. 218) Amends FISA to require an application for an electronic surveillance order or search warrant to certify that a significant purpose (currently, the sole or main purpose) of the surveillance is to obtain foreign intelligence information.

(Sec. 219) Amends rule 41 of the FRCrP to permit Federal magistrate judges in any district in which terrorism-related activities may have occurred to issue search warrants for searches within or outside the district.

(Sec. 220) Provides for nationwide service of search warrants for electronic evidence.

(Sec. 221) Amends the Trade Sanctions Reform and Export Enhancement Act of 2000 to extend trade sanctions to the territory of Afghanistan controlled by the Taliban.

(Sec. 222) Specifies that: (1) nothing in this Act shall impose any additional technical obligation or requirement on a provider of a wire or electronic communication service or other person to furnish facilities or technical assistance; and (2) a provider of such service, and a landlord, custodian, or other person who furnishes such facilities or technical assistance, shall be reasonably compensated for such reasonable expenditures incurred in providing such facilities or assistance.

(Sec. 223) Amends the Federal criminal code to provide for administrative discipline of Federal officers or employees who violate prohibitions against unauthorized disclosures of information gathered under this Act. Provides for civil actions against the United States for damages by any person aggrieved by such violations.

(Sec. 224) Terminates this title on December 31, 2005, except with respect to any particular foreign intelligence investigation beginning before that date, or any particular offense or potential offense that began or occurred before it.

(Sec. 225) Amends the Foreign Intelligence Surveillance Act of 1978 to prohibit a cause of action in any court against a provider of a wire or electronic communication service, landlord, custodian, or any other person that furnishes any information, facilities, or technical assistance in accordance with a court order or request for emergency assistance under such Act (for example, with respect to a wiretap).

Title III: International Money Laundering Abatement and Anti-Terrorist Financing Act of 2001—International Money Laundering Abatement and Financial Anti-Terrorism Act of 2001—Sunsets this Act after the first day of FY 2005 if Congress enacts a specified joint resolution to that effect.

Subtitle A: International Counter Money Laundering and Related Measures—Amends Federal law governing monetary transactions to prescribe procedural guidelines under which the Secretary of the Treasury (the Secretary) may require domestic financial institutions and agencies to take specified measures if the Secretary finds that reasonable grounds exist for concluding that jurisdictions, financial institutions, types of accounts, or transactions operating outside or within the United States, are of primary money laundering concern. Includes mandatory disclosure of specified information relating to certain correspondent accounts.

(Sec. 312) Mandates establishment of due diligence mechanisms to detect and report money laundering transactions through private banking accounts and correspondent accounts.

(Sec. 313) Prohibits U.S. correspondent accounts with foreign shell banks.

(Sec. 314) Instructs the Secretary to adopt regulations to encourage further cooperation among financial institutions, their regulatory authorities, and law enforcement authorities, with the specific purpose of encouraging regulatory authorities and law enforcement authorities to share with financial institutions information regarding individuals, entities, and organizations engaged in or reasonably suspected (based on credible evidence) of engaging in terrorist acts or money laundering activities. Authorizes such regulations to create procedures for cooperation and information sharing on matters specifically related to the finances of terrorist groups as well as their relationships with international narcotics traffickers. Requires the Secretary to distribute annually to financial institutions a detailed analysis identifying patterns of suspicious activity and other investigative insights derived from suspicious activity reports and investigations by Federal, State, and local law enforcement agencies.

(Sec. 315) Amends Federal criminal law to include foreign corruption offenses as money laundering crimes.

(Sec. 316) Establishes the right of property owners to contest confiscation of property under law relating to confiscation of assets of suspected terrorists.

(Sec. 317) Establishes Federal jurisdiction over: (1) foreign money launderers (including their assets held in the United States); and (2) money that is laundered through a foreign bank.

(Sec. 319) Authorizes the forfeiture of money laundering funds from interbank accounts. Requires a covered financial institution, upon request of the appropriate Federal banking agency, to make available within 120 hours all pertinent information related to anti–money laundering compliance by the institution or its customer. Grants the Secretary summons and subpoena powers over foreign banks that maintain a correspondent bank in the United States. Requires a covered financial institution to terminate within ten business days any correspondent relationship with a foreign bank after receipt of written notice that the foreign bank has failed to comply with certain judicial proceedings. Sets forth civil penalties for failure to terminate such relationship.

(Sec. 321) Subjects to record and report requirements for monetary instrument transactions: (1) any credit union; and (2) any futures commission merchant, commodity trading advisor, and commodity pool operator registered, or required to register, under the Commodity Exchange Act.

(Sec. 323) Authorizes Federal application for restraining orders to preserve the availability of property subject to a foreign forfeiture or confiscation judgment.

(Sec. 325) Authorizes the Secretary to issue regulations to ensure that concentration accounts of financial institutions are not used to prevent association of the identity of an individual customer with the movement of funds of which the customer is the direct or beneficial owner.

(Sec. 326) Directs the Secretary to issue regulations prescribing minimum standards for financial institutions regarding customer identity in connection with the opening of accounts. Requires the Secretary to report to Congress on: (1) the most timely and effective way to require foreign nationals to provide domestic financial institutions and agencies with appropriate and accurate information; (2) whether to require foreign nationals to obtain an identification number (similar to a Social Security or tax identification number) before opening an account with a domestic financial institution; and (3) a system for domestic financial institutions and agencies to review Government agency information to verify the identities of such foreign nationals.

(Sec. 327) Amends the Bank Holding Company Act of 1956 and the Federal Deposit Insurance Act to require consideration of the effectiveness of a company or companies in combating money laundering during reviews of proposed bank shares acquisitions or mergers.

(Sec. 328) Directs the Secretary to take reasonable steps to encourage foreign governments to require the inclusion of the name of the originator in wire transfer instructions sent to the United States and other countries, with the information to remain with the transfer from its origination until the point of disbursement. Requires annual progress reports to specified congressional committees.

(Sec. 329) Prescribes criminal penalties for Federal officials or employees who seek or accept bribes in connection with administration of this title.

(Sec. 330) Urges U.S. negotiations for international cooperation in investigations of money laundering, financial crimes, and the finances of terrorist groups, including record sharing by foreign banks with U.S. law enforcement officials and domestic financial institution supervisors.

Subtitle B: Bank Secrecy Act Amendments and Related Improvements—Amends Federal law known as the Bank Secrecy Act to revise requirements for civil liability immunity for voluntary financial institution disclosure of suspicious activities. Authorizes the inclusion of suspicions of illegal activity in written employment references.

(Sec. 352) Authorizes the Secretary to exempt from minimum standards for anti–money laundering programs any financial institution not subject to certain regulations governing financial recordkeeping and reporting of currency and foreign transactions.

(Sec. 353) Establishes civil penalties for violations of geographic targeting orders and structuring transactions to evade certain recordkeeping requirements. Lengthens the effective period of geographic targeting orders from 60 to 180 days.

(Sec. 355) Amends the Federal Deposit Insurance Act to permit written employment references to contain suspicions of involvement in illegal activity.

(Sec. 356) Instructs the Secretary to: (1) promulgate regulations requiring registered securities brokers and dealers, futures commission merchants, commodity trading advisors, and commodity pool operators, to file reports of suspicious financial transactions; (2) report to Congress on the role of the Internal Revenue Service in the administration of the Bank Secrecy Act; and (3) share monetary instruments transactions records upon request of a U.S. intelligence agency for use in the conduct of intelligence or counterintelligence activities, including analysis, to protect against international terrorism.

(Sec. 358) Amends the Right to Financial Privacy Act to permit the transfer of financial records to other agencies or departments upon certification that the records are relevant to intelligence or counterintelligence activities related to international terrorism. Amends the Fair Credit Reporting Act to require a consumer reporting agency to furnish all information in a consumer's file to a government agency upon certification that the records are relevant to intelligence or counterintelligence activities related to international terrorism.

(Sec. 359) Subjects to mandatory records and reports on monetary instruments transactions any licensed sender of money or any other person who engages as a business in the transmission of funds, including through an informal value transfer banking system or network (e.g., hawala) of people facilitating the transfer of money domestically or internationally outside of the conventional financial institutions system.

(Sec. 360) Authorizes the Secretary to instruct the United States Executive Director of each international financial institution to use his or her voice and vote to: (1) support the use of funds for a country (and its institutions) which contributes to U.S. efforts against international terrorism; and (2) require an auditing of disbursements to ensure that no funds are paid to persons who commit or support terrorism.

(Sec. 361) Makes the existing Financial Crimes Enforcement Network a bureau in the Department of the Treasury.

(Sec. 362) Directs the Secretary to establish a highly secure network in the Network that allows financial institutions to file certain reports and receive alerts and other information regarding suspicious activities warranting immediate and enhanced scrutiny.

(Sec. 363) Increases to $1 million the maximum civil penalties (currently $10,000) and criminal fines (currently $250,000) for money laundering. Sets a minimum civil penalty and criminal fine of double the amount of the illegal transaction.

(Sec. 364) Amends the Federal Reserve Act to provide for uniform protection authority for Federal Reserve facilities, including law enforcement officers authorized to carry firearms and make warrantless arrests.

(Sec. 365) Amends Federal law to require reports relating to coins and currency of more than $10,000 received in a nonfinancial trade or business.

(Sec. 366) Directs the Secretary to study and report to Congress on: (1) the possible expansion of the currency transaction reporting requirements exemption system; and (2) methods for improving financial institution utilization of the system as a way of reducing the submission of currency transaction reports that have little or no value for law enforcement purposes.

Subtitle C: Currency Crimes—Establishes as a bulk cash smuggling felony the knowing concealment and attempted transport (or transfer) across U.S. borders of currency and monetary instruments in excess of $10,000, with intent to evade specified currency reporting requirements.

(Sec. 372) Changes from discretionary to mandatory a court's authority to order, as part of a criminal sentence, forfeiture of all property involved in certain currency reporting offenses. Leaves a court discretion to order civil forfeitures in money laundering cases.

(Sec. 373) Amends the Federal criminal code to revise the prohibition of unlicensed (currently, illegal) money transmitting businesses.

(Sec. 374) Increases the criminal penalties for counterfeiting domestic and foreign currency and obligations.

(Sec. 376) Amends the Federal criminal code to extend the prohibition against the laundering of money instruments to specified proceeds of terrorism.

(Sec. 377) Grants the United States extraterritorial jurisdiction where: (1) an offense committed outside the United States involves an access device issued, owned, managed, or controlled by a financial institution, account issuer, credit card system member, or other entity within U.S. jurisdiction; and (2) the person committing the offense transports, delivers, conveys, transfers to or through, or otherwise stores, secrets, or holds within U.S. jurisdiction any article used to assist in the commission of the offense or the proceeds of such offense or property derived from it.

Title IV: Protecting the Border—Subtitle A: Protecting the Northern Border—Authorizes the Attorney General to waive certain Immigration and Naturalization Service (INS) personnel caps with respect to ensuring security needs on the Northern border.

(Sec. 402) Authorizes appropriations to: (1) triple the number of Border Patrol, Customs Service, and INS personnel (and support facilities) at points of entry and along the Northern border; and (2) INS and Customs for related border monitoring technology and equipment.

(Sec. 403) Amends the Immigration and Nationality Act to require the Attorney General and the Federal Bureau of Investigation (FBI) to provide the Department of State and INS with access to specified criminal history extracts in order to determine whether or not a visa or admissions applicant has a criminal history. Directs the FBI to provide periodic extract updates. Provides for confidentiality. Directs the Attorney General and the Secretary of State to develop a technology standard to identify visa and admissions applicants, which shall be the basis for an electronic system of law enforcement and intelligence sharing system available to consular, law enforcement, intelligence, and Federal border inspection personnel.

(Sec. 404) Amends the Department of Justice Appropriations Act, 2001 to eliminate certain INS overtime restrictions.

(Sec. 405) Directs the Attorney General to report on the feasibility of enhancing the Integrated Automated Fingerprint Identification System and other identification systems to better identify foreign individuals in connection with U.S. or foreign criminal investigations before issuance of a visa to, or permitting such person's entry or exit from, the United States. Authorizes appropriations.

Subtitle B: Enhanced Immigration Provisions—Amends the Immigration and Nationality Act to broaden the scope of aliens ineligible for admission or deportable due to terrorist activities to include an alien who: (1) is a representative of a political, social, or similar group whose political endorsement of terrorist acts undermines U.S. antiterrorist efforts; (2) has used a position of prominence to endorse terrorist activity, or to persuade others to support such activity in a way that undermines U.S. antiterrorist efforts (or the child or spouse of such an alien under specified circumstances); or (3) has been associated with a terrorist organization and intends to engage in threatening activities while in the United States.

(Sec. 411) Includes within the definition of "terrorist activity" the use of any weapon or dangerous device. Redefines "engage in terrorist activity" to mean, in an individual capacity or as a member of an organization, to: (1) commit or to incite to commit, under circumstances indicating an intention to cause death or serious bodily injury, a terrorist activity; (2) prepare or plan a terrorist activity; (3) gather information on potential targets for terrorist activity; (4) solicit funds or other things of value for a terrorist activity or a terrorist organization (with an exception for lack of knowledge); (5) solicit any individual to engage in prohibited conduct or for terrorist organization membership (with an exception for lack of knowledge); or (6) commit an act that the actor knows, or reasonably should know, affords material support, including a safe house, transportation, communications, funds, transfer of funds or other material financial benefit, false documentation or identification, weapons (including chemical, biological, or radiological weapons), explosives, or training for the commission of a terrorist activity; to any individual who the actor knows or reasonably should know has committed or plans to commit a terrorist activity; or to a terrorist organization (with an exception for lack of knowledge). Defines "terrorist organization" as a group: (1) designated under the Immigration and Nationality Act or by the Secretary of State; or (2) a group of two or more individuals, whether related or not, which engages in terrorist-related activities. Provides for the retroactive application of amendments under this Act. Stipulates that an alien shall not be considered inadmissible or deportable because of a relationship to an organization that was not designated as a terrorist organization prior to enactment of this Act. States that the amendments under this section shall apply to all aliens in exclusion or deportation proceedings on or after the date of enactment of this Act. Directs the Secretary of State to notify specified congressional leaders seven days prior to designating an organization as a terrorist organization. Provides for organization redesignation or revocation.

(Sec. 412) Provides for mandatory detention until removal from the United States (regardless of any relief from removal) of an alien certified by the Attorney General as a suspected terrorist or threat to national security. Requires release of such alien after seven days if removal proceedings have not commenced, or the alien has not been charged with a criminal offense. Authorizes detention for additional periods of up to six months of an alien not likely to be deported in the reasonably foreseeable future only if release will threaten U.S. national security or the safety of the community or any person. Limits judicial review to habeas corpus proceedings in the U.S. Supreme Court, the U.S. Court of Appeals for the District of Columbia, or any district court with jurisdiction to entertain a habeas corpus petition. Restricts to the U.S. Court of Appeals for the District of Columbia the right of appeal of any final order by a circuit or district judge.

(Sec. 413) Authorizes the Secretary of State, on a reciprocal basis, to share criminal- and terrorist-related visa lookout information with foreign governments.

(Sec. 414) Declares the sense of Congress that the Attorney General should: (1) fully implement the integrated entry and exit data system for airports, seaports, and land border ports of entry with all deliberate speed; and (2) begin immediately establishing the Integrated Entry and Exit Data System Task Force. Authorizes appropriations. Requires the Attorney General and the Secretary of State, in developing the integrated entry and exit data system, to focus on the use of biometric technology and the development of tamper-resistant documents readable at ports of entry.

(Sec. 415) Amends the Immigration and Naturalization Service Data Management Improvement Act of 2000 to include the Office of Homeland Security in the Integrated Entry and Exit Data System Task Force.

(Sec. 416) Directs the Attorney General to implement fully and expand the foreign student monitoring program to include other approved educational institutions like air flight, language training, or vocational schools.

(Sec. 417) Requires audits and reports on implementation of the mandate for machine readable passports.

(Sec. 418) Directs the Secretary of State to: (1) review how consular officers issue visas to determine if consular shopping is a problem; and (2) if it is a problem, take steps to address it, and report on them to Congress.

Subtitle C: Preservation of Immigration Benefits for Victims of Terrorism—Authorizes the Attorney General to provide permanent resident status through the special immigrant program to an alien (and spouse, child, or grandparent under specified circumstances) who was the beneficiary of a petition filed on or before September 11, 2001, to grant the alien permanent residence as an employer-sponsored immigrant or of an application for labor certification if the petition or application was rendered null because of the disability of the beneficiary or loss of employment due to physical damage to, or destruction of, the business of the petitioner or applicant as a direct result of the terrorist attacks on September 11, 2001 (September attacks), or because of the death of the petitioner or applicant as a direct result of such attacks.

(Sec. 422) States that an alien who was legally in a nonimmigrant status and was disabled as a direct result of the September attacks may remain in the United States until his or her normal status termination date or September, 11, 2002. Includes in such extension the spouse or child of such an alien or of an alien who was killed in such attacks. Authorizes employment during such period. Extends specified immigration-related deadlines and other filing requirements for an alien (and spouse and child) who was directly prevented from meeting such requirements as a result of the September attacks respecting: (1) nonimmigrant status and status revision; (2) diversity immigrants; (3) immigrant visas; (4) parolees; and (5) voluntary departure.

(Sec. 423) Waives, under specified circumstances, the requirement that an alien spouse (and child) of a U.S. citizen must have been married for at least two years prior to such citizen's death in order to maintain immediate relative status if such citizen died as a direct result of the September attacks. Provides for: (1) continued family-sponsored immigrant eligibility for the spouse, child, or unmarried son or daughter of a permanent resident who died as a direct result of such attacks; and (2) continued eligibility for adjustment of status for the spouse and child of an employment-based immigrant who died similarly.

(Sec. 424) Amends the Immigration and Nationality Act to extend the visa categorization of "child" for aliens with petitions filed on or before September 11, 2001, for aliens whose 21st birthday is in September 2001 (90 days), or after September 2001 (45 days).

(Sec. 425) Authorizes the Attorney General to provide temporary administrative relief to an alien who, as of September 10, 2001, was lawfully in the United States and was the spouse, parent, or child of an individual who died or was disabled as a direct result of the September attacks.

(Sec. 426) Directs the Attorney General to establish evidentiary guidelines for death, disability, and loss of employment or destruction of business in connection with the provisions of this subtitle.

(Sec. 427) Prohibits benefits to terrorists or their family members.

Title V: Removing Obstacles to Investigating Terrorism—Authorizes the Attorney General to pay rewards from available funds pursuant to public advertisements for assistance to DOJ to combat terrorism and defend the Nation against terrorist acts, in accordance with procedures and regulations established or issued by the Attorney General, subject to specified conditions, including a prohibition against any such reward of $250,000 or more from being made or offered without the personal approval of either the Attorney General or the President.

(Sec. 502) Amends the State Department Basic Authorities

Act of 1956 to modify the Department of State rewards program to authorize rewards for information leading to: (1) the dismantling of a terrorist organization in whole or significant part; and (2) the identification or location of an individual who holds a key leadership position in a terrorist organization. Raises the limit on rewards if the Secretary of State determines that a larger sum is necessary to combat terrorism or defend the Nation against terrorist acts.

(Sec. 503) Amends the DNA Analysis Backlog Elimination Act of 2000 to qualify a Federal terrorism offense for collection of DNA for identification.

(Sec. 504) Amends FISA to authorize consultation among Federal law enforcement officers regarding information acquired from an electronic surveillance or physical search in terrorism and related investigations or protective measures.

(Sec. 505) Allows the FBI to request telephone toll and transactional records, financial records, and consumer reports in any investigation to protect against international terrorism or clandestine intelligence activities only if the investigation is not conducted solely on the basis of activities protected by the first amendment to the U.S. Constitution.

(Sec. 506) Revises U.S. Secret Service jurisdiction with respect to fraud and related activity in connection with computers. Grants the FBI primary authority to investigate specified fraud and computer related activity for cases involving espionage, foreign counterintelligence, information protected against unauthorized disclosure for reasons of national defense or foreign relations, or restricted data, except for offenses affecting Secret Service duties.

(Sec. 507) Amends the General Education Provisions Act and the National Education Statistics Act of 1994 to provide for disclosure of educational records to the Attorney General in a terrorism investigation or prosecution.

Title VI: Providing for Victims of Terrorism, Public Safety Officers, and Their Families—Subtitle A: Aid to Families of Public Safety Officers—Provides for expedited payments for: (1) public safety officers involved in the prevention, investigation, rescue, or recovery efforts related to a terrorist attack; and (2) heroic public safety officers. Increases Public Safety Officers Benefit Program payments.

Subtitle B: Amendments to the Victims of Crime Act of 1984—Amends the Victims of Crime Act of 1984 to: (1) revise provisions regarding the allocation of funds for compensation and assistance, location of compensable crime, and the relationship of crime victim compensation to means-tested Federal benefit programs and to the September 11th victim compensation fund; and (2) establish an antiterrorism emergency reserve in the Victims of Crime Fund.

Title VII: Increased Information Sharing for Critical Infrastructure Protection—Amends the Omnibus Crime Control and Safe Streets Act of 1968 to extend Bureau of Justice Assistance regional information sharing system grants to systems that enhance the investigation and prosecution abilities of participating Federal, State, and local law enforcement agencies in addressing multijurisdictional terrorist conspiracies and activities. Authorizes appropriations.

Title VIII: Strengthening the Criminal Laws Against Terrorism—Amends the Federal criminal code to prohibit specific terrorist acts or otherwise destructive, disruptive, or violent acts against mass transportation vehicles, ferries, providers, employees, passengers, or operating systems.

(Sec. 802) Amends the Federal criminal code to: (1) revise the definition of "international terrorism" to include activities that appear to be intended to affect the conduct of government by mass destruction; and (2) define "domestic terrorism" as activities that occur primarily within U.S. jurisdiction, that involve criminal acts dangerous to human life, and that appear to be intended to intimidate or coerce a civilian population, to influence government policy by intimidation or coercion, or to affect government conduct by mass destruction, assassination, or kidnapping.

(Sec. 803) Prohibits harboring any person knowing or having reasonable grounds to believe that such person has committed or to be about to commit a terrorism offense.

(Sec. 804) Establishes Federal jurisdiction over crimes committed at U.S. facilities abroad.

(Sec. 805) Applies the prohibitions against providing material support for terrorism to offenses outside of the United States.

(Sec. 806) Subjects to civil forfeiture all assets, foreign or domestic, of terrorist organizations.

(Sec. 808) Expands: (1) the offenses over which the Attorney General shall have primary investigative jurisdiction under provisions governing acts of terrorism transcending national boundaries; and (2) the offenses included within the definition of the Federal crime of terrorism.

(Sec. 809) Provides that there shall be no statute of limitations for certain terrorism offenses if the commission of such an offense resulted in, or created a foreseeable risk of, death or serious bodily injury to another person.

(Sec. 810) Provides for alternative maximum penalties for specified terrorism crimes.

(Sec. 811) Makes: (1) the penalties for attempts and conspiracies the same as those for terrorism offenses; (2) the supervised release terms for offenses with terrorism predicates any term of years or life; and (3) specified terrorism crimes Racketeer Influenced and Corrupt Organizations statute predicates.

(Sec. 814) Revises prohibitions and penalties regarding fraud and related activity in connection with computers to include specified cyber-terrorism offenses.

(Sec. 816) Directs the Attorney General to establish regional computer forensic laboratories, and to support existing laboratories, to develop specified cyber-security capabilities.

(Sec. 817) Prescribes penalties for knowing possession in certain circumstances of biological agents, toxins, or delivery systems, especially by certain restricted persons.

Title IX: Improved Intelligence—Amends the National Security Act of 1947 to require the Director of Central Intelligence (DCI) to establish requirements and priorities for foreign intelligence collected under the Foreign Intelligence Surveillance Act of 1978 and to provide assistance to the Attorney General (AG) to ensure that information derived from electronic surveillance or physical searches is disseminated for efficient and effective foreign intelligence purposes. Requires the inclusion of international terrorist activities within the scope of foreign intelligence under such Act.

(Sec. 903) Expresses the sense of Congress that officers and employees of the intelligence community should establish and maintain intelligence relationships to acquire information on terrorists and terrorist organizations.

(Sec. 904) Authorizes deferral of the submission to Congress of certain reports on intelligence and intelligence-related matters until: (1) February 1, 2002; or (2) a date after February 1, 2002, if the official involved certifies that preparation and submission on February 1, 2002, will impede the work of officers or employees engaged in counterterrorism activities. Requires congressional notification of any such deferral.

(Sec. 905) Requires the AG or the head of any other Federal

department or agency with law enforcement responsibilities to expeditiously disclose to the DCI any foreign intelligence acquired in the course of a criminal investigation.

(Sec. 906) Requires the AG, DCI, and Secretary of the Treasury to jointly report to Congress on the feasibility and desirability of reconfiguring the Foreign Asset Tracking Center and the Office of Foreign Assets Control to provide for the analysis and dissemination of foreign intelligence relating to the financial capabilities and resources of international terrorist organizations.

(Sec. 907) Requires the DCI to report to the appropriate congressional committees on the establishment and maintenance of the National Virtual Translation Center for timely and accurate translation of foreign intelligence for elements of the intelligence community.

(Sec. 908) Requires the AG to provide a program of training to Government officials regarding the identification and use of foreign intelligence.

Title X: Miscellaneous—Directs the Inspector General of the Department of Justice to designate one official to review allegations of abuse of civil rights, civil liberties, and racial and ethnic profiling by government employees and officials.

(Sec. 1002) Expresses the sense of Congress condemning acts of violence or discrimination against any American, including Sikh-Americans. Calls upon local and Federal law enforcement authorities to prosecute to the fullest extent of the law all those who commit crimes.

(Sec. 1004) Amends the Federal criminal code with respect to venue in money laundering cases to allow a prosecution for such an offense to be brought in: (1) any district in which the financial or monetary transaction is conducted; or (2) any district where a prosecution for the underlying specified unlawful activity could be brought, if the defendant participated in the transfer of the proceeds of the specified unlawful activity from that district to the district where the financial or monetary transaction is conducted. States that: (1) a transfer of funds from one place to another, by wire or any other means, shall constitute a single, continuing transaction; and (2) any person who conducts any portion of the transaction may be charged in any district in which the transaction takes place. Allows a prosecution for an attempt or conspiracy offense to be brought in the district where venue would lie for the completed offense, or in any other district where an act in furtherance of the attempt or conspiracy took place.

(Sec. 1005) First Responders Assistance Act—Directs the Attorney General to make grants to State and local governments to improve the ability of State and local law enforcement, fire department, and first responders to respond to and prevent acts of terrorism. Authorizes appropriations.

(Sec. 1006) Amends the Immigration and Nationality Act to make inadmissible into the United States any alien engaged in money laundering. Directs the Secretary of State to develop a money laundering watchlist which: (1) identifies individuals worldwide who are known or suspected of money laundering; and (2) is readily accessible to, and shall be checked by, a consular or other Federal official before the issuance of a visa or admission to the United States.

(Sec. 1007) Authorizes FY 2002 appropriations for regional antidrug training in Turkey by the Drug Enforcement Administration for police, as well as increased precursor chemical control efforts in South and Central Asia.

(Sec. 1008) Directs the Attorney General to conduct a feasibility study and report to Congress on the use of a biometric identifier scanning system with access to the FBI integrated automated fingerprint identification system at overseas consular posts and points of entry to the United States.

(Sec. 1009) Directs the FBI to study and report to Congress on the feasibility of providing to airlines access via computer to the names of passengers who are suspected of terrorist activity by Federal officials. Authorizes appropriations.

(Sec. 1010) Authorizes the use of Department of Defense funds to contract with local and State governments, during the period of Operation Enduring Freedom, for the performance of security functions at U.S. military installations.

(Sec. 1011) Crimes Against Charitable Americans Act of 2001—Amends the Telemarketing and Consumer Fraud and Abuse Prevention Act to cover fraudulent charitable solicitations. Requires any person engaged in telemarketing for the solicitation of charitable contributions, donations, or gifts to disclose promptly and clearly the purpose of the telephone call.

(Sec. 1012) Amends the Federal transportation code to prohibit States from licensing any individual to operate a motor vehicle transporting hazardous material unless the Secretary of Transportation determines that such individual does not pose a security risk warranting denial of the license. Requires background checks of such license applicants by the Attorney General upon State request.

(Sec. 1013) Expresses the sense of the Senate on substantial new U.S. investment in bioterrorism preparedness and response.

(Sec. 1014) Directs the Office for State and Local Domestic Preparedness Support of the Office of Justice Programs to make grants to enhance State and local capability to prepare for and respond to terrorist acts. Authorizes appropriations for FY 2002 through 2007.

(Sec. 1015) Amends the Crime Identification Technology Act of 1998 to extend it through FY 2007 and provide for antiterrorism grants to States and localities. Authorizes appropriations.

(Sec. 1016) Critical Infrastructures Protection Act of 2001—Declares it is U.S. policy: (1) that any physical or virtual disruption of the operation of the critical infrastructures of the United States be rare, brief, geographically limited in effect, manageable, and minimally detrimental to the economy, human and government services, and U.S. national security; (2) that actions necessary to achieve this policy be carried out in a public-private partnership involving corporate and nongovernmental organizations; and (3) to have in place a comprehensive and effective program to ensure the continuity of essential Federal Government functions under all circumstances. Establishes the National Infrastructure Simulation and Analysis Center to serve as a source of national competence to address critical infrastructure protection and continuity through support for activities related to counterterrorism, threat assessment, and risk mitigation. Defines critical infrastructure as systems and assets, whether physical or virtual, so vital to the United States that their incapacity or destruction would have a debilitating impact on security, national economic security, national public health or safety, or any combination of those matters. Authorizes appropriations.

Quotations

Remember, remember always, that all of us . . . are descended from immigrants and revolutionists.

—Franklin D. Roosevelt

What, then, is this new man, the American? They are a mixture of English, Scotch, Irish, French, Dutch, Germans, and Swedes. From this promiscuous breed, that race, now called Americans, have arisen.

—J. Hector St. Josh de Crevecouer

In times of shrinking expectations . . . everyone feels like a victim and pushes away outsiders to defend his own corner.

—Oscar Handlin

Remember that when you say "I will have none of this exile and this stranger for his face is not like my face and his speech is strange," you have denied America with that word.

—Stephen Vincent Benet

Give me your tired, your poor, your huddled masses yearning to breathe free, the wretched refuse of your teeming shore, send these, the homeless, tempest-tossed, to me: I lift my lamp beside the golden door.

—Emma Larzarus

Everywhere immigrants have enriched and strengthened the fabric of American life.

—John F. Kennedy

One day our descendants will think it incredible that we paid so much attention to things like the amount of melanin in our skin or the shape of our eyes or our gender instead of the unique identities of each of us as complex human beings.

—Franklin Thomas

It is a great shock at the age of five or six to find that in a world of Gary Coopers you are the Indian.

—James Baldwin

We have become not a melting pot but a beautiful mosaic. Different people, different beliefs, different yearnings, different hopes, different dreams.

—Jimmy Carter

It were not best that we should all think alike; it is difference of opinion that makes horse races.

—Mark Twain

We send missionaries to China so the Chinese can get to heaven, but we won't let them into our country.

—Pearl S. Buck

Human diversity makes tolerance more than a virtue; it makes it a requirement for survival.

—René Dubos

We really are fifteen different countries and it's really remarkable that each of us thinks we represent the real America. The midwesterner in Kansas, the black American in Durham—both are certain they are the real American.

—Maya Angelou

America is woven of many strands. I would recognize them and let it so remain. Our fate is to become one, and yet many. This is not prophecy, but description.

—Ralph Ellison

I have a dream that my four little children will one day live in a nation where they will not be judged by the color of their skin but by the content of their character.

—Martin Luther King, Jr.,

No one is born hating another person because of the color of his skin, or his background, or his religion. If [people] can learn to hate they can be taught to love, for love comes more naturally to the human heart than its opposite.

—Nelson Mandela

We are a nation of many nationalities, many races, many religions—bound together by a single unity, the unity of freedom and equality. Whoever seeks to set one nationality against another, seeks to degrade all nationalities.

—Franklin D. Roosevelt

What sets worlds in motion is the interplay of differences, their attractions and repulsions; life is plurality, death is uniformity.

—Octavio Paz

7

Directory of Organizations

The World Wide Web (WWW), or the Internet, has opened a door to vast amounts of information and data. The Internet is rich with resources for persons interested in archival, organizational, and personal information. In many ways, the Internet is simply too rich: Search engines can identify thousands of Web sites on a single topic or subject, which can easily overwhelm a researcher. The purpose of this chapter is to identify Web sites that can assist persons interested in finding information on organizations focused on particular racial and ethnic populations in the United States. The directory of organizations in this chapter is by no means exhaustive of what is available on the Internet. The organizations have been selected because they meet the following criteria: (1) The organization serves as a general clearinghouse on a particular racial or ethnic population, (2) its Web site offers links to other Web sites, especially those of other organizations that are similar in scope and purpose, and (3) its Web address has been relatively stable. Readers are encouraged to use this chapter as a starting point in the construction of a framework for studying organizations that address specific issues regarding racial and ethnic populations in the United States.

African American

African American Literature Book Club
615 Warren Street
Brooklyn, NY 11217-2016

Phone: (718) 623-1628
Fax: (877) 415-3709
Web site: http://www.aalbc.com

The goal of the African American Literature Book Club is to increase knowledge of the diversity of African American literature, facilitate the exchange of opinions, and serve as a gateway to the work of aspiring and professional writers. One can learn about authors, read book excerpts, listen to poetry, and learn about popular new books and classic titles.

Asian American

Asian American Writers' Workshop
16 West Thirty-Second Street
Suite 10A
New York, NY 10001
Phone: (212) 494-0061
Fax: (212) 494-0062
Web site: www.aaww.org

The Asian American Writers' Workshop, Inc., is a nonprofit organization dedicated to the creation, development, publication, and dissemination of Asian American literature. The Workshop publishes books on Asian America, *The Asian Pacific American Journal,* and the literary magazine *Ten;* sponsors readings; offers creative-writing workshops; presents performances; offers fellowships to aspiring Asian American writers; produces the youth program CreateNow; presents the Annual Asian American Literary Awards; and operates the Asian American Bookseller, the most comprehensive collection of Asian American books and magazines in the country. The Workshop's Programs Division is devoted to promoting Asian American writers and their work. It provides writers with opportunities to further develop writing skills and advance their careers through creative-writing workshops, readings, a performance series, and the national Asian American Literary Caravan. It offers a variety of writing workshops ranging from screenwriting and performance poetry to prose narrative and technical assistance. The workshops are facilitated by award-winning artists who have extensive publishing and teaching backgrounds. Workshop facilitators have included MacArthur Genius Awardee Han Ong, Pulitzer Prize winner

Jhumpa Lahiri and American Book Award recipient Kimiko Hahn. Since 1992, the literary caravan has brought Asian American writers to college campuses, community centers, national arts institutions, and bookstores. The goal of the Caravan is to bring Asian American literature to areas with minimal or no exposure to this segment of literature. New audiences are especially eager to hear the voices of such underrepresented groups as South Asian Americans, Filipinos, Pacific Islanders, and Vietnamese Americans.

Asian Pacific American Legal Center (APALC) of Southern California

1145 Wilshire Boulevard
2nd floor
Los Angeles, CA 90017
Phone: (213) 977-7500
Fax: (213) 977-7595
Web site: http://apalc.org

The Asian Pacific American Legal Center (APALC) has become the largest organization in southern California providing Asian and Pacific Islander (API) and other communities with multilingual, culturally sensitive services and legal education. In-house attorneys and paralegals have developed expertise in a variety of areas, such as immigration and naturalization, workers' rights, family law and domestic violence, immigrant welfare, and voting rights and antidiscrimination, and the organization has also worked toward building interethnic relations. APALC language capacity includes Chinese (Cantonese and Mandarin), Hindi, Japanese, Korean, Spanish, Tagalog, Thai, Urdu, and Vietnamese.

Association of Asian Pacific Community Health Organizations (AAPCHO)

439 Twenty-Third Street
Oakland, CA 94612
Phone: (510) 272-9536
Fax: (510) 272-0817
Web site: http://aapcho.org

The Association of Asian Pacific Community Health Organizations (AAPCHO) is a national association representing community health organizations. It is dedicated to promoting advocacy, collaboration, and leadership to improve the health status and access to health care of Asian Americans, Native Hawaiians, and Pacific Islanders within the United States, its territories, and freely associated states, primarily through member community health clinics. Formed in 1987, AAPCHO advocates for policies and programs that will improve the provision of health care services that are community driven, financially affordable, linguistically accessible, and culturally appropriate. AAPCHO shares its collective knowledge and experiences with policymakers at the national, state, and local levels. Working collaboratively with its members throughout the continental United States, Hawaii, and U.S. territories, AAPCHO promotes policy and program needs as they affect the health status of Asian and Pacific Islander (API) populations. It serves as a conduit for the exchange and distribution of ideas, information, and service models to improve health care delivery to API populations. It develops and tests health-education and promotion programs across the nation and evaluates those nationwide programs already in existence. It also offers technical assistance and training to promote the establishment and expansion of services for medically underserved API communities.

Chinese American Political Association (CAPA)
P.O. Box 4313
Walnut Creek, CA 94596-0314
Phone: (510) 538-2791
Fax: (925) 938-2961
Web site: http://www.capa-news.org

The Chinese American Political Association (CAPA) has been serving the Chinese American community in the San Francisco and East Bay Area since 1984. It is a nonprofit, nonpartisan political association dedicated to political education. Its mission is to raise the political awareness of Chinese Americans and to encourage and promote their participation in the political processes of the United States. Its objectives are to assure Chinese Americans the same inherent social privileges and constitutional rights that are provided all U.S. citizens; to provide an effective voice on issues and events of concern to Chinese Americans; to endorse candidates for local, state, and national offices; to support and promote local, state, and national issues that are in the best interests of Chinese Americans; and to oppose prejudice and discrimination against Chinese Americans.

Japanese American Citizens League (JACL)
1765 Sutter Street
San Francisco, CA 94115
Phone: (415) 921-5225
Web site: http://www.jacl.org

The Japanese American Citizens League (JACL) is a membership organization whose mission is to secure and maintain the human and civil rights of Americans of Japanese ancestry and others victimized by injustice. The JACL has 112 chapters nationwide and eight regional districts with more than 24,000 members in twenty-three states. In addition to its national headquarters in San Francisco, the JACL has five regional offices (in Los Angeles, Fresno, and San Francisco, California; Seattle, Washington; and Chicago, Illinois) and an office in Washington, D.C. Its organizational newspaper, the *Pacific Citizen,* is distributed nationally from its office in Los Angeles. The JACL, the nation's oldest and largest Asian American civil rights organization, was founded in 1929 to address issues of discrimination targeted specifically at persons of Japanese ancestry residing in the United States. It was established to fight for the civil rights primarily of Japanese Americans but also for the benefit of Chinese Americans and other peoples of color. Its programs include advocacy, education, leadership development, legacy grants, and scholarships.

Japanese American National Museum
369 East First Street
Los Angeles, CA 90012
Phone: (213) 625-0414
Fax: (213) 625-1770
National School Project (NSP) Coordinator: (213) 830-5626
Web site: http://www.janm.org

The mission of the Japanese American National Museum is to promote understanding and appreciation of America's ethnic and cultural diversity by preserving, interpreting, and sharing the experiences of Japanese Americans. It shares the story of Japanese Americans because it honors the nation's diversity and strives to provide a voice for Japanese Americans and a forum that enables all people to explore their own heritage and culture.

The National School Project (NSP) is an undertaking of the museum to establish a national and international presence by creating a network of educators dedicated to developing classroom curriculum materials that reflect the story of Japanese Americans against the backdrop of the United States and to developing a training program for educators that emphasizes good pedagogical processes. The NSP provides workshops on cultural awareness for teachers. Another major task of the NSP is to try to develop or create a curriculum that can be used by teachers to help students make connections to Japanese Americans.

Korean American Historical Society (KAHS)
10303 N. Meridian Avenue, Suite 200
Seattle, WA 98133-9483
Phone: (206) 528-5784
Fax: (206) 523-4340
Web site: http://www.kahs.org

Founded in 1985, the Korean American Historical Society (KAHS) is a nonprofit organization dedicated to enriching the collective memory of Korean Americans through collecting, maintaining, and transmitting the heritage and achievements of Koreans living in the United States and abroad. KAHS projects include *Occasional Papers,* an annual scholarly journal of oral histories, community research, book reviews, critical essays, and reports. This journal is intended to present information and material for primary researchers as well as general readers. KAHS conducts and archives oral history interviews on the history of Korean expatriates in general and Korean Americans in particular; maintains a library of books, photographs, and materials pertinent to its mission; organizes and conducts seminars and symposia; encourages the development of Korean American studies as an academic discipline; and coordinates activities with other Korean community organizations for historical purposes.

European American

American Irish Historical Society
991 Fifth Avenue
New York, NY 10028
Phone: (212) 288-2263
Fax: (212) 628-7927
E-mail: info@aihs.org

The American Irish Historical Society, founded at the close of the nineteenth century to inform the world of the achievements of the Irish in the United States, is today a national center of scholarship and public education. From its home on New York's Fifth Avenue, across from the Metropolitan Museum of Art, it is a focus of contemporary Irish experience where current public issues are explored and where the great renaissance in Irish culture is celebrated in lectures, music recitals, art exhibits, and a literary journal. The society is nonpartisan and nonpolitical and welcomes new members. Its offices are open to the public during the week. Members have access to the society's large collection of rare Irish books, manuscripts, newspapers, and memorabilia.

American Scandinavian Foundation (ASF)
58 Park Avenue
New York, NY 10016
Phone: (212) 879-9779
Web site: http://www.amscan.org

The American Scandinavian Foundation (ASF) promotes international understanding through educational and cultural exchange between the United States and Denmark, Finland, Iceland, Norway, and Sweden. Founded in 1910, the ASF is a publicly supported, nonprofit organization that carries on an extensive program of fellowships, grants, trainee placement, publishing, membership offerings, and cultural activities. It is headquartered in New York City and has alumni, donors, and associate members worldwide.

Over the years, more than 26,000 young Americans and Scandinavians have participated in ASF's exchange programs of study, research, or practical training. Through these programs, the ASF cultivates enduring academic, professional, and personal ties between the United States and the Scandinavian countries. Its training program enables young Americans and Scandinavians to receive practical working experience while living abroad. Scandinavian trainees participate in the program in the United States in fields such as engineering, shipping, law, business administration, agriculture, and cabinetmaking. A smaller number of Americans also find training assignments in Scandinavia, mostly in technological fields. The ASF presents a wide range of cultural programs at its Scandinavia House: The Nordic Center in America. Most programs are open to the public, though some are restricted to ASF members. The ASF helps bring American and

Scandinavian life, art, and thought to public audiences by giving financial support to other institutions through its Public Project Grants program. A special effort is made to reach audiences outside the ASF's home base in New York City.

The ASF provides information on Scandinavian topics to a broad audience through the publication of its magazine, *Scandinavian Review,* which has been published continuously since 1913. The magazine, issued three times a year, is an English-language publication devoted to contemporary Scandinavian affairs and culture. The ASF also publishes a quarterly newsletter, *Scan,* which features news from Scandinavia, provides information on Scandinavian events throughout the United States, and reports on the ASF's activities. Other ASF publications include the annual guide *Study in Scandinavia* and *The Longboat,* an annual newsletter for ASF fellows.

American Swedish Institute (ASI)

2600 Park Avenue
Minneapolis, MN 55407
Phone: (612) 871-4907
Fax: (612) 871-8682
Web site: http://www.swedishamericanhist.org

The American Swedish Institute (ASI), founded in 1929 by Swan J. Turnblad, is a historic house/museum offering a variety of programs designed to celebrate Swedish culture. The museum showcases the institute's collection of Swedish glass, decorative and fine arts, textiles, and items from Sweden. The permanent exhibit "Swedish Life in the Twin Cities" explores the local Swedish American community through photographs, diaries, vintage recordings, and immigrant artifacts. The archives and library of the ASI serve as a reference and research facility for ASI staff, ASI members, and the public. Collections of books, papers, photographic materials, microforms, and sound recordings are focused on the following areas: (1) the history of the Turnblad family, the *Svenska Amerikanska Posten (Swedish-American Post),* and the American Swedish Institute; (2) the history of Swedish immigration to the United States, particularly to Minnesota; (3) Swedish American life and culture; and (4) the history and culture of Sweden, especially as it has influenced Swedish America.

Library Forum, a lecture series focusing on Swedish American history, art, music, and culture, presents speakers January through May and September through October. The ASI offers various educational opportunities that include Swedish language courses and courses in wood carving and knyppling (making Swedish bobbin lace) and in Swedish painting, history, and folk dance.

National Italian American Foundation (NIAF)
1860 Nineteenth Street, NW
Washington, DC 20009
Phone: (202) 387-0600
Web site : http://www.niaf.org

The National Italian American Foundation (NIAF) is the major advocate in Washington, D.C., for nearly 25 million Italian Americans, the nation's fifth-largest ethnic group. Its mission is to preserve and protect Italian American heritage and culture. Through its many programs, NIAF helps young Italian Americans with their education and careers. It works closely with Congress and the White House to promote the appointment of Italian Americans in government. It encourages the teaching of Italian language and culture in U.S. schools and monitors the portrayal of Italian Americans by the news and entertainment industries. It strengthens cultural and economic ties between Italy and the United States.

OSIA Italian American Culture and Heritage
219 E Street, NE
Washington, DC 20002
Phone: (202) 547-2900
Fax: (202) 546-8168
Web site: http://www.osia.org

Through a variety of philanthropic and social programs, OSIA represents the interests of Italian Americans and cooperates with U.S. and Italian officials to strengthen trade, diplomatic, cultural, and educational opportunities. OSIA also works with other organizations to unite all Americans in a multicultural society so that people may live in greater harmony. Its objectives include enrolling all men and women of Italian heritage under one banner in order to preserve and disseminate the rich cultural heritage of Italy. It seeks to promote and advance Italian Americans' progress everywhere within the framework of U.S. society. OSIA meets its objectives through a wide variety of community, cultural, social, charitable, educational, youth, and civic activities.

Polish American Association
(Zrzeszenie Amerykansko Polskie)
3834 North Cicero Avenue
Chicago, Illinois 60641
Phone: (773) 282-8206
Fax: (773) 282-1324
Web site: http://www.polish.org

The Polish American Association, founded in 1922 as the Polish Welfare Association, is the nation's only human services agency offering a comprehensive range of bilingual and bicultural services to the Polish community. The mission of the Polish American Association is to serve the diverse needs of the Polish community in the Chicago metropolitan area by providing resources for changing lives, with emphasis on assisting immigrants. Major program areas are education, employment, immigration, and social services. The philosophy of the Polish American Association reflects the belief that all people, but especially those who are in the process of change and adjustment, must be treated with sensitivity and respect.

The Polish American Association provides social services such as senior casework services; information, counseling, and advocacy assistance in obtaining benefits; battered-women's counseling; crisis intervention and counseling; court escort services; emergency housing placement; and a homeless day shelter. Employment services include job development and placement, employee recruitment for companies, homemaker services, and physical and environmental assistance for homebound or disabled persons. The association gives immigration assistance by preparing Immigration and Nationalization Services applications for visas, family reunification, extension of visas, student visas, fiancée visas, and U.S. passports and by conducting citizenship programs (including holding preliminary hearings and arranging oath ceremonies), classes, and seminars and community-education, information, and outreach programs. Educational programs include English classes and vocational classes in various work skills.

Polish American Congress (PAC)
5711 North Milwaukee Avenue
Chicago, IL 60646
Phone: (773) 763-9944

Fax: (773) 763-7114
Web site: http://pacchgo@www.polamcon.org
or
1612 K Street, NW
Suite 410
Washington, DC 20006
Phone: (202) 296-6955
Fax: (202) 835-1565
Web site: http://pacwash@www.polamcon.org

The Polish American Congress (PAC) is a national umbrella organization representing Americans of Polish descent and origin. The Polish American community prides itself on its deeply rooted commitment to the values of family, faith, democracy, hard work, and fulfillment of the American dream. PAC is a federation of more than 3,000 Polish American organizations and clubs. These groups include national fraternal benefit societies, such as the Polish National Alliance, Polish Women's Alliance, Polish Roman Catholic Union, Polish Falcons, and others, as well as veterans', cultural, professional, religious, and social associations. It has an aggregate membership of more than 1 million persons. PAC bylaws also provide for individual membership and associate membership. PAC promotes civic, educational, and cultural programs designed not only to further the knowledge of Polish history, language, and culture but also to stimulate Polish American pride in accomplishments.

Latina/Latino

ASPIRA Association
1444 Eye Street, NW
Suite 800
Washington, DC 20005
Phone: (703) 998-8045, (202) 835-3600
Fax: (202) 835-3613
E-mail: info@aspira.org
Web site: http://www.aspira.org/

The ASPIRA Association is the only national nonprofit organization devoted solely to the education and leadership development of Puerto Rican and other Latino youth. ASPIRA takes its name from the Spanish verb *aspirar*, "to aspire." All of ASPIRA's goals and activities spring from one basic belief: Puerto Ricans and Latinos have the collective potential to move their communities forward. ASPIRA looks at Latino youth and sees this potential: leaders waiting to emerge. Based on this philosophy, the ASPIRA Association has defined its mission as being to empower the Puerto Rican and Latino community through advocacy and through the education and leadership development of its youth.

The ASPIRA Association promotes the empowerment of the Puerto Rican and Latino community by developing and nurturing the leadership, intellectual, and cultural potential of its youth so that they may contribute their skills and dedication to the fullest development of Puerto Rican and Latino communities everywhere. With community-based offices in major cities in six states and Puerto Rico, ASPIRA's five hundred staff members work with more than 25,000 youth and their families each year to develop that potential. These youth—who will become educated, committed leaders for the community's future benefit—are called Aspirantes. Since its founding in 1961, ASPIRA has provided one-quarter of a million youth with the personal resources they need to remain in school and contribute to their communities. Most mainland Puerto Rican leaders today were encouraged by AS-PIRA during their adolescence.

ASPIRA News is a quarterly newsletter that covers local AS-PIRA activities, interviews, legislation, statistics, research, and commentary on local and national education issues. ASPIRA also publishes manuals and information guides on such issues as parental involvement in their children's schools, making the most of a child's education, and college and community empowerment.

Bilingual Review
Hispanic Research Center
Arizona State University
P.O. Box 872702
Tempe, AZ 85287-2702
Phone: (480) 965-3867
Fax: (480) 965-8309
E-mail: brp@asu.edu

The *Bilingual Review,* which has been published since 1974, features articles in the areas of bilingualism, bilingual education, and ethnic scholarship as well as the best creative literature by established and emerging Hispanic writers. It also contains book reviews, publication notices, and a section of professional announcements of upcoming events.

Cuban American National Foundation (CANF)
1312 South West Twenty-Seventh Avenue
Miami, FL 33145
Phone: (305) 592-7768
Fax: (305) 592-7889
Web site: http://www.canfnet.org

The Cuban American National Foundation (CANF) is a nonprofit organization dedicated to advancing freedom and democracy in Cuba. CANF is the largest Cuban organization in exile, with thousands of members across the United States and in other countries, representing a cross section of the Cuban exile community. CANF conducts and supports numerous and diverse activities, programs, and initiatives to advance human rights in Cuba, to inform public opinion on the plight of the Cuban people, to dispel prejudice and intolerance against Cubans in exile, and to promote Cuban culture and creative achievements.

Regular contact with independent groups and journalists and opposition figures as well as extensive information gathering and analysis allow CANF to offer an updated and comprehensive view of the situation in Cuba. Likewise, CANF provides a window to the outside world for Cubans on the island. In addition to having its own radio station, La Voz de la Fundación, for transmissions to the island, it led the effort to establish the U.S. Information Agency's Radio Martí (established in 1985) and TV Martí (established in 1990), the official U.S. operations broadcasting news and programming to the Cuban people. CANF's research, education, and information efforts are designed to enlighten the media, academia, policymakers, and public opinion—domestically and abroad—on Cuban issues. Numerous humanitarian programs provide active assistance to Cuba's people and help break down barriers that separate free Cubans and those on the island.

Latino Music and Books
P.O. Box 1104
De Soto, TX 75115
Phone: (972) 230-6204
Fax: (801) 991-6054
Web site: http://www.ritmoymas.com

Latino Music and Books specializes in Tejano music and Chicano literature. Its purpose is to make the Latino American experience available in music, literature, and music videos. It stocks Latino American literature published by Arte Publico Press, Bilingual Press Review, Children's Books Press, Curbstone Press, and other publishers that specialize in Latino American literature. These publishers feature the works of U.S. Latino authors such as Sandra Cisneros, Rudolfo Anaya, Denise Chavez, Pat Mora, and R. Hinojosa. Latino Music and Books stocks bilingual children's books, and the majority of the books stocked are written by Latinos for the Latino market.

**Mexican American Legal Defense
and Educational Fund (MALDEF)**
634 South Spring Street
Los Angeles, CA 90014
Phone: (213) 629-2512
Web site: http://www.maldef.org

The Mexican American Legal Defense and Educational Fund (MALDEF) is the leading nonprofit Latino litigation, advocacy, and educational outreach institution in the United States. Its mission is to protect and promote the civil rights of the Latinos living in the United States. MALDEF works to secure the rights of Latinos, primarily in the areas of employment, education, immigrants' rights, political access, language, and public resource equity. Its goals are to foster sound public policies, laws, and programs that safeguard the rights of Latinos and to expand the opportunities of Latinos to participate fully in society and to make a positive contribution toward their well-being. MALDEF achieves its objectives through advocacy, community education, collaboration with other groups and individuals, the awarding of higher education scholarships in law and communications, and, when necessary, the legal system.

Over the years, MALDEF has been at the forefront of civil rights litigation, setting precedent in many cases and establishing new systems to elect officials, hire and promote employees, and educate children. On the nonlitigation side, MALDEF works extensively on the issues of redistricting and census adjustment, and through its leadership-development programs, it trains and empowers Latinos to serve on policy-making boards and commissions at the local, state, and national levels. Through the skills and training taught in its parent leadership programs, MALDEF also provides parents with the knowledge and tools necessary to advocate for a high-quality education for their children.

Mexican American Political Association (MAPA)
P.O. Box 1744
Fresno, CA 93717
Fax: (559) 888-0210
Web site: http://www.mapa.org

The Mexican American Political Association (MAPA) is dedicated to the constitutional and democratic principle of political freedom and representation for the Mexican and Hispanic people of the United States. MAPA's goals are to (1) recruit and advise Latino and Latina candidates for offices at every level of government, (2) work with MAPA committees to raise money and contribute to Hispanic sensitive campaigns, (3) lobby and testify for legislation responsive to Hispanic needs, (4) monitor the judicial selection process, (5) support qualified Latinos and Latinas for governmental appointments, (6) affect all levels of the educational system, and (7) develop voter-registration and education programs in Hispanic communities.

**National Association for Chicana
and Chicano Studies (NACCS)**
P.O. Box 720052
San Jose, CA 95172-0052
Web site: http://www.naccs.org

The National Association for Chicana and Chicano Studies (NACCS) was founded to encourage research to further the political actualization of the Chicana and Chicano community. From its inception, NACCS has encouraged research that diverges from mainstream academic research. It holds that mainstream research, which is based on an integrationist perspective emphasizing consensus, assimilation, and the legitimacy of society's institutions, has obscured and distorted the significant historical roles that class, race, gender, sexuality, and group interests have played in shaping Chicana and Chicano existence as a people. Its research confronts these perspectives and challenges the structures and ideologies of inequality based on classist, racist, sexist, and heterosexist privileges in society. In shaping the form of this challenge, NACCS contends that its research generates new knowledge about the Chicana and Chicano community.

The NACCS's purpose is to (1) facilitate dialogue about Chicana and Chicano experiences among scholars, students, and community members; (2) encourage, promote, and assist the development of Chicana and Chicano studies centers, programs, and departments; (3) facilitate the recruitment of Chicanas and Chicanos at all levels of education; (4) promote and develop curriculum and the integration of Chicana and Chicano studies from kindergarten to college; (5) provide mentorship for undergraduate and graduate students to facilitate their entrance and success in the academy and the community; and (6) provide mentorship to faculty to facilitate their entrance and success in the academy.

National Puerto Rican Coalition (NPRC)
1700 K Street, NW
Suite 500
Washington, DC 20006
Phone: (202) 223-3915
Fax: (202) 429-2223
E-mail: nprc@nprcinc.org

The mission of the National Puerto Rican Coalition (NPRC) is to strengthen and enhance the social, political, and economic well-being of Puerto Ricans throughout the United States and in Puerto Rico with a special focus on the most vulnerable. The National Puerto Rican Coalition, Inc., was incorporated as a membership organization in 1977. The NPRC's public policy analyses of issues concerning the Puerto Rican and Latino community is recognized by national organizations and advocates as being valuable to the work they perform. Working in coalition with other national policy groups and advocates, NPRC serves as a convener, catalyst, facilitator, and resource for the community at large. It provides leadership and a voice on national policy to address the needs of the Puerto Rican community, and it empowers the Puerto Rican community to become an effective participant in the formulation of public policies. This work has included developing a national public policy agenda, preparing reports on the impact of legislative changes to federal benefit programs, issuing demographic profiles of ninety-two congressional districts with significant Puerto Rican populations, and publishing the 1999 *National Directory of Puerto Rican Elected Officials*, which identifies ninety-five officials of Puerto Rican heritage elected to federal, state, and municipal legislative offices on the mainland.

The NPRC has been serving the developmental needs of the Puerto Rican community through a set of training and technical-assistance services that make up NPRC's Community Building Initiative (CBI). Through the CBI, nonprofit civic organizations are provided hands-on assistance in developing and implementing solutions to social, economic, and political problems. NPRC assists community-based organizations with strategic planning, capacity-building training, access to vital resources, and financing of community housing and economic-development projects. The CBI is focused on individual improvement, the promotion of opportunity, and the advancement of quality of life through holistic approaches that are community driven and that have broad participation and collaborative linkages. Through the CBI program, NPRC has worked with community leaders in more than two hundred communities to advance economic and social agendas, to address community-development issues, and to move citizens to develop agendas for change.

Native American

Native American Journalists Association (NAJA)
3359 Thirty-Sixth Avenue South
Minneapolis, MN 55406
Phone: (612) 729-9244
Fax: (612) 729-9373
Web site: http://infor@naja.com

The Native American Journalists Association (NAJA) serves Native journalists through programs designed to enrich journalism and promote Native cultures. This organization recognizes Native Americans as distinct peoples, based on tradition and culture. It seeks to educate and unify its membership through journalism programs that promote diversity and defend freedom of expression. The goal of the NAJA is the improvement of communications among Native people and between Native Americans and the general public. The work of the association addresses the spectrum of Native communications and encompasses a wide range of issues and concerns affecting the survival and development of the Native media. Its programs include professional-development fellowships and scholarship funds, job listings, and media resources.

North American Indian Legal Services
Brenda Bellonger, Manager/Attorney
Phone: (303) 988-2611
Web site: www.nailsinc.org

This organization responds to the need for legal services and advocacy for low-income American Indian families in the Colorado Front Range urban Indian community (the four-county area of Denver, Jefferson, Adams, and Arapahoe Counties). It is currently undertaking two focus projects, the Permanency Planning for Indian Children Project and the Juvenile Justice Advocacy Service. The Permanency Planning for Indian Children Project is an Indian child-welfare mediation program that attempts to ensure timely resolution of Indian child-welfare cases. The Juvenile Justice Advocacy Service provides legal services in cases involving American Indian youth that are heard in juvenile courts. The goal is to create an effective partnership among the courts, service agencies, and American Indian communities to service the needs of low-income American Indian youth and their families. Client services are free for families with incomes less than 125 percent of the federal poverty level, and a sliding scale of fees are charged for those with incomes above that level.

8

Print Resources

The topic of racial and ethnic relations in the United States is extremely broad and is characterized by a large array of comparative issues. The print resources I have identified in this chapter are intended to communicate both the richness of the topic for interested readers and the range of subtexts within discussions of race and ethnicity. In this chapter, I have tried to avoid duplicating the references in Chapters 1, 2 and 3. Together, the references in Chapters 1, 2, and 3 and those in this chapter provide the reader with an extensive range of materials—books, chapters in books, journal articles, and Internet sites—for studying racial and ethnic relations in the United States.

I have also tried to provide the reader with references in this chapter congruent with the topics discussed in Chapters 1, 2, and 3. For example, I used the following descriptors for organizing the reference materials in this chapter: *diversity, nativism, immigration, hate crimes, racial profiling, immigration, affirmative action,* and *racial inequality.* I have supplemented the reference materials in this chapter with studies focused on particular racial or ethnic groups in the United States. I have also included references to textbooks on race and ethnic relations for readers interested in a textbook approach to the study of racial and ethnic relations in the United States.

Finally, the reader must keep in mind that the list of print resources in this chapter is not comprehensive. Rather, the print resources listed in this chapter should be used as a starting point for further study of a particular topic, for example, racial profiling as a discriminatory practice. I have attempted to provide the reader with a range of topics in the print references to arouse interest in the study of racial and ethnic relations in the United States. It is up to the reader to utilize the print resources as a catalyst in his or her exploration of racial and ethnic relations in the United States.

Adams, David W. 1988. **"Fundamental Considerations: The Deep Meaning of Native American Schooling, 1880–1900."** *Harvard Educational Review* 58: 1–28.

According to the author, by the late nineteenth century, in light of the American Indians' loss of land and traditional ways of life, U.S. policymakers undertook a massive campaign directed at American Indian education. The author argues that these efforts represented much more than an attempt to assimilate American Indians into white culture. The historical significance of the crusade to school American Indians is explored, with emphasis on three interpretive perspectives: the Protestant ideology, the civilization-savagism paradigm, and the quest for land by whites.

Allen, Walter R., and Angie Y. Chung. 2000. **"Your Blues Ain't Like My Blues: Race, Ethnicity, and Social Inequality in America."** *Contemporary Sociology* 29: 796–805.

This article reviews and evaluates the research on racial and ethnic inequality. The authors argue that racial and ethnic inequality in the United States is unique because of the history of slavery, the subjugation of American Indians and Mexicans, and the unfair treatment of Asian and other ethnic laborers. Years of slavery and years of legally sanctioned segregation have left social practices that deny opportunities to minority groups. According to the authors, white females, some Asian American groups, and middle-class African Americans have made some progress in overcoming inequality. However, their progress has resulted in the perception that all racial and ethnic groups have equal opportunities. The authors argue that the perception is narrow and overly simplified because white males are still the most privileged members of American society.

Andrews, William L., and Henry Louis Gates Jr., eds. 1998. *The Civitas Anthology of African American Slave Narratives.* New York: Basic Civitas Books.

The slave narrative forms the foundation of the African American literary tradition. From the late-eighteenth-century narratives by Africans who endured the harrowing Middle Passage through the classic U.S. fugitive-slave narratives of the mid–nineteenth century, slave narratives have provided some of the most graphic and damning documentary evidence of the horrors of slavery. Riveting, passionate, and politically charged, the slave narrative blends personal memory and rhetorical attacks on slavery to create powerful literature and propaganda. In this anthology, the editors present seven classic antislavery narratives of the antebellum period in their entirety: (1) *The History of Mary Prince*, a West Indian slave, the first slave narrative published by a woman in the Americas; (2) *The Confessions of Nat Turner,* written when Turner was asked to record his motivation for leading the bloodiest slave revolt in U.S. history; (3) *The Narrative of the Life of Frederick Douglass,* an international best-seller and the first narrative to fashion the male fugitive slave into an African American cultural hero; (4) *The Narrative of William W. Brown,* an account that explored with unprecedented realism the slave's survival ethic and the art of the slave trickster; (5) *The Narrative of the Life of Henry Bibb,* the story of the struggles of the most memorable family man among the classic slave narrators; (6) *Running a Thousand Miles for Freedom,* a gripping chronicle of one of the most daring and celebrated slave escapes ever recorded; and (7) *Incidents in the Life of Slave Girl,* a dramatic text that exposed the sexual abuse of female slaves and pioneered the image of the fugitive slave woman as an articulate resister and survivor.

Asumah, Seth N., and Matthew T. Bradley. 2001. **"Making Sense of U.S. Immigration Policy and Multiculturalism."** *Western Journal of Black Studies* 25: 82–92.

According to the authors of this article, antagonism toward multiculturalism continues to adversely affect superordinate and subordinate group relationships in the United States. The authors argue that this antagonism manifests itself in various ways, such as the unicultural notion that immigration has reached epidemic proportions in the United States. The authors examine how the cleavages between the advocates and opponents of immigration have been exacerbated by the unfounded suggestion that newly arrived immigrants (neo-sojourners) are "taking more than they are giving" to the "American way of life."

Bartkowski, John, Frank Howell, and Shu-Chuan Lai. 2002. **"Spatial Variations in Church Burnings: The Social Ecology of Victimized Communities in the South."** *Rural Sociology* 67: 578–602.

In recent years, church burnings in the U.S. South have attracted a great deal of attention. Many commentators have charged that they are a product of strained race relations throughout the South, particularly of severe racial tensions in southern rural areas. In this study, the authors evaluate these claims. They begin by mapping the spatial coordinates of recorded church burnings from 1990 to 1997 and find that church arsons are concentrated in the South. Church burnings, however, are more an urban phenomenon than popular media accounts suggest. The authors then explore the influence of contextual factors—population and locale, racial composition and inequality, socioeconomic conditions, local religious ecology, and patterns of reported crime—on church burnings in counties located in the study region. They use statistical models to show that church arsons are most likely to occur in small metropolitan statistical areas (MSAs) and non-MSA counties containing a city of a least 10,000 residents. Church burnings are also especially likely in counties with a higher percentage of black residents, a larger number of churches relative to the rest of the state, and a higher arson rate.

Bass, Sandra. 2001. **"Policing Space, Policing Race: Social Control Imperatives and Police Discretionary Decisions."** *Social Justice* 27: 156–176.

In this examination of the relationship between race and policing in the United States, the author notes that discriminatory policies embedded in police practices have resulted in a strained relationship between police agencies and racial minorities. She argues that the experiences of African Americans with police illustrate the practice of racism and discrimination by police officers. She also argues that the "war on drugs," the crackdown on gang violence, and the resultant emergence of condoned racial profiling demonstrate that the police continue to use race as a determination of criminality. She suggests that police reform is necessary and can only be accomplished when the police begin to conceive of a new role for themselves, one that is compatible with the ideals upheld by a multicultural democracy.

Bean, Frank D., and Marta Tienda. 1987. *The Hispanic Population of the United States.* New York: Russell Sage Foundation.

The authors use U.S. census data to construct a portrait of the social and demographic features of the Hispanic population in the United States. They use detailed population statistics from the 1960, 1970, and 1980 U.S. censuses to examine trends in educational, occupational, and income outcomes for Hispanics. In addition, they compare and contrast the three major groups in the Hispanic population—Puerto Ricans, Cubans, and Mexicans—across social and demographic characteristics. Hispanics are compared on select dimensions to other racial populations in the United States.

Beck, E. 2000. **"Guess Who's Coming to Town: White Supremacy, Ethnic Competition, and Social Change."** *Sociological Focus* 33: 153–174.

This article attempts to provide a better understanding of the dynamics of white racist movements by exploring the socioeconomic factors associated with communities targeted by the Ku Klux Klan for its publication activities. Ethnic competition theory is utilized to provide clues for understanding which social environments are conducive to the formation of racist and white-nationalist movements. The author examines data on almost nine hundred incidents of white-supremacist activity in the U.S. South between 1980 and 1990 to explore the empirical relationship between competition, social change, and white supremacy. The author found that in static models, there was no support for linking ethnic competition to Klan activity, but that in dynamic models, there was evidence that linked white-supremacist activity to communities where Asians and Hispanics were increasing their relative share of resources.

Benei, Veronique. 2000. **"Nation, Diaspora, and Area Studies: South Asia from Great Britain to the United States."** *L'Homme* 156: 131–160.

This study describes the relations between national identities and the tradition of research on South Asia in Great Britain and the United States during the twentieth century. According to the author, academic disciplines were reinforced as the British Empire waned, while area studies were started in the United

States. Such studies later developed in Great Britain owing to a national commitment. Political and intellectual rivalry between the two nations occurred over the Indian subcontinent when a wave of Indian immigrants arrived in the United States in the 1960s. By the 1980s, these immigrants' children had found a place on U.S. college campuses, resulting in the placement of South Asian studies in the context of U.S. multiculturalism.

Brown, Dee. 2001. *Bury My Heart at Wounded Knee: An Indian History of the American West.* New York: Henry Holt.

This book was first published in 1970, and it changed the way Americans think about the original inhabitants of the United States. The author begins with the Long Walk of the Navajos in 1860 and ends thirty years later with the massacre of Sioux men, women, and children at Wounded Knee in South Dakota. The book tells how American Indians lost their land and lives to a dynamically expanding white society. The author shows how promises made to the Indians fell victim to the ruthlessness and greed of white settlers pushing westward to make new lives. The Indians were herded off their ancestral lands into ever-shrinking reservations and were starved and killed if they resisted. This book is unique in describing the opening of the West from the Indian's viewpoint and in its account of how Indian leaders and their peoples suffered the West's opening to white settlers.

Bullard, Robert D. 2000. *Race, Class, and Environmental Quality.* 3rd ed. Boulder, CO: Westview Press.

According to the author, to be poor, working-class, or a person of color in the United States often means bearing a disproportionate share of the country's environmental problems. Bullard examines the premise that all Americans have a basic right to live in a healthy environment by documenting the efforts of five African American communities, empowered by the civil rights movement, to link environmentalism with issues of social justice. He speaks to the reader from the front lines of the environmental justice movement about new developments in environmental racism, different organizing strategies, and success stories in the struggle for environmental equity.

Button, J., and B. Rienzo. 2003. **"The Impact of Affirmative**

Action: Black Employment in Six Southern Cities." *Social Science Quarterly* 84: 1–14.

There have been numerous claims about the current role and impact of affirmative action, one of the most controversial public policies in U.S. society. This article examines data on affirmative action and black employment in six representative Florida cities. Data were gathered on 167 randomly selected businesses through personal interviews with employers. The authors utilized statistical models to explore the independent effects of affirmative action in a multivariate path model of employment-related predictors. The study's results show that employer support for affirmative action has a significant and positive influence on black employment, particularly at higher job levels. The authors conclude that affirmative action has developed a constituency among employers who value diversity in employment due to demographic changes that have altered labor and consumer markets.

Comas-Diaz, Lillian. 2001. **"Hispanics, Latinos, or Americanos: The Evolution of Identity."** *Cultural Diversity and Ethnic Minority Psychology* 7: 115–120.

In this essay, the author identifies and categorizes terms used to designate the Hispanic/Latino population in the United States. Her analysis frames the process of ethnic self-designation within an ethnopolitical and psychosocial context. She concludes the analysis by presenting mestizaje (the culture of mixed-blood Latinos and indigenous peoples) and transculturation as processes involved in the evolution of Latino identity.

Conyers, James, Jr. 1997. **"The Problems of the Twenty-First Century: Black Studies Locating a Niche in the Public Sphere of Higher Education."** *Western Journal of Black Studies* 21(2): 117–123.

The author reviews the research literature on black studies to show that the Eurocentric hegemonic perspective in education has proven to be "inept." According to the author, conceptual problems in the literature illustrate the absence of an alternative epistemology to allow the examination of African phenomena from an interdisciplinary perspective. The author argues that Africana scholars must collectively accept the challenge of intellectual rigor and academic integrity in the pursuit of providing critical studies that seek to describe and evaluate the historical and cultural experiences of African Americans.

Danquah, Meri Nana-Ama, ed. 2000. *Becoming American: Personal Essays by First Generation Immigrant Women.* New York: Hyperion.

The editor asked twenty-three first-generation immigrant women a simple question: "What does it mean to become American?" The women's responses are captured in twenty-three essays that reveal the dual lives many immigrants lead. The duality in the women's life experiences revolves around two issues: appreciating the freedom and opportunity in the United States while remaining ambivalent about the superficiality of the U.S. lifestyle, and wanting to fit in while fearing that assimilating means losing some part of one's self. The diversity of the women's homelands—Latin America, Africa, Asia, and Europe—makes each story unique. One interesting feature of these essays is that most of them are by immigrants from middle-class and privileged backgrounds. As such, they open a window to observing the difficulties experienced by nonpoor immigrants pursuing a better life in the United States.

Delgado, Richard, and Jean Stefancic, eds. 1998. *The Latino Condition: A Critical Reader.* New York: New York University Press.

The editors have assembled a collection of essays that address the historical origins of Spanish-speaking people in the United States, how the Spanish-speaking people were viewed by the dominant culture, how those views were magnified into stereotypes by the media, and the growth of efforts in the Latino community for self-definition. Other topics include legal reform and resistance to prejudice, divisions within the civil rights movement, gender- and class-based divisions within the Latino community, issues of assimilation and bilingualism, and border theory.

Deloria, Vine, Jr. 1981. **"Native Americans: The American Indian Today."** *Annals of the American Academy of Political and Social Science* 454: 139–149.

The author describes factors in the emergence of American Indians as a distinctive ethnic group. He details dislocations within reservation communities by focusing on (1) urbanization and the dropping median age of reservation residents, (2) technology and transport innovations, (3) fragmentation of federal American Indian policy and programs, and (4) experimentation and the influence of the civil rights movement. He identifies issues important to American Indians: the continued lack of economic access, particularly as both a cause and a result of lack of educational opportunities; the question of developing energy and mineral resources on American Indian lands; conservation-minded agricultural projects; political activism and tribal organization; and areas of increasing cultural development and visibility.

————. 1992. **"Secularism, Civil Religion, and the Religious Freedom of American Indians."** *American Indian Culture and Research Journal* 16: 9–206.

According to the author, although the anti–American Indian nature of decisions by the U.S. Supreme Court and Congress is clear, court rulings also reveal an antireligious inclination. The notion of "free religious practice" is discussed in historical perspective. Forms of modern U.S. religiosity are examined, particularly the superficial and politically oriented nature of fundamentalist Christian movements. The author argues that the animosity toward American Indian religiosity is related to the fact that American Indians are a fundamentally religious and consistent tribal community desiring freedom to practice values higher than those of the state.

Dinnerstein, Leonard, Roger L. Nichols, and David M. Reimers. 1996. *Natives and Strangers: A Multicultural History of Americans.* New York: Oxford University Press.

The authors examine the role of immigrants, African Americans, and American Indians in U.S. history. They argue that changes in the demographic character of U.S. society, especially the increasing numbers of immigrants, has increased the need for awareness of the contributions of immigrants, African Americans, and American Indians in the building of U.S. society.

Dinnerstein, Leonard, and David M. Reimers. 1999. *Ethnic Americans: A History of Immigration.* 4th ed. New York: Columbia University Press.

This book provides a concise and comprehensive overview of immigration from Europe, Asia, and Latin America from 1607 to the present. Principal topics addressed by the authors are ethnic conflict and assimilation in American society, the increasing numbers of refugees arriving in the United States during the 1980s, the asylum crisis of the 1990s, and the changing demographics of immigration to the United States. The authors also examine the rise of nativism in response to the "new immigrants"—for example, the passage of English-only laws, the attack on bilingual education, and the end of bilingual ballots.

Essed, Philomena, and David T. Goldberg, eds. 2002. *Race Critical Theories: Text and Context.* Malden, MA: Blackwell.

This anthology brings together major critical race theorizing over the last twenty years and provides significant insights into the use of race for political, legal, and cultural purposes. Each essay is accompanied by a reflection, usually written by the contributor, about the original essay's political context and the author's personal motivations. Seminal writings are joined by more recent essays that assess the impact of the critical past on the scope and depth of current thinking on race.

The book is divided into two parts. The essays in the first part are organized in chronological order to illustrate the lines of conceptual influence, as well as the types of theoretical influences, that prevailed in racial studies at different moments in its development. The essays in the second part are conceptually driven to show the impact of past texts on understanding and transforming conditions. The editors draw on the essays to bring fresh insights to the discourse on critical theories about race and racism that have been generated in multiple localities.

Feagin, Joe R., and Karyn D. McKinney. 2003. *The Many Costs of Racism.* Lanham, MD: Rowman and Littlefield.

The authors of this book argue that racism is not a thing of the past, that it is, rather, a persistent feature in U.S. society. In order to demonstrate the pervasiveness of discrimination against blacks by whites in the United States, the authors draw on previous research and data from focus groups conducted in the mid-1990s with two groups of economically successful African Americans (a total of thirty-seven participants). Supplementary data were drawn from interviews with more than two hundred middle-class African Americans conducted by one of the authors in the 1990s.

The authors argue that although most Americans are acquainted with the more visible forms of racism and discriminatory practices, it is the subtle, more covert forms that continue to create problems in society. The costs of racism and discriminatory practices for African Americans, as individuals and as a group, are identified by the authors in several contexts: psychological, economic, physical, health care, and community. The authors review strategies used by African Americans to fight against oppression and discrimination, strategies ranging from private, psychological coping techniques to active resistance behaviors.

Feagin, Joe R., Hernan Vera, and Pinar Batur. 2001. *White Racism: The Basics.* 2nd ed. New York: Routledge.

The authors present a series of case studies focused on the topics of cross burnings and white supremacy, antiblack attitudes on a college campus, racial discrimination in restaurants, racial victimization, racial profiling by criminal justice agencies, negative perceptions of nonwhite minorities in private and government sectors, white views of African Americans, and the struggles of social justice against antiblack racism.

Flippen, Chenoa. 2001. **"Residential Segregation and Minority Home Ownership."** *Social Science Research* 30: 337–362.

The author analyzes the impact of residential segregation on the home ownership of black, white, and Hispanic preretirement adults. By combining individual and household-level data from the Health and Retirement Study, a nationally representative longitudinal survey of the preretirement age population (e.g., 51–61 years of age) administered every two years since the initial survey in 1992. Using metropolitan-level characteristics from the 1990 census, the author identifies the unique effect of metropolitan residential segregation on minority home ownership. By considering the disparate impact of five dimensions of segregation on home ownership, the author illustrates the mechanisms through which metropolitan residential segregation operates. The results clearly demonstrate the negative effect of segregation on minority home ownership and key differences between blacks and Hispanics and across dimensions of segregation that highlight the contextual nature of housing stratification and the importance of urban population dynamics to racial and ethnic housing inequality.

Fredrickson, Darin D., and Raymond P. Siljander. 2002. *Racial Profiling: Eliminating the Confusion between Racial and Criminal Profiling and Clarifying What Constitutes Unfair Discrimination and Persecution.* Springfield, IL: Charles C. Thomas.

The authors discuss how the practice of profiling criminals is differentiated from acts of racial profiling in order to illustrate which practices constitute legitimate or discriminatory acts of profiling. They examine the origins of criminal profiling, the differences between criminal and racial profiling, instances in which law enforcement agencies apply profiling strategies, and the constitutionality of pretext stops. The authors also discuss difficulties in monitoring law enforcement agencies' use of profiling and problems with systems that collect racial profiling data, for example, the U.S. Supreme Court's decision in *U.S. v. Armstrong* (1996).

Glazer, Nathan. 2001. **"From Multiculturalism to Diversity."** *Hedgehog Review* 3: 24–39.

The author discusses the shift from the word *multiculturalism* to the less intimidating word *diversity* to describe the different racial and ethnic groups in the United States. The assumption is that differences will not only persist but will enjoy a significant amount of public support. The author argues that since the change in emphasis from assimilation to a celebration of diversity, controversies no longer focus on formal political equality for immigrants but instead now focus on the meaning of full acceptance. An exploration of the historical context that promoted the development of multiculturalism stresses the importance of the civil rights movement, noting that the increased political and social influence of the black population, as well as the introduction of black studies departments in colleges and universities, led to similar changes for Latinos, Asian groups, and American Indians. The author explores attitudinal changes that occurred in the United States during the 1960s and 1970s and reasons why multiculturalism has been so successful in U.S. schools in spite of considerable criticism by the intellectual elite. He also discusses the meaning of multiculturalism for the future of the United States.

Goodman, Greg S. 2002. *Reducing Hate Crimes and Violence among American Youth: Creating Transformational Agency through Critical Praxis.* New York: Peter Lang.

This book discusses how educators and school boards can develop and implement strategies for promoting transformational agency for those students most at risk. According to the author, developing alternative schools that foster strong relationships through supportive communities for disaffected youth can develop hope and trust within those youth as they continue their educational and social development. Alternative schools effectively build transformative agency within their students by genuinely caring about their success.

Green, Donald, Robert Abelson, and Margaret Garnett. 1999. **"The Distinctive Political Views of Hate-Crime Perpetrators and White Supremacists."** In *Cultural Divides: Understanding and Overcoming Group Conflict,* ed. Deborah Prentice and Dale Miller, 429–464. New York: Russell Sage Foundation.

This essay focuses on the role of social psychological causes of hate crimes, suggesting that discomfort with social change, not increased economic resentment, is what distinguishes white supremacists and hate-crime perpetrators from the general public. The authors explore the values of white-supremacist groups by obtaining questionnaire data from eighty-two persons suspected of being involved in hate-crime activity in North Carolina between 1986 and 1995 and from a comparison sample of seven hundred members of the general population. The findings show that hate-crime perpetrators and white supremacists are not notably more economically frustrated and pessimistic about financial prospects than other people. However, they are significantly more likely to hold reactionary political views, to fear diversity, and to feel threatened by immigration, race-mixing, or the blurring of gender roles. The fear of social change distinguishes hate-crime perpetrators and white supremacists and makes them more susceptible to participation in harassment or violent action as a means of preventing encroachment on what they perceive as their territory and familiar way of life.

Hamm, Mark. 1993. *American Skinheads: The Criminology and Control of Hate Crime.* Westport, CT: Praeger.

The author explores the role of Nazism in modern developments in crime and delinquency, noting the prevalence of neo-Nazi skinhead movements in diverse cities and among a wide spectrum of the population. The book is divided into three parts. Part I, "Idiots with Ideology" includes four chapters: Chapter 1, "The Neo-Nazi Skinheads of North America," describes the types of ideologically motivated violent crimes committed by skinhead youths in the United States and explores the social perceptions of skinheads. Chapter 2, "A History of the Skinhead Nation," explores the development of the skinhead movement since the 1950s (in London, England) to explain how it became an international youth subculture that developed around the punk rock music movement. Chapter 3, "From Haight-Ashbury to Plymouth Rock: The Rise of the American Neo-Nazi Skinheads," traces the development of several U.S. skinhead gangs during the late 1970s and early 1980s. It offers a glimpse of the leaders and lifestyles of these gangs and focuses special attention on the life of Tom Metzger and his White Aryan Resistance movement. Chapter 4, "The Internal Structure of a Terrorist Youth Subculture," explains that U.S. neo-Nazi skinheads differ from traditional juvenile gangs because of their overt racism, political violence, and international connections, arguing that, for the purposes of devising public policies to control their violence, they should be defined as a terrorist youth subculture.

Part II, "Inside the Skinhead Subculture," consists of eight chapters. Chapter 5, "Sociological Perspectives on Terrorist Youth Subcultures," provides an overview of functionalist, neo-Marxist, and differential identification-reinforcement models, each of which offers insight into explanations for the development of the skinhead subculture in the United States. Chapter 6, "Entering the Skinhead Subculture," describes the data for this study, which came from thirty-six interviews with racist skinheads throughout the United States. They were asked questions regarding family issues, lifestyle, drugs, criminal records, recruitment, indoctrination, hate crimes, Nazism, and Satanism. Chapter 7, "Terrorism, Rebellion, and Style," reports the findings of the interviews, offers a discussion of the background characteristics of the skinheads and the social organization of the groups, and compares these findings to commonly held assumptions about skinheads. Chapter 8, "Terrorism and Racist Media Images," argues that white youths are attracted to the skinhead movement not because of socioeconomic disadvantage but, rather, because of the subculture's emotional appeal of white power rock and the skinhead style. Chapter 9, "The Social Organization of Terrorist Youth Subcultures," analyzes diverse patterns of organization, the role of the group, and group processes to reveal how values, music preferences, and styles differ between terrorist and nonterrorist skinheads. Chapter 10, "Antifeminism and the Orthodoxy of Domestic Terrorism," discusses the communal nature of most skinhead organizations, offering case studies to investigate social roles, gender differences, and the role of women in sustaining subcultural homology. Chapter 11, "Beer, Bonding, and the Ceremony of Berserking," shows that skinheads are almost complete abstainers from hard drugs. However, beer plays a large role in their social life, with most reporting that they were intoxicated with beer when carrying out acts of racial violence. Chapter 12, "Chaos in the Soul: Nazi Occultism and the Morality of Vengeance," argues that Satanic beliefs are not prevalent among skinheads. Instead, they are devotees of Nazi occultism, believing in vengeance and selective compassions.

Part III, "Conclusions and Recommendations," consists of a final chapter, Chapter 13, "The Criminology and Control of Domestic Terrorism," which offers a theory of terrorist youth subcultures and an assessment of various measures to control these movements.

Henderson, Eric. 1997. **"Indian Gaming: Social Consequences."** *Arizona State Law Journal* 29: 205–250.

The author examines historical and ethnographic materials in order to discuss the social consequences of gaming for American Indian communities. According to the author, games and gaming activities were a central part of American Indian life prior to contact with European immigrants. The passage of the Indian Gaming Regulatory Act, however, has resulted in the development and expansion of a gaming industry in American Indian communities that has the potential to create "problem gambling" among tribal members.

———. 1998. **"Ancestry and Casino Dollars in the Formation of Tribal Identity."** *Race and Ethnic Ancestry Law Journal* 4: 7–24.

This paper explores the implications of the Indian Gaming Regulatory Act for tribal polities and their constituent members. The author argues that scrutiny of tribal membership by the U.S. government is an infringement on tribal sovereignty. In particular, U.S. governmental scrutiny of tribal membership is an erosion of Indian self-identity in the United States.

Hine, Darlene. 1997. *Hine Sight: Black Women and the Re-Construction of American History.* Bloomington: Indiana University Press.

The essays in this collection, written and previously published by Darlene Hine over a fourteen-year period, investigate the role of African American women in U.S. history. Several of the essays challenge historians of the black experience and of women to pay more attention to African American women. The typical explanation for their exclusion is the paucity of historical records and documents that might reveal their historical circumstances. However, the author identifies a number of themes and topics pertaining to African American women that can be usefully investigated, including the history of black women in slavery, particularly the female slave's use of sexual resistance as a method of challenging the slave order. Another topic of importance is the relationship between lynching and rape as an avenue to exploring the power dynamics among black and white men and women. Attention is also paid to the need for black and white female historians to engage in crossover studies as a step toward better understanding one another. Other forms of black women's resistance are also examined, especially in the context of the great black migration to the urban Midwest during the first half of the twentieth century.

Horton, John. 1995. *The Politics of Diversity: Immigration, Resistance, and Change in Monterey Park, California.* Philadelphia: Temple University Press.

This book chronicles the change in Monterey Park, California, a suburb eight miles east of downtown Los Angeles, from a predominantly white, middle-class bedroom community in the 1970s to a thriving Pacific Rim boomtown populated by immigrants from Hong Kong and Taiwan in the 1980s. The book examines the response of white residents in Monterey Park to the increasing numbers of Asian immigrants: the implementation of anti-Asian initiatives designed to "take back the community," such as the passage by the city council of an English-only language restriction for business and public signs or advertisements. Monterey Park attracted national attention as a result of the hostilities between white and Asian residents.

Hutner, Gordon, ed. *Immigrant Voices: Twenty-Four Narratives on Becoming an American.* New York: Signet Classic, 1999.

Narratives about the immigrant experience in early America are instructional because they serve as a window to a life experience of adjustment to new social settings and the emergence of a new cultural lifestyle. This book presents a collection of such narratives.

Jacobson, Cardell K. 1984. **"Internal Colonialism and Native Americans: Indian Labor in the United States from 1871 to World War II."** *Social Science Quarterly* 65: 158–171.

Theories of internal colonialism and dual labor markets have been used to describe black, Mexican American, and American Indian conditions in the United States. However, according to the author, what is missing in the research record is a systematic examination of the history of American Indian labor in the United States to document the labor-exploitation aspects of colonialism. The author presents a history of American Indian labor from 1871, the end of the treaty-making period, to World War II.

Jenness, Valerie, and Kenal Broad. 1997. *Hate Crimes: New Social Movements and the Politics of Violence.* New York: de Gruyter.

This book addresses a timely set of questions about the politics and dynamics of intergroup violence manifested as discrimination. It explores such issues as why injuries against some groups of people have increasingly captured notice, whereas similar acts of bias-motivated violence continue to go unnoticed. According to the authors, new social movements have converged of late to sustain public discussions that put into question issues of "rights" and "harm" as they relate to a variety of minority constituencies. The authors couple their general discussion with close attention to many particular antiviolence projects. They present a theoretical argument about the social processes through which new social problems emerge, social policy is developed and diffused, and new cultural forms are institutionalized.

Kibria, Nazli. 1996. **"Not Asian, Black, or White? Reflections on South Asian American Racial Identity."** *Amerasia Journal* 22: 77–86.

In this article, the author explores and discusses the difficulty of delineating racial boundaries among South Asians. South Asians are usually classified as Asian American, yet there are some racial differences between South Asians (for example, Bangladeshis) and East Asians (for example, Chinese). According to the author, South Asians are marginalized in the pan-Asian movements, Asian studies, and the Asian American racial identity. The author concludes that open dialogue on racial and cultural issues must be encouraged between South Asians and members of the wider Asian American community and that the study of South Asia must be incorporated into pan-Asiatic scholarly studies.

Killenbeck, M. 1999. **"Pushing Things Up to Their First Principles: Reflections on the Values of Affirmative Action."** *California Law Review* 87: 1299–1407.

The author examines the constitutionality of college and university affirmative action admissions programs that seek to foster and preserve a diverse learning environment. The author explores the major assumptions informing the higher education community's belief in the need for and value of diversity. The author discusses what the concept of affirmative action has come to mean in U.S. society, showing how a system originally conceived of as a mandate for procedural fairness has been transformed into the functional equivalent of a system of substantive entitlements. The author argues that certain types of affirmative actions are constitutionally permissible given the Supreme Court's recognition that schools may employ affirmative measures, in particular, race-conscious measures, when they reflect the pursuit and appropriate attainment of a compelling educational interest.

Kilty, Keith, and Maria Vidal de Haymes. 2000. **"Racism, Nativism, and Exclusion: Public Policy, Immigration, and the Latino Experience in the United States."** *Journal of Poverty* 4: 1–25.

Although population growth for the Latino population has surged since the middle of the twentieth century, people of Spanish origin have been part of the American fabric since the nation's earliest days. Since the Treaty of Guadalupe Hidalgo, which ended the Mexican War in 1848 and ceded to the United States most of what is now the U.S. Southwest, Hispanics in the United States, whether born within or outside U.S. borders, have been affected in various ways by the exclusionary and restrictive nature of U.S. immigration laws and policies. The authors point out that most Latinos living in the United States are citizens, 62 percent by birth and an additional 7 percent by naturalization, but those who are citizens often have family members residing in the United States who are not. They argue that anti-immigrant and exclusionary sentiments are on the rise in the United States, with most of those sentiments focused incorrectly on Latinos. Public policy is a critical matter for minorities, who typically occupy positions toward the bottom of the social hierarchy. In response to the need to address public policy issues for minorities, the authors examine the impact of social policy on the lives of Hispanics, including recent immigration and border legislation, welfare reform, and official language policy and educational programs. According to the authors, much of the rhetoric used to justify policy changes and proposals is based on misperceptions, misrepresentations, and misunderstandings.

King, C. Richard, and Charles F. Springwood. 2001. *Beyond the Cheers: Race as Spectacle in College Sport.* Albany: SUNY Press.

Focusing on the racial tensions present in college sport, the authors argue that revenue-producing college sports are inherently exploitative. American Indians and African Americans are stereotyped as either delinquents or superstars, whereas white coaches and players are portrayed in positive images. As a result, viewers of college sports events come to embrace a distorted understanding of racial difference and race relations in general. To support their arguments, the book's authors examine the effects of Jim Crow laws and racial discrimination on college sports, especially the symbolism associated with team mascots.

King, Joyce. 2002. *Hate Crime: The Story of a Dragging in Jasper, Texas.* New York: Pantheon.

On June 7, 1998, in Jasper, Texas, James Byrd Jr., a forty-nine-year-old black man, was dragged to death behind a pickup truck. It was a crime of racial hatred. Byrd was killed by three young white men simply because of the color of his skin. This book is an in-depth analysis of the social forces that created the context for Byrd's killing and of how the Jasper community responded to his death.

Kleg, Milton. 1993. *Hate, Prejudice, and Racism.* Albany: SUNY Press.

The author provides comprehensive background information and concepts to help educators address the contemporary problems of racial and ethnic discrimination. He considers the effect of prejudice from casual racist jokes to lynch mobs, the nature of ethnicity, stereotyping, the beliefs and activities of specific racist and anti-Semitic groups and individuals, implications for teachers and cultural workers, and approaches to studying and combating such attitudes.

Lambert, Wallace E., and Donald M. Taylor. 1990. *Coping with Cultural and Racial Diversity in Urban America.* New York: Praeger.

This book examines U.S. attitudes regarding pluralism, acculturation, and ethnic or race relations. The book is divided into seven topics, each of which receives a separate chapter in the book. Chapter 1, "The American Challenge: Assimilation or Multiculturalism," describes Americans' feelings toward the fine line that exists between retaining one's ethnic identity and being considered un-American. Chapter 2, "Methodological Approach," describes the research strategy used to conduct interviews concerning attitudes and feelings about cultural and racial diversity with parents of public school students in the Michigan cities of Hamtramck and Pontiac. The 360 respondents in the study represented Polish, Arab, Albanian, black, Mexican, Puerto Rican, working-class white, and middle-class white Americans.

Chapter 3, "Ethnic Immigrant Groups in Hamtramck: Polish, Albanian, and Arab Americans," shows that all three groups favor multiculturalism over assimilation. Arab Americans have the strongest feelings, Polish Americans the weakest, and Albanian Americans are in the middle. Chapter 4, "Ethnic Immigrant Groups in Pontiac: Mexican and Puerto Rican Americans," shows that Puerto Rican Americans are as strongly pro-multiculturalism as are Arab Americans and that Mexican Americans feel less strongly about multiculturalism than do Albanian Americans. Chapter 5, "The Perspectives of Mainstream White Americans," shifts the discussion from ethnic immigrant minorities to "host" Americans. Both working-class and middle-class white Americans, especially the latter, are pro-multiculturalism, but to a substantially lesser degree than are the ethnic immigrant groups. Chapter 6, "The Perspectives of Black Americans," shows that black Americans in Hamtramck are three times as pro-multiculturalistic as are black Americans in Pontiac, suggesting that blacks are influenced by the prevailing attitudes in their respective communities. Chapter 7, "Two Faces of Multiculturalism: Sobering Reflections and Exciting Possibilities!" discusses the social significance of the major themes covered in the authors' investigation.

Lee, Brant. 2002. **"Liars, Traitors, and Spies: Wen Ho Lee and the Racial Construction of Disloyalty."** *Asian American Policy Review* 10: 1–16.

This article discusses the historical recurrence of interrogations of Asian Americans with the assumption that all Asians are liars, traitors, and spies. According to the author, the prevailing attitude seems to be that any Asian person, regardless of citizenship, activities, and character, is presumed to be loyal first to his or her Asian homeland. Accusations against Wen Ho Lee, a U.S. citizen for twenty-five years who was accused of stealing nuclear secrets from the Los Alamos lab, have a long-standing historical precedent that raises skepticism about their validity. The author argues that racial profiling creates disenchantment and low morale among the entire group, exacting a price from the entire society and weakening U.S. research capacity. According to the author, since patriots stand up to injustice, Asian Americans who fight for their right to be considered full-fledged loyal citizens become opponents of the American system, and the accusation becomes self-fulfilling and self-reinforcing. Economic recession, national security risks, or war further turn the U.S. vision of its Asian American citizens into that of the enemy.

Leonard, Rebecca, and Don Locke. 1988. **"Communication Stereotypes in the 1980s: How Do Blacks and Whites See Themselves and Each Other?"** *Educational and Psychological Research* 8: 73–82.

The authors asked one hundred white and one hundred black college students to characterize the communication behavior of their own racial group by choosing from a checklist of communication traits. According to the authors, white students most frequently chose friendly to describe their own communication behavior, whereas black students perceived themselves as caring. Both black and white students perceived themselves as active, caring, critical, emotional, friendly, individualistic, intelligent, and talkative. Most of the top twelve terms chosen by each group were favorable. The authors also found that black students' perceptions of themselves and white students' perceptions of black students were more similar than were the perceptions of white students of themselves and by black students.

Lobo, Arun, Ronald Flores, and Joseph Salvo. 2002. **"The Impact of Hispanic Growth on the Racial/Ethnic Composition of New York City Neighborhoods."** *Urban Affairs Review* 37: 703–727.

According to the authors, between 1970 and 1990, a surging Hispanic population succeeded whites across New York City, resulting in major increases in both all minority and multiethnic neighborhoods. Puerto Rican and Dominican flows resulted in transitions to all minority neighborhoods, whereas South Americans showed a more integrated pattern of settlement. The authors argue that the unique settlement patterns of Hispanic sub-groups need to be understood in the context of larger political, social, and economic forces operating in the city. In the post-1990 period, newer Hispanic groups have begun to succeed Puerto Ricans. Thus, earlier patterns of white-to-Hispanic transitions now have been supplemented by ethnic succession among Hispanics.

Lomotey, Kofi, ed. 1990. *Going to School: The African-American Experience.* Albany: SUNY Press.

The essays in this volume address a number of key issues related to the education of African Americans. The authors go beyond merely discussing the issues and suggest remedies in several areas related to improving the academic achievement of African American students. Some of the issues addressed by the authors are the deculturalization of African American children in the public school system, literacy and schooling in subordinate cultures, limitations of current academic achievement measures, standardized test scores and the black college environment, and qualities shared by African American principals in effective schools.

Luhman, Reid. 2002. *Race and Ethnicity in the United States.* Belmont, CA: Thomson/Wadsworth.

This text emphasizes ethnic group interactions using an institutional perspective. It combines historical, theoretical, and comparative approaches to the study of race and ethnicity. It provides an understanding of the origin of contemporary racial and ethnic groups and the importance of the past for understanding all groups.

Marger, Martin. 2002. *Race and Ethnic Relations: American and Global Perspectives.* Belmont, CA: Wadsworth.

Although focusing on issues in the United States, this book also integrates and juxtaposes conditions in other multiethnic societies around the world. It outlines the field's principal theories and basic concepts, discusses racial and ethnic relations in the United States, and compares management of diversity in the United States with that of South Africa, Brazil, Canada, Northern Ireland, and the former Yugoslavia.

Martinez, George. 2000. **"The Legal Construction of Race: Mexican-Americans and Whiteness."** Latino Studies Series, occasional paper no. 54. East Lansing: Michigan State University, Julian Samora Research Institute.

According to the author, Mexican Americans were legally defined as whites as a result of treaty obligations with Mexico that expressly allowed Mexicans to become U.S. citizens. Federal laws of the time required that an alien be white to become a U.S. citizen. The government of Mexico and the U.S. Department of State pressured the U.S. Census Bureau to reclassify Mexican Americans as white. In a Texas school-desegregation case, the court held that Mexican American children could not be segregated on a racial basis but did permit segregation on the basis of linguistic difficulties or migrant status. Historically, institutions controlled by dominant groups have determined the legal definitions of racial groups and imposed those definitions in ways that maintained the status quo. The author argues that the law recognizes racial group identity when such identity is a basis for exclusion and subordination but often refuses to recognize group identity when asserted as a basis for affirming rights and resisting subordination. He provides examples from a Texas court ruling that imposed a definition of "white" on Mexican Americans protesting their exclusion from grand and petit juries as a distinct group and from a court rejection of Mexican American claims for class representation in a class-action suit seeking equal educational opportunities. Although Mexican Americans have been legally constructed as white, this legal status has had only marginal impact on daily life because of colonial discourses constructing Mexican Americans as racially "other."

McDade, Jeffrey R. 1999. **"Social Control and the Native American: The Nineteenth Century Manual Labor Boarding School."** *Research in Social Movements, Conflicts, and Change* 21: 249–270.

This article compares the nineteenth-century establishment and diffusion of the American Indian manual-labor boarding school by Christian missionary societies to other U.S. institutions established in this period. The author reviews literature on the history of missions to American Indians and archival data from missions in Kansas to argue that the manual-labor boarding school arose in the context of a larger social movement in the nineteenth century based on an "ideological shift" regarding the appropriate method of social control for "problem populations." According to the author, the roots of the manual-labor boarding school are found in the same ideology that gave birth to the prison.

Million, Dian. 2000. **"Policing the Rez: Keeping No Peace in Indian Country."** *Social Justice* 27: 101–119.

According to the author, American Indians, especially those living on reservations, are subject to conflicting issues that make sovereignty and basic rights unattainable. In particular, they face serious obstacles when dealing with U.S. courts of law. Jurisdictional disputes over historically indigenous land have weakened Native American attempts at self-governance and protection. The author argues that racist organizations perpetuate anti–American Indian legislation and that discriminatory individuals have contributed to increasingly racialized nation-states. As non-native immigrants continue to pour into the United States from Mexico and South America and as the American Indian population continues to grow, federal-Indian relations will become progressively more strained.

Mitchell, Gary D. 1992. **"The Impact of U.S. Immigration Policy on the Economic 'Quality' of German and Austrian Immigrants in the 1930s."** *International Migration Review* 26: 940–967.

This article discusses whether the "likely to become a public charge" (LPC) clause was effective in raising the economic "quality" of German and Austrian immigrants to the United States in the 1930s. Data from a 1945 official study of 11,500 immigrants arriving in the United States between 1933 and 1944 are used to compare LPC immigrants and those admitted after the clause was revoked in March 1938. The authors conclude that the LPC clause did not result in the selection of a superior group of immigrants, thus raising concerns about the ethnocentric motives of the creators of the clause.

Nabokov, Peter, and Vine Deloria Jr., eds. 1999. *Native American Testimony: A Chronicle of Indian-White Relations from 1492 to 2000.* New York: Penguin.

The editors present Native American and white relations as seen through American Indian eyes and told through American Indian records spanning more than five hundred years of interchange between the two peoples. The editors use a wide range of sources: traditional narratives, American Indian autobiographies, government treaties, and firsthand interviews. The editors use the materials in the book to present an alternative history of North America.

Oliver, William. 2001. **"Cultural Racism and Structural Violence: Implications for African Americans."** *Journal of Human Behavior in the Social Environment* 4: 1–26.

The author discusses the importance of considering how cultural racism contributes to the construction of motives and justifications among individuals who have committed acts of structural violence, including lynchings, hate crimes, and police violence against African Americans. Cultural racism is also discussed as a factor that contributes to interpersonal structural violence in situations involving black offenders and victims.

Patchen, Martin. 1998. *Diversity and Unity: Relations between Racial and Ethnic Groups.* Chicago: Nelson-Hall.

This text provides a comprehensive overview of the relevant theory and evidence to help readers understand the processes and outcomes of the development of ethnic diversity. Rather than describing a succession of specific ethnic groups, the author focuses on the general forces and processes—such as the formation of ethnic attitudes, intergroup contacts, economic competition, and demographic changes—that lead to such central outcomes as prejudice, segregation, and discrimination. It presents a theoretical overview that links individual attitudes and behavior to societal institutions and processes. Two alternative visions of a multiethnic society are systematically discussed: one promoting assimilation and the other encouraging pluralism. The advantages and problems associated with each approach, the necessary conditions needed to produce this type of society, and possible ways to reduce its problems are outlined. Policy aims and techniques such as ways to reduce prejudice, income inequality, and housing are also examined.

Patterson, Orlando. 1999. *Rituals of Blood: Consequences of Slavery in Two American Centuries.* New York: Basic Civitas Books.

The author focuses on three themes in this collection of essays: First, he analyzes the very latest survey data to delineate the different attitudes, behaviors, and circumstances of African American men and women, dissecting both the external and internal causes for the great disparities he finds. Second, he focuses on the lynching of African American boys and men during the decades after Reconstruction, particularly on the substantial number of cases that constituted apparent ritual human sacrifice. He reveals how the complex interplay between Christian sacrificial symbolism and the deep recesses of postbellum southern culture resulted in some of the most shameful, barbaric events in U.S. history. Third, he takes the reader into the late twentieth century, with an investigation of the various images of African American men portrayed by the media.

Perry, Barbara. 2002. **"Defending the Color Line: Racially and Ethnically Motivated Hate Crime."** *American Behavioral Scientist* 46: 72–92.

Drawing on structured action theory, the author examines the ways racially and ethnically motivated hate crimes emerge as a forceful means of constructing identity and difference. The author summarizes the trends in racially and ethnically motivated violence nationwide and examines hate crimes as readily available means of establishing difference. The author argues that racially motivated violence is not an aberration associated with a lunatic or extremist fringe. Instead, she states it is a normative means of asserting racial identity relative to the victimized "other" because it is an enactment of the racism that allocates privilege along racial lines.

Petrosino, Carolyn. 1999. **"Connecting the Past to the Future: Hate Crime in America."** *Journal of Contemporary Criminal Justice* 15: 22–47.

The author argues that hate crimes are not a modern-day phenomenon but, rather, extend throughout the history of the United States. Using a definition based on intrinsic justice rather than codified law, the author examines selected events in the seventeenth through early nineteenth centuries. A comparative analysis of the events indicated similarities and differences between historical and modern events. The distillation of conditions surrounding the dynamics of hate crimes, both past and present, suggests the following summary factors: (1) Racism is a primary predictor of hate crime through time; (2) the efficiency and degree of harm potential in hate crime is a function of opportunity and technology; (3) hate crimes will occur more frequently and be more difficult to prevent; (4) notwithstanding the repugnant nature of hate crimes, many Americans are becoming more sympathetic to hate-crime perpetrators' causes; and (5) hate crime, on some levels, is becoming indistinguishable from domestic terrorism.

Ramos-Zayas, Ana. 2001. **"Racializing the 'Invisible' Race: Latino Constructions of 'White Culture' and Whiteness in Chicago."** *Urban Anthropology* 30(4): 341–380.

In this essay, the author examines how Latinos construct "white culture" and generate ideas of whiteness. According to the author, Latinos have developed complex conceptions of "white culture" shaped in the context of demographic and economic change, urban gentrification, and face-to-face interactions. Drawing from ethnographic research in a Chicago Latino neighborhood, the author argues that Latinos construed and articulated whiteness as a function of power and privilege, as a multi-layered "ladder" of whiteness.

Reimers, David M. 1999. *Unwelcome Strangers: American Identity and the Turn against Immigration.* New York: Columbia University Press.

This book charts the history of U.S. immigration policy and public reaction to newcomers, from the Puritan colonists to World War II refugees. The author shows how immigrant groups have historically been targeted, whether for ethnic, racial, or religious reasons.

The history of prejudice directed at immigrants is examined within a context of actions that diminished the incorporation of immigrants into U.S. society. This context is shaped, for example, by the public response to the Cuban refugee crisis, the growing proportion of Third World immigrants, and the relationship between legal and illegal immigration that served as a battleground for Proposition 187 in California. The author challenges anti-immigration arguments that the increasing numbers of immigrants are creating an environmental crisis in the United States, taking jobs away from Americans, and threatening American culture.

Rose, William. 2002. **"Crimes of Color: Risk, Profiling, and the Contemporary Racialization of Social Control."** *International Journal of Politics, Culture, and Society* 16: 179–205.

According to the author, racial profiling has emerged in the United States as an important and controversial issue within political and criminal justice policy debates. For the most part, these debates have assumed a sort of racism at work in order to explain law enforcement's use of criminal profiles largely determined by racial classifications. Accordingly, many have worked to expose this allegedly racist behavior in the hopes that such exposure will bring an end to the practice. In this essay, the author argues that racial profiling is embedded in much larger social developments that must be explored in order to understand the role race now plays in the maintenance of social order in contemporary U.S. society.

San Juan, E., Jr. 1998. *From Exile to Diaspora: Versions of the Filipino Experience in the United States.* Boulder, CO: Westview Press.

As the largest contingent of Asian/Pacific Islanders in the United States, Filipinos are "invisible," "forgotten," and "marginal others" in U.S. society. They are often overlooked in studies of Asians/Pacific Islanders. In this book, the author challenges stereotypic images of Filipinos in the United States before and after World War II. According to the author, with the Philippines undergoing a revolutionary transformation, the Filipino diaspora—about 6 million "overseas contract workers" scattered around the planet—is radically configuring the Filipino presence and potential for change in the United States. The author argues that until now Filipinos have been subsumed in the category of immigrants, exiles, or refugees but that they now claim a nation-alitarian, uniquely political and ethical identity removed from panethnic racializing generalities. As a result, Filipinos in their singular diversity are reassessing their colonial past, engaging in projects of popular-democratic resistance to the transnational system of global commodification, and engaging in discourse regarding their assimilation and acculturation in U.S. society.

Schafer, Richard T. 2003. *Racial and Ethnic Groups.* Upper Saddle River, NJ: Prentice Hall.

This book is a comprehensive survey of racial and ethnic groups in the United States. It explores such topics as the economic impact of immigration, economic development of Native Americans, and changes in affirmative action programs. It also includes a chapter on overcoming exclusion, which looks at three groups—the aged, people with disabilities, and lesbians and gays—and explores the challenges all groups face.

Simon, Barbara. 1992. **"U.S. Immigration Policies, 1798–1992: Invaluable Texts for Exploring Continuity and Change in Racism and Xenophobia."** *Journal of Multicultural Social Work* 2: 53–63.

The author discusses the change and continuity in governmental resistance to the growth of a multicultural population in the United States via an analysis of U.S. immigration policy since 1798. These policies clearly document the historical traditions of nativism, racism, and xenophobia in the United States. The author argues that two centuries of immigration policies, in combination with case records of social-work agencies that served immigrants, constitute excellent texts from which to teach social-work students about U.S. ambivalence regarding "others."

Snipp, C. Matthew. 1989. *American Indians: The First of This Land.* New York: Russell Sage Foundation.

Using data from the 1980 U.S. census, the author provides a comprehensive analysis of the living conditions and demographic features of the American Indian population. The book is unique in its presentation of population data and its coverage of topics—housing, family structure, labor-force participation, language and education, and occupation and income—in discussions of which American Indians are often ignored.

Takaki, Ronald. 1993. *A Different Mirror: A History of Multicultural America*. Boston: Little, Brown.

The author combines stories with the personal narratives of people previously ignored in America's historical record to "re-vision" America's past. He begins with the seventeenth-century arrival of the English settlers as witnessed by the Powhatans in Virginia and the Wampanoags in Massachusetts. He then recounts the forced arrival of African slaves in America, the arrival of Irish women in the United States as factory workers and maids, the arrival of Chinese and Japanese immigrants to fill the demand for mine and rail workers in the West, the arrival of Jews fleeing the shtetls of Russia, and the journey of Latino immigrants into the United States.

———. 1999. **"Multiculturalism: Battleground or Meeting Ground."** In *Race and Ethnic Conflict: Contending Views on Prejudice, Discrimination, and Ethnoviolence*, ed. Fred Pincus and Howard Ehrlich, 2nd ed., 305–315. Boulder, CO: Westview Press.

The author examines and discusses the struggle over cultural diversity taking place on U.S. college and university campuses to argue that the consequences will define education and help determine what a person should learn about the United States and the world. He argues that the two perspectives underpinning the struggle, called "particularism" and "pluralism," are not totally antagonistic but instead complement each other in several ways. Understanding the similarities and valid aspects of both viewpoints prevents being forced into an either-or situation. The benefits of curriculum innovations offering a comparative and integrative approach are examined, along with the shift from integration to separatism and the tendency of some members of minorities to view their civil rights in terms of cultural pluralism and group identities. Outstanding critiques of multiculturalism are reviewed in order to show that many of the arguments are based on an unrealistic fear of the loss of U.S. culture.

———. 2000. *Iron Cages: Race and Culture in Nineteenth-Century America*. Rev. ed. New York: Oxford University Press.

The author provides a comparative and contrastive analysis of white attitudes toward Asians, blacks, Mexicans, and American Indians in nineteenth-century U.S. society. He argues that the experiences of nonwhite racial and ethnic groups illustrate the presence of racist beliefs and attitudes among white Americans. According to the author, the primary purpose of the book is to understand how the domination of people of color in U.S. society had cultural and economic bases that involved race.

Talwar, Jennifer Parker. 2002. *Fast Food, Fast Track: Immigrants, Big Business, and the American Dream.* Boulder CO: Westview Press.

The author examines the role of immigrants from China, the Caribbean, Latin America, and India as counter workers in the U.S. fast-food industry. According to the author, immigrants have become a vital link between the growing service sector in U.S. ethnic enclaves and the multibillion dollar global fast-food industry. For four years, the author went behind the counter herself and listened to immigrant fast-food workers in New York City's ethnic communities. They talked about balancing their low-paying jobs and monotonous daily reality with keeping the faith that these very jobs could be the first step on the path to the American Dream. The author asserts that, contrary to those who argue that the fast-food industry only represents an increasing homogenization of the U.S. workforce, fast-food chains in immigrant communities must and do adapt to their surroundings. Rather than focusing on how ethnic communities become relatively sealed off from the larger economy, she discusses the interplay between globalizing mainstream forces like fast-food chains and the immigrant communities of our largest and most diverse cities.

Tatum, Beverly. 1979. *Assimilation Blues: Black Families in White Communities—Who Succeeds and Why.* New York: Basic Books.

This book addresses the question "What does it mean to be black in a white, middle-class community?" Is it the ultimate symbol of success? Or will one pay in isolation, alienation, or rootlessness? What price must one pay for paradise? Is the price too high? The author interviewed black families in depth to identify the sacrifices and achievements necessary to survive and prosper in a white community. For the black citizens of "Sun Beach," dual-income households, religious affiliation, and extended families help maintain stability. But with assimilation comes an insidious hidden racism, subtly communicated when black children are not called on in class and revealed more fully in incidents of racial name-calling. By listening to the individual voices of these children and their parents, the author examines questions of identity that arise for a visible people rendered invisible by their surroundings.

Taylor, Jared, and Glayde Whitney. 1999. **"Crime and Racial Profiling by U.S. Police: Is There an Empirical Basis?"** *Journal of Social, Political, and Economic Studies* 24: 485–510.

The authors investigate the disparity between public sensibilities and empirical data in U.S. criminology. The article's principal focus is on racial profiling, that is, the practice of systematically stopping minority motorists for search based on the belief that they are more likely than whites to commit certain crimes.

Torpy, Sally J. 2000. **"Native American Women and Coerced Sterilization: On the Trail of Tears in the 1970s."** *American Indian Culture and Research Journal* 24: 1–22.

This article examines the forced sterilization of American Indian women during the 1970s as a civil rights violation: the abuse of women's reproductive freedom. The author describes the 1970s U.S. socioeconomic and sociocultural climate that contributed to American Indian women's vulnerability to sterilization. She presents two case studies of American Indian women subjected to forced sterilization and the social forces—poverty, patriarchy, racism—that rendered them victims.

Torres, Sam. 1999. **"Hate Crimes against African Americans: The Extent of the Problem."** *Journal of Contemporary Criminal Justice* 15: 48–63.

This article examines hate crimes against African Americans in the United States by reviewing 1990–1996 FBI data. Based on Uniform Crime Report data on hate crimes, African Americans are most often the victims of race-motivated crimes. The data show that from 1992 to 1996, there was a 52 percent increase in the number of hate crimes reported against African Americans. The author discusses African American hate-crime victimization trends since the passage of the Hate Crime Statistics Act of 1990, the factors that contribute to hate crimes against African Americans, and some of the recommendations that have been put forward for dealing with this growing problem. The author con-

cludes that there is a climate of increasing intolerance and a growing acceptability of racial prejudice in the United States.

Trapassi, Francesco. 2001. **"American Nativism of the Late
Twentieth Century: The Case of Mexican Immigrants in
California."** *Studi Emigrazione/Etudes Migrations* 38: 95–113.

In the late 1990s, conservative sectors of California society
adopted legislation reducing the social rights of immigrants who
were not U.S. citizens. Limitations on the citizenship rights of
immigrants in California were imposed by Propositions 187, 227,
and 209. The propositions were promoted by conservative sectors, passed by a majority of voters, and challenged in the courts.
The author argues that nativist feeling has always emerged during economic crises, such as the recession of the early 1990s,
which clearly affected the politics of propositions.

Ward, James D. 2002. **"Race, Ethnicity, and Law Enforcement
Profiling: Implications for Public Policy."** *Public Administration
Review* 62: 726–735.

The proposed Traffic Stops Statistics Study Act of 2001, Title II of
Senate Bill 19 of the 107th Congress, was the third consecutive
legislative proposal aimed at addressing the problems of racial
profiling and police abuse in the detention of minority motorists
for allegedly unjustifiable reasons. The measure followed Senate
Bill 821 from the 106th Congress and House Bill 118 from the
105th Congress. The author discusses the purpose of these bills
and examines the reasons used to support federal policy mandat-
ing that law enforcement agencies collect racial data on motorists
who are stopped or detained. He also discusses public policy
questions that such an act might raise.

Williams, Robert A., Jr. 1990. *The American Indian in Western
Legal Thought: The Discourses of Conquest.* New York: Oxford
University Press.

This book is an examination of western legal thought and its
application to American Indians from 1500 to 1800. The author
argues that the colonizing nations—Spain, England, and the
United States—of the New World used law as an instrument for
imposing their version of truth on the American Indian. The
imposition of western legal theory on American Indians, in turn,

created the image of the American Indian as a distinct problem in western legal thought. As a result, European colonizing law, as the framework for western legal theory, is interpreted by the author as a "discourse of conquest" that served to define the rights and status of American Indians.

Woo, Deborah. 2000. *Glass Ceilings and Asian Americans: The New Face of Workplace Barriers.* Walnut Creek, CA: AltaMira Press.

The author examines the research literature regarding the glass ceiling and labor-market discrimination against Asian American ethnic groups. She uses an in-depth analysis of two institutional settings—a high-tech firm and higher education—to illustrate the operation of a glass ceiling for Asian Americans. She uses the in-depth analysis to discuss the complex interaction between ethnicity and organizational culture in economic institutions and labor markets.

Wu, Frank H. 2001. *Yellow: Race in America beyond Black and White.* New York: Basic Books.

The author offers a unique perspective on how changing ideas of racial identity will affect race relations in the new century. Often provocative and always thoughtful, this book addresses some of the most controversial of contemporary issues: discrimination, immigration, diversity, globalization, and the mixed-race movement. The author focuses on Asian Americans to shed new light on the current debates regarding racial identity. He combines personal anecdotes, social science research, legal cases, history, and original journalistic reporting to discuss such damaging Asian American stereotypes as "the model minority" and "the perpetual foreigner." By offering new ways of thinking about race in U.S. society, Wu's work challenges us to make good on our great democratic experiment.

Yamamoto, Eric K., Margaret Chon, Carol L. Izumi, Jerry Kang, and Frank H. Wu. 2001. *Race, Rights, and Reparation: Law and the Japanese American Internment.* New York: Aspen.

This book is a comprehensive compilation of oral histories and the legal, sociological, and historical materials needed to understand the legal, ethical, and social ramifications of the internment of Japanese American citizens during World War II.

Yee, Albert. 1973. **"Myopic Perceptions and Textbooks: Chinese Americans' Search for Identity."** *Journal of Social Issues* 29: 99–113.

According to the author, Americans have perpetuated inaccurate images and attitudes concerning the Chinese. Narrow stereotypic perceptions of and prejudice toward the Chinese have been so pervasive that Americans of Chinese ancestry do not perceive themselves with a meaningful identity. The author examines U.S. social studies textbooks for elementary and secondary schools to show that Asian studies and the involvement of Asians in U.S. history are barely mentioned or are neglected completely. According to the author, the information provided in the textbooks reinforces stereotypic images of the Chinese. He argues that there is rising protest and counterresponse to these restrictive perceptions among younger Asian Americans, who seek the identity they have been denied by others.

9

Nonprint Resources

Distributors of Films and Videos

American Indian Film Institute (AIFI)
333 Valencia Street, Suite 322
San Francisco, CA 94103
Contact: Michael Smith
Phone: (415) 554-0525
Fax: (415) 554-0542
Web site: http://www.aifisf.com

The American Indian Film Institute (AIFI) is a media arts center whose mission is "to foster understanding of the culture, traditions and issues of contemporary Native Americans . . . [and to] encourage American Indian filmmakers to bring to the broader media culture the native voices, viewpoints and stories that have been historically excluded." It sponsors programs that provide mentors to American Indian youngsters interested in learning about film and video, a quarterly cinema journal, a year-round exhibition program, and the annual American Indian Film Festival, now in its twenty-third year. AIFI's open-submission festival presents features, documentaries, live-action and animated shorts, music video, and works focusing on indigenous cultures throughout the United States and Canada.

Asian Cinevision
32 East Broadway, 4th Floor

New York, NY 10002
Contact: Bill Gee
Phone: (212) 925-8685
Fax: (212) 925-8157

This nonprofit organization publishes the *Asian American Media Reference Guide* and a newsletter, *Cinevue*. It also promotes film and video produced by Asian Americans through its exhibition, Videoscape, and the annual Asian American International Film Festival.

Black Film Center/Archive (BFC/A)
Indiana University
Smith Research Center
2805 East 10th Street, Suites 180-181
Bloomington, IN 47408
Contact: Audrey T. McCluskey, Director
Phone: (812) 855-6041
Fax: (812) 856-5832
Web site: http://www.indiana.edu\~bfcal

Founded in 1981, the Black Film Center/Archive (BFC/A) publishes the biannual newsletter *Black Camera* as well as *Frame by Frame II: A Filmography of the African American Image, 1978–1994.* This nonprofit research center also maintains a diverse collection of films, tapes, and manuscripts on African American cinema and holds public screenings. BFC/A maintains a database of almost 5,000 films and runs database searches for a small fee.

Cine Acción
346 Ninth Street, 2nd Floor
San Francisco, CA 94103
Contact: Rosalia Valencia
Phone: (415) 553-8135
Fax: (415) 553-8137

In addition to publishing a monthly bulletin and quarterly newsletter, Cine Acción distributes *Cineworks*, a catalog of members' film and video works addressing Latino cultural identity, politics, and imagery. The organization screens film and video year-round and produces the annual Festival Cine Latino, a major showcase of animated films, documentaries, experimental work, and fiction features and shorts.

National Asian American Telecommunications Association (NAATA)
346 Ninth Street, 2nd Floor
San Francisco, CA 94103
Contact: Eddie Wong
Phone: (415) 863-0814, ext. 103
Fax: (415) 863-7428
Web site: http://www.naatanet.org

The National Asian American Telecommunications Association (NAATA) supports the production and distribution of film, video, and radio programs by and about Asian-Pacific Americans. Its purpose is to introduce this group's perspectives about what it means to be "American." Distribution outlets include public television, public radio, theaters, and classrooms. NAATA also publishes a catalog of Asian American film and video materials called *CrossCurrents Media*. NAATA presents the annual San Francisco International Asian American Film Festival as well as a children's film program.

National Museum of the American Indian (NMAI)
Smithsonian Institution Film and Video Center
One Bowling Green
New York, NY 10004
Contact: Elizabeth Weatherford
Phone: (212) 514-3730
Fax: (212) 514-3725
Web site: www.si.edu/nmai

The National Museum of the American Indian (NMAI) Film and Video Center is a major exhibitor of film and video by and about Inuit and American Indian people of North, Central, and South America. The center provides information and services to U.S. film and video makers, tribal media organizations, television producers, scholars, and programmers. It maintains collections (mostly documentaries) and generates touring film and video programs. The centerpiece of its programming work is the biannual Native American Film and Video Festival.

University of California Extension
Center for Media and Independent Learning
2000 Center Street, 4th Floor
Berkeley, CA 94704

Contact: Kate Spohr or Daniel Bickley
Phone: (510) 643-2788 or (510) 642-1340
Fax: (510) 643-9271
E-mail: cmil@uclink.berkeley.edu
Web site: http://www-cmil.unex.berkeley.edu/media

One of the most extensive media collections in the country, the University of California–Berkeley's media center houses an excellent bibliographic and video reference library that includes such collections as Native Americans in Film and Television; Indigenous Peoples of North and Central America; Chicano/Latino Studies; and The Movies, Race and Ethnicity (a large collection of videotapes by and about African Americans, Asian Americans, and Latinos).

Films and Videos

***Multicultural Peoples of North America* video series**
Type: Video
Length: 30 minutes each
Date: 1993
Cost: $39.95
Source: Library Video Company
             P.O. Box 580
             Wynnewood, PA 19096
             Phone: (800) 843-3620
             Fax: (610) 645-4040
             Web site: http://www.libraryvideo.com

This is a fifteen-volume video series that looks at the heritage of different cultural groups, tracing the history of their emigration to North America, their unique traditions, and their significant contributions. Three generations of a family from each culture are interviewed. Interviews with leading historians examine the impact of each ethnic group on the growth of the United States and the effects of contemporary immigration policies. The titles in this series include *African Americans, Central Americans, Chinese Americans, Irish Americans, Italian Americans, Japanese American, Korean Americans, Mexican Americans, Polish Americans,* and *Puerto Ricans.*

African American

Black Is . . . Black Ain't
Type: Video
Length: 86 minutes
Date: 1994
Cost: $195.00
Source: California Newsreel/Resolution Inc.
P.O. Box 2284
South Burlington, VT 05407
Phone: (877) 811-7495
Fax: (802) 846-1850
Web site: http://www.newsreel.org

This video asks, "Is there a *real* black man or a *true* black woman?" It crisscrosses the country with encounters with black people—young and old, rich and poor, rural and urban, gay and straight—grappling with the numerous contested definitions of blackness. The video also presents commentary by cultural critics such as Angela Davis, bell hooks, and Cornel West. It is a critique of sexism, patriarchy, homophobia, colorism, and cultural nationalism in the black family, church, and other institutions.

The Black Press: Soldiers without Swords
Type: Video
Length: 86 minutes
Date: 1998
Cost: $195.00
Source: California Newsreel/Resolution Inc.
P.O. Box 2284
South Burlington, VT 05407
Phone: (877) 811-7495
Fax: (802) 846-1850
Web site: http://www.newsreel.org

This video is a historical account of the birth, evolution, and impact of African American newspapers and journalism. Historical footage and photos and interviews with pioneering black newspapermen and women help to chronicle the black press from the first pre–Civil War independent black newspapers through the rise of the southern black press during Reconstruction to the continuing growth of the black press in the early part of the twentieth century. This video reveals the role of these papers both in encouraging African migration out of the South and in establishing new northern urban communities.

The Civil Rights Movement: Primary Sources
Type: Video
Length: Six part series, 57 minutes each
Date: 1999
Cost: $486
Source: Films for the Humanities and Sciences
              P.O. Box 2053
              Princeton, NJ 08543-2053
              Phone: (800) 257-5126
              Fax: (609) 275-3767
              Web site: http://www.films.com

In this six-part series of newscasts filmed during the 1950s and 1960s, broadcast journalists of the day cover the viewpoints and issues that shaped the civil rights dialogue. This video series is compiled by CBS News from their film archives. The individual videos are *Desegregation in Clinton, Tennessee* (1957); *Mississippi and the Black Vote* (1962); *The Color Line on Campus* (1963); *Ten Years after Brown: The Court and the Schools* (1964); *Segregation, Northern Style* (1964); *Black Power, White Backlash* (1966).

Forgotten Fires
Type: Video
Length: 57 minutes
Date: 1999
Cost: $295; rental, $95
Source: University of California Extension
              Center for Media and Independent Learning
              2000 Center Street, 4th Floor
              Berkeley, CA 94704
              Contact: Kate Spohr or Daniel Bickley
              Phone: (510) 643-2788 or (510) 642-1340
              Fax: (510) 643-9271
              E-mail: cmil@uclink.berkeley.edu
              Web site: http://www-cmil.unex.berkeley.edu/media

This film investigates the burning of two African American churches in rural South Carolina by a young convert to the Ku Klux Klan. Told through interviews with both the victims and the perpetrators of these racial crimes, the film puts a human face on racism, transforming a simple story of blacks and whites into a complex tale filled with shades of gray. What begins as an investigation into the church burnings becomes a meditation on race relations in America today.

Found Voices: The Slave Narratives
Type: Video
Length: 22 minutes
Date: 1999
Cost: $90
Source: Films for the Humanities and Sciences
                 P.O. Box 2053
                 Princeton, NJ 08543-2053
                 Phone: (800) 257-5126
                 Fax: (609) 275-3767
                 Web site: http://www.films.com

This video explores the question "How did it feel to be bought and sold like cattle, only to be liberated with nowhere to go and no one to turn to for help?" It presents the African American slave experience in the voices of those who knew it firsthand. It includes interviews from the 1930s and 1940s with ex-slaves who give their recollections of life before emancipation and during Reconstruction.

Homecoming
Type: Video
Length: 56 minutes
Date: 1998
Cost: $195.00
Source: California Newsreel/Resolution Inc.
                 P.O. Box 2284
                 South Burlington, VT 05407
                 Phone: (877) 811-7495
                 Fax: (802) 846-1850
                 Web site: http://www.newsreel.org

This film explores the rural roots of African American life. It chronicles the generations-old struggle of African Americans for land of their own, which pitted them against both the southern white power structure and the federal agencies responsible for helping Blacks gain the land. The Black farmers' story is one of perseverance in the face of prejudice and perjured promises.

Homecoming is also a meditation on the unfinished work of redeeming the land African Americans worked as slaves for hundreds of years. This film argues that black farms, though few in number today, can continue to provide African Americans with a sense of cultural stability and family unity in the 1990s.

Legacy
Type: Video
Length: 90 minutes
Date: 2000
Cost: $195.00
Source: California Newsreel/Resolution Inc.
            P.O. Box 2284
            South Burlington, VT 05407
            Phone: (877) 811-7495
            Fax: (802) 846-1850
            Web site: http://www.newsreel.org

This video chronicles three generations of African American women as they struggle to free themselves from welfare and poverty. This longitudinal study, filmed over a five-year period, makes visible the underlying economic, social, psychological, and bureaucratic difficulties faced by the urban poor. This video illustrates that new programs addressing drugs, violence, teen pregnancy, and race and gender discrimination are needed for real welfare reform.

Racial Profiling and Law Enforcement:
America in Black and White
Type: Video
Length: 44 minutes
Date: 1998
Cost: $130
Source: Films for the Humanities and Sciences
            P.O. Box 2053
            Princeton, NJ 08543-2053
            Phone: (800) 257-5126
            Fax: (609) 275-3767
            Web site: http://www.films.com

This video investigates the issue of racial profiling from the victims' points of view and also through the eyes of the police, with special commentary by law professor and former prosecutor Christopher Darden.

The Rise and Fall of Jim Crow

Type:	Video
Length:	224 minutes (4 cassettes)
Date:	2002
Cost:	$295.00
Source:	California Newsreel/Resolution Inc.
	P.O. Box 2284
	South Burlington, VT 05407
	Phone: (877) 811-7495
	Fax: (802) 846-1850
	Web site: http://www.newsreel.org

This video is a comprehensive look at race relations in the United States between the Civil War and the civil rights movement. This four-part series documents an era rooted in the growing refusal of many southern states to grant slaves freed in the Civil War equal rights with whites. The life of southern blacks was defined by legal segregation known as Jim Crow, which shaped the social, political, and legal history of the period. The story of the struggle through this period is told through the eyes of those who experienced it, both historical figures and nonfamous African Americans.

The Road to **Brown**

Type:	Video
Length:	56 minutes
Date:	1990
Cost:	$195.00
Source:	California Newsreel/Resolution Inc.
	P.O. Box 2284
	South Burlington, VT 05407
	Phone: (877) 811-7495
	Fax: (802) 846-1850
	Web site: http://www.newsreel.org

This film is the story of segregation and the legal assault on it, which launched the civil rights movement. It is also a tribute to a black lawyer, Charles Hamilton Houston, "the man who killed Jim Crow." Moving from slavery to civil rights, this film provides a concise history of how African Americans finally won full legal equality under the Constitution. Its depiction of the interplay between race, law, and history adds a crucial dimension to courses in U.S. history, black studies, constitutional law, law and society, social movements, and government. The film explores the world of Jim Crow, which robbed former slaves of the rights granted by the Fourteenth and Fifteenth Amendments. Under the "separate but equal" doctrine of the Supreme Court's 1896 *Plessy v. Ferguson* decision, black citizens were denied the right to vote, to attend white schools, to be sick in white hospitals, or to be buried in white cemeteries. Those who objected were liable to be lynched. Charles Houston, the first black editor of the *Harvard Law Review*, dean of Howard University Law School, and chief counsel to the National Association for the Advancement of Colored People, launched a number of precedent-setting cases that targeted segregated education as the key to undermining the entire Jim Crow system. The film recapitulates the arguments before the Court, Chief Justice Earl Warren's opinion striking down *Plessy*, the reactions of black America, and the string of legal and legislative victories that followed.

Asian American

Abandoned: The Betrayal of America's Immigrants
Type: Video
Length: 55 minutes
Date: 2000
Cost: $250
Source: Bullfrog Films
             P.O. Box 149
             Oley, PA 19547
             Phone: (610) 779-8226
             Fax: (610) 370-1978
             Web site: http://www.bullfrogfilms.com

This video looks at the most recent wave of anti-immigrant sentiment in the United States and at the personal impact of new immigration laws, focusing on the severity of current detention and deportation policies. Legal residents find themselves torn away from their U.S. families and sent to countries they barely know while political asylum seekers are kept for years in county jails that profit from their incarceration.

American Sons
Type: Video
Length: 28 minutes

Date: 1995
Cost: $150
Source: National Asian American Telecommunications
Association (NAATA)
346 Ninth Street, 2nd Floor
San Francisco, CA 94103
Contact: Eddie Wong
Phone: (415) 863-0814, ext. 103
Fax: (415) 863-7428
Web site: http://www.naatanet.org

American Sons is a provocative examination of how racism shapes the lives of Asian American men. Actors Yuji Okumoto, Kelvin Han Yee, Lane Nishikawa, and Ron Muriera tell real stories based on interviews with Asian Americans throughout the country. They express the issues of hate violence, the stereotypes placed on Asian men, the "model minority" myth, and the deep psychological damage that racism causes over generations. The film presents a painful and angry view of U.S. life never before explored in a film or television program.

The Americans
Type: Video
Length: 90 minutes
Date: 1997–2000
Cost: $19.95
Source: PBS
Phone: (800) 344-3337
Web site: http://ShopPBS.com/teachers

This video traces the history and contributions of Chinese Americans in the United States. Using vintage film footage, stories, and family photos, it traces where Chinese Americans came from, where they are now, and what the future may hold for them.

Ancestors in the Americas: Coolies, Sailors, Settlers
Type: Video
Length: 62 minutes
Date: 1996; revised 2002
Cost: $265
Source: Center for Educational Telecommunications
Video Order Department
22 Hollywood Avenue, Suite D

Hohokus, NJ 07423
Phone: (800) 343-5540
Fax: (201) 652-1973

This film is the untold story of how Asians—Filipino, Chinese, Asian Indian—first arrived in the Americas. The film crosses centuries and oceans from the sixteenth-century Manila-Acapulco trade to the Opium War to the nineteenth-century plantation coolie labor in South America and the Caribbean.

The Asianization of America
Type: Video
Length: 26 minutes
Date: 1998
Cost: $89.95
Source: Films for the Humanities and Sciences
              P.O. Box 2053
              Princeton, NJ 08543-2053
              Phone: (800) 257-5126
              Web site: http://www.films.com

Asians are among the nation's fastest-growing ethnic groups. Stereotypes have been revised, and condescension has given way to admiration and jealousy. This program examines the role of Asian Americans half a century after the repeal of the Chinese Exclusion Act, seeking to determine what accounts for Asians' startling successes in academia and to what extent they can, should, or want to blend into the American melting pot.

Becoming American
Type: Video
Length: 30 minutes
Date: 1983
Cost: $150
Source: University of California Extension
              Center for Media and Independent Learning
              2000 Center Street, 4th Floor
              Berkeley, CA 94704
              Contact: Kate Spohr or Daniel Bickley
              Phone: (510) 643-2788 or (510) 642-1340
              Fax: (510) 643-9271
              E-mail: cmil@uclink.berkeley.edu
              Web site: http://www-cmil.unex.berkeley.edu/media

The video traces the relocation path of a refugee family as they leave their native Laos, journey temporarily to Thailand, then finally resettle in Seattle, Washington.

Becoming American—The Chinese Experience
Type: Video
Length: Three-part series, 90 minutes each
Date: 2003
Cost: $130 each
Source: Films for the Humanities and Sciences
P.O. Box 2053
Princeton, NJ 08543-2053
Phone: (800) 257-5126
Fax: (609) 275-3767
Web site: http://www.films.com

This three-part video series answers the questions "What does it mean to become American?" "What is lost and gained when one sheds part of one's heritage to make way for a new self-identity?" It explores these questions through interviews with historians, descendants of immigrants, and recent immigrants from China.

Between Two Worlds: A Documentary
Type: Video C5846
Length: 29 minutes
Date: 1998
Cost: $150
Source: University of California Extension
Center for Media and Independent Learning
2000 Center Street, 4th Floor
Berkeley, CA 94704
Contact: Kate Spohr or Daniel Bickley
Phone: (510) 643-2788 or (510) 642-1340
Fax: (510) 643-9271
E-mail: cmil@uclink.berkeley.edu
Web site: http://www-cmil.unex.berkeley.edu/media

This documentary video examines the difficulties experienced by first-generation Asian American youth who struggle with "living in two worlds": the Asian family culture and the U.S. culture. Chinese American, Japanese American, and Korean American young adults and members of their families expound upon the generational and cultural gaps existing in Asian American families and stereotypical perceptions of Asians in U.S. society.

Chinese Americans: Living in Two Worlds
Type: Video
Length: 22 minutes
Date: 2001
Cost: $89.95
Source: Films for the Humanities and Sciences
              P.O. Box 2053
              Princeton, NJ 08543-2053
              Phone: (800) 257-5126
              Fax: (609) 275-3767
              Web site: http://www.films.com

What is the immigrant experience like for second-generation Americans? This ABC News program tells the story of a young Chinese American woman, her siblings, and her parents. Armed with a college degree and facing a life in which she is sometimes considered too Chinese to be American and too American to be Chinese, where should she begin her career? In Manhattan, or in Hong Kong, where there are even better opportunities?

The Color of Honor
Type: Video
Length: 90 minutes
Date: 1988
Cost: $129
Source: National Asian American Telecommunications
              Association
              346 Ninth Street, 2nd Floor
              San Francisco, CA 94103
              Contact: Eddie Wong
              Phone: (415) 863-0814, ext. 103
              Fax: (415) 863-7428
              Web site: http://www.naatanet.org

Interviews, dramatic reenactments, archival footage, and photographs recount the discrimination and hardship faced by Japanese Americans in the wake of the bombing of Pearl Harbor and acknowledges the contributions of the Nisei (second-generation Japanese American) soldiers in World War II. The film examines the policies invoked against Japanese Americans, including confiscation of businesses and property and internment in the U.S. detention camps.

A Family Gathering

Type: Video
Length: 57 minutes
Date: 1988
Cost: $175
Source: National Asian American Telecommunications
Association
346 Ninth Street
2nd Floor
San Francisco, CA 94103
Contact: Eddie Wong
Phone: (415) 863-0814, ext. 103
Fax: (415) 863-7428
Web site: http://www.naatanet.org

This video tells the dramatic story of the consequences of the U.S. internment policy on Japanese Americans during World War II and one family's long battle to reclaim their place as Americans.

Filipino Americans: Discovering Their Past for the Future

Type: Video
Length: 54 minutes
Date: 1994
Cost: $175
Source: National Asian American Telecommunications
Association
346 Ninth Street, 2nd Floor
San Francisco, CA 94103
Contact: Eddie Wong
Phone: (415) 863-0814, ext. 103
Fax: (415) 863-7428
Web site: http://www.naatanet.org

This video presents an in-depth history of Filipino Americans through interviews with historians, archival photos, and documents. It offers a 400-year chronicle of one of the largest ethnic groups in the U.S. Asian/Pacific Islander population.

From a Different Shore: The Japanese-American Experience

Type: Video

Length: 50 minutes
Date: 1994
Cost: $129
Source: Films for the Humanities and Sciences
P.O. Box 2053
Princeton, NJ 08543-2053
Phone: (800) 257-5126
Fax: (609) 275-3767
Web site: http://www.films.com

This program explores the distinct experience of Japanese Americans, from the first immigrants from Japan, the Issei, to the experiences of their children, the Nisei, who were confined in camps during World War II, and their grandchildren. The program explores these experiences through the lives of three families, whose members span all of the generations. They offer their view of the United States and what it means and has meant to be an American of Japanese ancestry.

Korean Americans
Type: Video
Length: 50 minutes
Date: 1998
Cost: $175
Source: Films for the Humanities and Sciences
P.O. Box 2053
Princeton, NJ 08543-2053
Phone: (800) 257-5126
Fax: (609) 275-3767
Web site: www.films.com

This program examines a group that is seeking to retain its traditional cultural values while adjusting to life in the United States. Korean Americans have come into frequent and violent conflict with inner-city African Americans, and they have sought, through their own ethnic civic organizations, to overcome the rejection of the community around them.

Mississippi Triangle
Type: Video
Length: 120 minutes
Date: 1984
Cost: $225

Source: Third World Newsreel
           545 Eighth Avenue, 10th Floor
           New York, NY 10018
           Phone: (212) 947-9277
           Fax: (212) 594-6417
           Web site: http://www.twn.org

This video documents the interethnic relations in the U.S. South, specifically the Mississippi Delta region, where Chinese Americans, African Americans, and whites live in a world of cotton, work, and racial conflict.

The New Generation: Vietnamese Americans Today

Type: Video
Length: 50 minutes
Date: 2001
Cost: $129
Source: Films for the Humanities and Sciences
           P.O. Box 2053
           Princeton, NJ 08543-2053
           Phone: (800) 257-5126
           Fax: (609) 275-3767
           Web site: http://www.films.com

Through interviews with first- and second-generation Vietnamese Americans, this program documents the process of assimilation into U.S. culture of refugees from the former Republic of Vietnam. Vu-Duc Vuong, of the University of California–Berkeley, college students, professionals, and clergy explore what it means to be of Vietnamese descent in the United States today. Topics include stresses on the family unit caused by cultural and generational differences, gang membership and drug abuse among the young, anti-Vietnamese racial bias, and feelings about relations between the United States and Vietnam.

The Polynesians—The New Americans Series

Type: Video
Length: 30 minutes
Date: 1994
Cost: $125
Source: National Asian American Telecommunications
           Association
           346 Ninth Street, 2nd Floor

San Francisco, CA 94103
Contact: Eddie Wong
Phone: (415) 863-0814, ext. 103
Fax: (415) 863-7428
Web site: http://www.naatanet.org

This video explores identity issues among Polynesian communities in the United States today. It features discussions about stereotyping, generational differences between children and first-generation immigrant parents, and identity questions.

The Stories of Maxine Hong Kingston
Type: Video
Length: 55 minutes
Date: 1990
Cost: $59.95
Source: PBS
             Phone: (800) 344-3337
             Web site: http://ShopPBS.com/teachers

This video is a two-part interview with Maxine Hong Kingston, author of *The Woman Warrior* and *China Men*, who discusses new images of America as a melting pot where dutiful notions of the Puritan blend with the Monkey Spirit of the Orient to produce a new American consciousness.

Tatau: What One Must Do
Type: Video
Length: 27 minutes
Date: 1997
Cost: $175
Source: University of California Extension
             Center for Media and Independent Learning
             2000 Center Street, 4th Floor
             Berkeley, CA 94704
             Contact: Kate Spohr or Daniel Bickley
             Phone: (510) 643-2788 or (510) 642-1340
             Fax: (510) 643-9271
             E-mail: cmil@uclink.berkeley.edu
             Web site: http://www-cmil.unex.berkeley.edu/media

This documentary video examines the ancient art of Samoan tattooing, its traditional place in Samoan culture, and its current renaissance, both in Samoa and in the large Samoan community in Los Angeles. Samoans are the only Polynesians who never abandoned their tattooing traditions and ceremonies. To the Samoans, tattooing—its symbols, its legends, its traditional instruments—is at the heart of their culture and represents a civilizing process through which a man gains the virtues and values of his society.

Who Killed Vincent Chin?

Type: Video
Length: 82 minutes
Date: 1988
Cost: $250
Source: Filmmakers Library
             Linda Gottesmand
             124 East Fortieth St., Suite 901
             New York, NY 10016
             Phone: (212) 808-4980
             E-mail: info@filmakers.com

This video documents the murder of Vincent Chin, a twenty-seven-year-old Chinese American. Chin was celebrating in a Detroit bar when an argument broke out, ethnic insults were shouted, and Chin was killed by a man with a baseball bat.

European American

European Americans

Type: Video
Length: 60 minutes
Date: 2001
Cost: $139
Source: Insight Media
             2162 Broadway
             New York, NY 10024-0621
             Phone: (800) 233-9910
             Fax: (212) 799-5309
             E-mail: cs@insight-media.com
             Web site: http://www.insight-media.com

This video documents the impact of European American culture both nationally and globally. It looks at the role and significance of European languages and religions in the United States and around the world. It features examples from the history and experiences of Polish Americans and Italian Americans.

The Irish in America: Long Journey Home

Type:	Video
Length:	6 hours
Date:	1998
Cost:	$79.99
Source:	PBS
	Phone: (800) 344-3337
	Web site: http://ShopPBS.com/teachers

This video series spans a hundred-year journey from the Great Potato Famine to the White House, tracing the struggles and successes of the 1 million Irish immigrants who left Ireland for the United States. It weaves stories of families, workers, churches, athletes, and entertainers into a portrait of Irish achievement. It contains Irish music and folk rhythms, black-and-white photos and film footage, drawings, and interviews with Irish Americans. Part 1 of the series explores the early Irish roots in the New World before and after the Great Potato Famine. Part 2 traces the building of lives as the United States itself took shape. Part 3 explores the "golden age" as the Irish made inroads into theater, sports, music, labor, Wall Street, and politics. Part 4 covers Irish American history from World War II to the present.

The Italian Gardens of South Brooklyn

Type:	Video
Length:	26 minutes
Date:	1997
Cost:	$175
Source:	University of California Extension
	Center for Media and Independent Learning
	2000 Center Street, 4th Floor
	Berkeley, CA 94704
	Contact: Kate Spohr or Daniel Bickley
	Phone: (510) 643-2788 or (510) 642-1340
	Fax: (510) 643-9271
	E-mail: cmil@uclink.berkeley.edu
	Web site: http://www-cmil.unex.berkeley.edu/media

This documentary video illustrates how "a mixture of old-world values and new world horse sense" invigorates the traditional

Italian American community of South Brooklyn and infuses it with a strong respect for family, friends, and neighborhood.

Little Italy

Type:	Video
Length:	60 minutes
Date:	1995
Cost:	$79
Source:	Insight Media
	2162 Broadway
	New York, NY 10024-0621
	Phone: (800) 233-9910
	Fax: (212) 799-5309
	E-mail: cs@insight-media.com
	Web site: http://www.insight-media.com

This video explores the issues of immigration, assimilation, and cultural identity through an examination of the Italian American experience. It blends archival footage, contemporary documentation, and interviews with well-known Italian Americans.

Multicultural Peoples of North America video series

Type:	Video
Length:	30 minutes
Date:	1993
Cost:	$39.95
Source:	Library Video Company
	Phone: (800) 843-3620
	Fax: (610) 645-4040
	Web site: http://www.libraryvideo.com

This video series examines the heritage of different European cultural groups, tracing the history of their emigration to North America, their unique traditions, and their significant contributions. Each video explores a family from a particular culture, meeting three generations who share their memories of their country of origin and their motivations for coming to the United States. The videos discuss the importance of cultural identity, how it is maintained, and how it changes. Interviews with leading historians examine the impact of each ethnic group on the growth of the United States and Canada and the effects of contemporary immigration policies.

Latina/Latino

Americano as Apple Pie
Type: Video
Length: Two parts, 30 minutes each
Date: 2001
Cost: $129 each
Source: Films for the Humanities and Sciences
            P.O. Box 2053
            Princeton, NJ 08543-2053
            Phone: (800) 257-5126
            Fax: (609) 275-3767
            Web site: http://www.films.com

This two-part video series looks at a variety of issues concerning the Latino cultures in America, including the size and history of different Hispanic populations and the effects of current U.S. immigration laws. The videos examine Latino identity in both thriving urban neighborhoods and isolated rural towns and feature prominent figures in the greater Hispanic community.

The Americans
Type: Video
Length: 90 minutes
Date: 1997–2000
Cost: $19.95 each
Source: PBS
            Phone: (800) 344-3337
            Web site: http://ShopPBS.com/teachers

This is a documentary series that traces the history and contributions of Mexican Americans, Cubans, and Puerto Ricans within the United States. Each video contains vintage footage, stories, and family photos. The series traces where these groups came from, where they are now, and what the future may hold for them. Each ethnic group is documented in a separate video.

Biculturalism and Acculturation among Latinos
Type: Video
Length: 28 minutes each
Date: 1991
Cost: $149.59
Source: Films for the Humanities and Sciences

P.O. Box 2053
Princeton, NJ 08543-2053
Phone: (800) 257-5126
Fax: (609) 275-3767
Web site: http://www.films.com

Many Latinos struggle with pressures to reclaim and reaffirm their heritage while simultaneously facing pressures to assimilate into the dominant U.S. culture. This program examines the question of what part of their culture Latinos feel they should keep and what they should leave behind, explores some commonly held beliefs and misperceptions about who Latinos are today in the United States, and probes the relationship of ethnic identity to entrepreneurial success in the changing mosaic of the U.S. marketplace.

Black and White in Exile
Type: Video
Length: Six-part series, 30 minutes each
Date: 1997
Cost: $299.95
Source: Edge Video
Ray Blanco
P.O. Box 430
Fanwood, NJ 97923
Phone: (980) 769-3250
Fax: (908) 769-3252
E-mail: ceetv@aol.com

This six-part documentary chronicles the experiences of Cuban and Haitian exiles in the United States since the 1960s. Using photographic images, the video deals with the themes of assimilation and immigration. The series explores the quest for equality in government treatment, economic opportunities, and access to political power. It discusses interracial and cross-cultural hostility, followed by cooperation and coalition. It reviews coverage of immigration and political refugees by the national media and brings up such issues as the government's reception of the exiles and prospects for peaceful coexistence between exiles and residents.

The Blending of Culture: Latino Influence on America
Type: Video
Length: 30 minutes

Date: 2001
Cost: $155
Source: Films for the Humanities and Sciences
             P.O. Box 2053
             Princeton, NJ 08543-2053
             Phone: (800) 257-5126
             Fax: (609) 275-3767
             Web site: http://www.films.com

This program looks at the "Three Houses of Latino Culture"—Cuban, Puerto Rican, and Mexican American—and their widespread influence in areas ranging from entertainment to politics to economics. Key issues include how long Hispanics have been in America and how U.S. immigration has affected their assimilation. Interviews with Latino community leaders bring home the diversity and achievement of this rapidly expanding segment of the U.S. population.

Chicano!
Type: Video
Length: Four-part series, 60 minutes each
Date: 1996
Cost: $175
Source: National Latino Communications
             Jose Ruiz
             Educational Media
             Los Angeles, CA 90039
             Phone: (323) 663-8294
             Web site: http://www.nlcc.org

This four-part series explores Mexican American social activism spanning the years 1965–1975. Combining archival footage and current interviews, the series charts the struggles of Mexican Americans to reclaim the name *Chicano* and fashion it into a term of pride and self-determination. Part 1 examines events that sparked a national movement for social justice. Part 2 chronicles the efforts of farmworkers to form a national labor union. Part 3 documents the struggle to reform an educational system that failed to educate Chicano students properly. Part 4 focuses on the emergence of Mexican American political power and the creation of the political party, La Raza Unida.

Cultural Bias in Education
Length: 28 minutes
Date: 2002
Cost: $90
Source: Films for the Humanities and Sciences
P.O. Box 2053
Princeton, NJ 08543-2053
Phone: (800) 257-5126
Fax: (609) 275-3767
Web site: http://www.films.com

This video examines roadblocks to Latino academic advancement as well as productive educational models, explores the relationship of standardized testing and cultural diversity and questions whether cultural bias can be eliminated from standardized testing, and looks at early-childhood education programs and the factors that deter Latino families from participating in them.

Growing Up Hispanic American
Type: Video
Length: 23 minutes
Date: 1998
Cost: $139
Source: Insight Media
2162 Broadway
New York, NY 10024-0621
Phone: (800) 233-9910
Fax: (212) 799-5309
E-mail: cs@insight-media.com
Web site: http://www.insight-media.com

This video focuses on cultural roots and the contributions made to U.S. culture by generations of Hispanic Americans in a wide range of fields.

Hero Hispanos
Type: Video
Length: 150 minutes
Date: 1993
Cost: $29.95 each
Source: Teacher's Video Company
P.O. Box 4455
Scottsdale, AZ 85261

Phone: (800) 262-8837
Web site: http://www.teachersvideo.com

The History Channel created this program on famous U.S. leaders of Hispanic descent. This film documents Hispanic Americans' participation in the American Revolution, the Civil War, the Rough Rider campaigns, World War I, World War II, and other major events.

Hispanic Americans
Type: Video
Length: 90 minutes (3 volumes)
Date: 1993
Cost: $149
Source: Insight Media
            2162 Broadway
            New York, NY 10024-0621
            Phone: (800) 233-9910
            Fax: (212) 799-5309
            E-mail: cs@insight-media.com
            Web site: http://www.insight-media.com

This series documents the cultural heritage of Central Americans, Mexican Americans, and Puerto Ricans. It examines the unique traditions of each group and discusses when and why each group immigrated to the United States. It also explores how they have preserved their cultural identities.

The Hispanic Americans
Type: Video
Length: Seven-part series, 44 minutes each
Date: 1995
Cost: $567 (or $90 each)
Source: Films for the Humanities and Sciences
            P.O. Box 2053
            Princeton, NJ 08543-2053
            Phone: (800) 257-5126
            Fax: (609) 275-3767
            Web site: http://www.films.com

This series explores what it means to be Hispanic. It is hosted by Jimmy Smits and Hector Elizondo. Many Hispanics—some famous, some average people—are interviewed in seeking answers to this question. The videos explore issues pertaining to cross-cultural understanding, education, gender roles, media, second-generation acculturation, economics, and cultural differences among different Hispanic groups.

Hispanic/Latino Americans

Type:	Video
Length:	120 minutes (2 tapes)
Date:	2001
Cost:	$199
Source:	Insight Media
	2162 Broadway
	New York, NY 10024-0621
	Phone: (800) 233-9910
	Fax: (212) 799-5309
	E-mail: cs@insight-media.com
	Web site: http://www.insight-media.com

This series examines the wide variety of cultural groups classified as Hispanic/Latino Americans. It features conversations among a group of students who discuss the fact that Latinos will soon be the largest ethnic group in the United States. It explores some of the Hostos Community College programs designed to serve a primarily Latino community in New York City.

Issues of Latino Identity: The Yearning to Be . . .

Type:	Video
Length:	30 minutes
Date:	2001
Cost:	$155
Source:	Films for the Humanities and Sciences
	P.O. Box 2053
	Princeton, NJ 08543-2053
	Phone: (800) 257-5126
	Fax: (609) 275-3767
	Web site: http://www.films.com

This program takes a detailed look at the fastest-growing minority in the United States and at what it means to be Latino and American. The documentary contrasts the experience of being a Latino in a flourishing ethnic neighborhood of a big city with the experience of living in a small town, where many Latinos feel isolated. Interviews with individuals occupying roles of leadership in the Hispanic community cover such subjects as social services, churches, business, and the arts.

The Latino Family
Length: 28 minutes
Date: 2001
Cost: $150
Source: Films for the Humanities and Sciences
P.O. Box 2053
Princeton, NJ 08543-2053
Phone: (800) 257-5126
Fax: (609) 275-3767
Web site: http://www.films.com

This video shows both the changes in and the endurance of traditional Latino families. It follows the paths of three generations of one Mexican American family. It traces the patterns of migration and cultural change. It shows how the traditional roles of the Latino elderly are being altered by their families' needs, and also how the traditional pleasures can still be celebrated.

The Mexican Americans
Type: Video
Length: 90 minutes
Date: 2000
Cost: $19.95
Source: PBS
Phone: (800) 344-3337
Web site: http://ShopPBS.com/teachers

Across 2,000 miles of border and hundreds of years of history, this film explores traditions and cultural connections among Mexican Americans. Actor Ricardo Montalban, comedian Paul Rodriguez, singers Vikki Carr and Tish Hinojosa, director Luis Valdez, and many others share their personal stories about Mexican culture north of the border. Archival film and photos and modern footage celebrate the men and women whose hard work, determination, strength, and faith have contributed so much to the United States.

Palante, Siempre Palante! The Young Lords
Type: Video
Length: 48 minutes
Date: 1996

Cost: $225
Source: Third World Newsreel
           545 Eighth Avenue, 10th Floor
           New York, NY 10018
           Phone: (212) 947-9277
           Fax: (212) 594-6417
           Web site: http://www.twn.org

This video concerns young Puerto Ricans in Chicago and New York City during the civil rights struggle of the 1960s and 1970s who organized into a group called the Young Lords Organization. Their purpose was to achieve economic and social justice for Puerto Rican Americans. Through archival footage, photographs, music, and interviews with former members of the group, this video documents their activities and philosophy and the eventual demise of the organization.

Seven Little-Known Truths about Latino History
Type: Video
Length: 20 minutes
Date: 1998
Cost: $139
Source: Insight Media
           2162 Broadway
           New York, NY 10024-0621
           Phone: (800) 233-9910
           Fax: (212) 799-5309
           E-mail: cs@insight-media.com
           Web site: http://www.insight-media.com

This video explores the history of Latinos in the United States. It focuses on some of their significant but lesser-known contributions to U.S. culture.

Yo Soy Chicano
Type: Video
Length: 60 minutes
Date: 1972
Cost: $199
Source: Insight Media
           2162 Broadway
           New York, NY 10024-0621
           Phone: (800) 233-9910

Fax: (212) 799-5309
E-mail: cs@insight-media.com
Web site: http://www.insight-media.com

This video traces the history of the Chicano experience, from its roots in pre-Columbian history to the political struggles of the early 1970s.

Multiracial Identities

An American Love Story
Type: Video
Length: 500 minutes
Date: 1999
Cost: $108
Source: First Run/Icarus
             Tom Hyland
             32 Court Street, 21st Floor
             Brooklyn, NY 11201
             Phone: (714) 488-8900
             Fax: (800) 876-1710
             E-mail: mail@frif.com

This video documentary is condensed from 1,000 hours of filming the biracial Wilson Sims family: Karen Wilson, a white woman, Bill Sims, a black man, and their two daughters: daughter Cicily's entrance to college, her semester in Nigeria, and her job search; daughter Chaney's first date; Karen Wilson's solitary visit to her mother and ill health; Bill Sims's visit to his past life and career struggles; and Karen and Bill's decision, twenty-five years after their first meeting, to attend her high school reunion to face people who had ostracized them in the past.

Between Worlds
Type: Video
Length: 57 minutes
Date: 1998
Cost: $225
Source: University of California Extension
             Center for Media and Independent Learning
             2000 Center Street, 4th Floor
             Berkeley, CA 94704

Contact: Kate Spohr or Daniel Bickley
Phone: (510) 643-2788 or (510) 642-1340
Fax: (510) 643-9271
E-mail: cmil@uclink.berkeley.edu
Web site: http://www-cmil.unex.berkeley.edu/media

This unique documentary explores the lives of several Vietnamese Amerasians (children of Vietnamese women and American servicemen) and their families who left Vietnam in 1992 through the Orderly Departure Program. Each of the families was sent to a refugee camp in the Philippines for six months of English-as-a-Second-Language instruction and cultural orientation. The film details their experiences in the camp and their arrival in different regions of this country. It then follows their lives for five more years as they struggle to learn English, find jobs, and pursue their educations, and for one Amerasian, to be reunited with his American father.

Children of Mixed Race=Who You Wanna Be?

Type: Video
Length: 38 minutes
Date: 1997
Cost: $225
Source: University of California Extension
             Center for Media and Independent Learning
             2000 Center Street, 4th Floor
             Berkeley, CA 94704
             Contact: Kate Spohr or Daniel Bickley
             Phone: (510) 643-2788 or (510) 642-1340
             Fax: (510) 643-9271
             E-mail: cmil@uclink.berkeley.edu
             Web site: http://www-cmil.unex.berkeley.edu/media

This video is a study of the various types of identities that interracial people have had to invent for themselves. It is based on interviews with racially mixed students at the University of California–Berkeley, who speak about their perceptions of their own personal identities.

Do Two Halves Really Make a Whole?

Type: Video
Length: 30 minutes
Date: 1993

Cost: $125
Source: National Asian American Telecommunications
Association
346 Ninth Street, 2nd Floor
San Francisco, CA 94103
Contact: Eddie Wong
Phone: (415) 863-0814, ext. 103
Fax: (415) 863-7428
Web site: http://www.naatanet.org

This video features the diverse viewpoints of people with multiracial Asian heritages. African and Japanese American poet and playwright Velina Hasu Houston lives an "amalgamated existence" and encourages others to take pride in all that they are. Performance artist Dan Kwong constantly struggles with two strong and often conflicting Asian heritages, Japanese and Chinese American. Chinese Japanese Chicana Scots storyteller, actress, and performance artist Brenda Wong Aoki uses her unique ethnic mix to intersect social circles.

Domino: Interracial People and the Search for Identity
Type: Video
Length: 45 minutes
Date: 1994
Cost: $150
Source: Films for the Humanities and Sciences
P.O. Box 2053
Princeton, NJ 08543-2053
Phone: (800) 257-5126
Fax: (609) 275-3767
Web site: http://www.films.com

This video portrays the stories of six interracial people, exploring issues of identity, cultural isolation, and the search for community. Through these personal stories, each person recounts how his or her identity is affected by parental history, hierarchies of race, gender roles, and class. Ultimately, these six individuals demonstrate how living intimately with two cultures can be a source of strength and enrichment.

En Ryo Identity
Type: Video
Length: 23 minutes

Date: 1991
Cost: $125
Source: National Asian American Telecommunications
            Association
            346 Ninth Street, 2nd Floor
            San Francisco, CA 94103
            Contact: Eddie Wong
            Phone: (415) 863-0814, ext. 103
            Fax: (415) 863-7428
            Web site: http://www.naatanet.org

This video addresses the complexities of establishing and asserting a "biracial identity." It also juxtaposes mainstream media constructions of Asian American identity with Hollywood represen-
tations of Asians.

Interracial Marriage: Blending the Races in America
Type: Video
Length: 52 minutes
Date: 1993
Cost: $150
Source: University of California Extension
            Center for Media and Independent Learning
            2000 Center Street, 4th Floor
            Berkeley, CA 94704
            Contact: Kate Spohr or Daniel Bickley
            Phone: (510) 643-2788 or (510) 642-1340
            Fax: (510) 643-9271
            E-mail: cmil@uclink.berkeley.edu
            Web site: http://www-cmil.unex.berkeley.edu/media

This video examines how and why couples of different colors, religions, and ethnic roots are drawn to one another, how their differences affect their marriages, and how they deal with their
friends and family.

Mixed Blood
Type: Video
Length: 20 minutes
Date: 1992
Cost: $125
Source: National Asian American Telecommunications
            Association

346 Ninth Street, 2nd Floor
San Francisco, CA 94103
Contact: Eddie Wong
Phone: (415) 863-0814, ext. 103
Fax: (415) 863-7428
Web site: http://www.naatanet.org

This experimental documentary takes a personal view of interracial relationships between Asian Americans and non–Asian Americans. The video skillfully combines interviews with couples, text, and clips from scientific films and classic miscegenation dramas to explore the complexities of intimate emotional and sexual choices. The video illustrates how such choices have public and political implications.

Mixed Feelings
Type: Video
Length: 45 minutes
Date: 1998
Cost: $195
Source: National Asian American Telecommunications
             Association
             346 Ninth Street, 2nd Floor
             San Francisco, CA 94103
             Contact: Eddie Wong
             Phone: (415) 863-0814, ext. 103
             Fax: (415) 863-7428
             Web site: http://www.naatanet.org

Through interviews with five University of California–Berkeley students and teachers of mixed ethnic heritage, this video illuminates the experience of growing up part Asian in U.S. society. The students offer personal anecdotes detailing how their parents met, what it was like growing up, how they initially perceived their own cultural identities, and how they see themselves today. Humorous and revelatory, this experimental documentary manages to tackle difficult issues of racial reconciliation while celebrating difference and diversity.

One Drop
Type: Video
Length: 45 minutes
Date: 2001

Cost: $195
Source: California Newsreel/Resolution Inc.
P.O. Box 2284
South Burlington, VT 05407
Phone: (877) 811-7495
Fax: (802) 846-1850
Web site: http://www.newsreel.org

This video explores the recurring and divisive issue in African American communities of skin color. The film intercuts intimate interviews with darker-skinned African Americans, lighter-skinned African Americans, and interracial children of black and white parents. It investigates the sensitive topic of color consciousness within the African American community with great tact and a clear commitment to healing divisions.

Native American

Boomtown
Type: Video
Length: 53 minutes
Date: 2002
Cost: $295; rental, $95
Source: University of California Extension
Center for Media and Independent Learning
2000 Center Street, 4th Floor
Berkeley, CA 94704
Contact: Kate Spohr or Daniel Bickley
Phone: (510) 643-2788 or (510) 642-1340
Fax: (510) 643-9271
E-mail: cmil@uclink.berkeley.edu
Web site: http://ucmedia.berkeley.edu

This video documents the lives of the Native Americans living on the Port Madison Indian Reservation in Suquamish, Washington. At the start of every summer, tribal members from the Suquamish Nation transform their seaside village into a marketplace devoted to the sale of fireworks for the upcoming Fourth of July. This documentary chronicles the many challenges faced by Suquamish families in the fireworks business. It also explores the complex and controversial issues of tribal sovereignty, treaty rights, and the pursuit of life, liberty, and happiness on this reservation.

Children of the Long-Beaked Bird
Type: Video
Length: 29 minutes
Date: 1976
Cost: $40
Source: Bullfrog Films
             P.O. Box 149
             Oley, PA 19547
             Phone: (610) 779-8226
             Fax: (610) 370-1978
             Web site: http://www.bullfrogfilms.com

This film presents a portrait of a modern Native American family that erases the stereotypes made infamous by westerns. It shows the daily life of twelve-year-old Dominic Old Elk, who is proud of his Indian heritage but is part of young America, too. Dominic is a Crow Indian. His great-great-grandfather was one of the scouts who warned George Armstrong Custer not to attack the large force of Sioux and Cheyenne camped by the banks of the Little Big Horn. The video begins with a concise review of Native American life and history and then follows the daily activities of Dominic Old Elk at a throbbing hand game and an all-Indian rodeo, riding in a pickup truck to the sacred mountains, rounding up horses in springtime, scraping teepee poles, and studying in school.

Dancing in Moccasins: Keeping Native American Traditions Alive
Type: Video
Length: 48 minutes
Date: 2002
Cost: $149
Source: Films for the Humanities and Sciences
             P.O. Box 2053
             Princeton, NJ 08543-2053
             Phone: (800) 257-5126
             Fax: (609) 275-3767
             Web site: http://www.films.com

This program examines the needs and problems of today's Native Americans, both those who live on reservations and those who have chosen the mainstream. The film focuses on celebration and survival as reflected in the continuing tradition of the Pow Wow.

Growing Up Native American

Type:	Video
Length:	22 minutes
Date:	1998
Cost:	$139
Source:	Insight Media

2162 Broadway
New York, NY 10024-0621
Phone: (800) 233-9910
Fax: (212) 799-5309
E-mail: cs@insight-media.com
Web site: http://www.insight-media.com

This video traces the legacy left by earlier generations of Native Americans. It emphasizes the importance of respect for cultural roots and recognition of their relevance to contemporary culture.

Homeland

Type:	Video
Length:	57 minutes
Date:	2000
Cost:	$295; rental, $90
Source:	University of California Extension

Center for Media and Independent Learning
2000 Center Street, 4th Floor
Berkeley, CA 94704
Contact: Kate Spohr or Daniel Bickley
Phone: (510) 643-2788 or (510) 642-1340
Fax: (510) 643-9271
Web site: http://ucmedia.berkeley.edu

This video documents the stories of four Lakota Indian families on the Pine Ridge Indian Reservation in South Dakota. Shot over several years, this film provides a portrait of contemporary Native American life as well as a depiction of the vitality of Native culture. The film balances the troubles that beset the reservation system with the resilience of Lakota culture and spirituality.

In the Light of Reverence

Type:	Video
Length:	73 minutes
Date:	2001
Cost:	$295

Source: Bullfrog Films
P.O. Box 149
Oley, PA 19547
Phone: (610) 779-8226
Fax: (610) 370-1978
Web site: http://www.bullfrogfilms.com

This video offers a portrait of land-use conflicts over Native American sacred sites on public and private land around the West. Across the United States, Native Americans are struggling to protect their sacred places. Every year, more sacred sites are being destroyed. This film tells the story of three indigenous communities and the land they struggle to protect: the Lakota of the Great Plains, the Hopi of the Four Corners area, and the Wintu of northern California.

Native American Influence on the United States
Type: Video
Length: 21 minutes
Date: 1998
Cost: $109
Source: Insight Media
2162 Broadway
New York, NY 10024-0621
Phone: (800) 233-9910
Fax: (212) 799-5309
E-mail: cs@insight-media.com
Web site: http://www.insight-media.com

This video documents the influence on the United States of the indigenous cultures that occupied the Americas before the arrival of the Europeans. It shows how U.S. agriculture, medicine, and language as well as the U.S. government, economy, and legal system still reflect the influence of Native Americans.

The Native Americans
Type: Video
Length: 47 minutes
Date: 1996
Cost: $130
Source: Films for the Humanities and Sciences
P.O. Box 2053
Princeton, NJ 08543-2053

Phone: (800) 257-5126
Fax: (609) 275-3767
Web site: http://www.films.com

This video explores the many similarities among tribal nations, including a profound respect for nature, myth, and tradition; matriarchal governance; a communal lifestyle; a belief in an afterlife; and the use of pictographs, symbols, and patterns rather than an alphabet-based writing system. Also included are brief scenes of re-created warfare. The near extinction of Native Americans is discussed, along with the renewal of Native American culture.

Native Americans: Celebrating Traditions

Type:	Video
Length:	30 minutes
Date:	2001
Cost:	$129
Source:	Films for the Humanities and Sciences
	P.O. Box 2053
	Princeton, NJ 08543-2053
	Phone: (800) 257-5126
	Fax: (609) 275-3767
	Web site: http://www.films.com

By presenting the experiences of Native Americans from a wide array of fields, including artisans, performers, and teachers, this program shows how many tribes are returning to the traditions and spirituality of their ancestors. Among those interviewed are Kevin Locke, award-winning Native American vocalist; Wilma Mankiller, the first woman in modern history to lead a tribe; and Richard West, director of the Smithsonian Institution's National Museum of the American Indian.

On and Off the Reservation: A Native American

Type:	Video
Length:	18 minutes
Date:	1997
Cost:	$159
Source:	Insight Media
	2162 Broadway
	New York, NY 10024-0621
	Phone: (800) 233-9910
	Fax: (212) 799-5309

E-mail: cs@insight-media.com
Web site: http://www.insight-media.com

This video explores the lives of contemporary Native Americans who strive to protect their culture and heritage while succeeding in the mainstream of the United States. It examines the roles of education, family, and tribal affiliation. It presents examples of traditional Native American practices and considers the economic issues that complicate reservation life. It also addresses some of the common stereotypes that surround Native American culture.

Savagery and the American Indian: "Civilization"
Type: Video
Length: 50 minutes
Date: 1991
Cost: 129
Source: Films for the Humanities and Sciences
           P.O. Box 2053
           Princeton, NJ 08543-2053
           Phone: (800) 257-5126
           Fax: (609) 275-3767
           Web site: http://www.films.com

This program documents the struggle of the scattered indigenous nations to reclaim and retain their language, history, and identity in the face of historical revisionism, coercive evangelism, and forcible assimilation. Indian-rights advocate Vine Deloria Jr.; members of the Oglala, Hunkpapa, and Sans Arc Sioux; and others describe the misguided practices, unscrupulous dealings, and outright cruelties of the United States against them and their peoples.

Teaching Indians to Be White
Type: Video
Length: 28 minutes
Date: 1997
Cost: $90
Source: Films for the Humanities and Sciences
           P.O. Box 2053
           Princeton, NJ 08543-2053
           Phone: (800) 257-5126
           Fax: (609) 275-3767

Web site: http://www.films.com

This video delves into the problem that schools represent for native children. Whether they are religious schools with native teachers, residential schools that tear children away from their families and traditional values, or public day schools where native children find it nearly impossible to balance the white view they are taught with the language and values they learn at home, these schools create tension and conflict. This film documents some of the consequences of this conflict: The Seminole Indians of Florida resisted being integrated, the Miccosukee Indians decided not to fight but to join the mainstream, and the Cree Indians took back their own schools.

Internet Resources

African American Biographical Database (AABD)
Web site: http://aabd.chadwyck.com

The African American Biographical Database (AABD) is a resource of first resort for anyone looking for biographical information, including photographs and illustrations, about African Americans. From the well-known to the everyday person, AABD includes profiles with biographical details and illuminating narratives of the lives of black Americans. Each text used in the AABD has been fully digitized, so not only can researchers search for specific biographical sketches, but they also have direct access to a rich collection of African American reference works, many of which are rare books.

The AABD can be used to find accounts of life as a slave, a religious leader in the U.S. South, a reformer, or a business person in the nineteenth-century United States; to verify names or birth records of family members for a genealogical search; to locate historical photographs or illustrations; to discover geographic and familial links vital to genealogical research; to explore the history of local black elites from Baltimore to Seattle; to collect information for a book, paper, or other scholarly endeavor; and to research the Abolitionist movement, the National Association for the Advancement of Colored People (NAACP), and many other political movements and organizations.

The AABD brings together in one resource the biographies of

thousands of African Americans, many not to be found in any other reference source. These sketches have been carefully assembled from biographical dictionaries and other sources. This collection contains extended narratives of African American activists, business people, former slaves, performing artists, educators, lawyers, physicians, writers, church leaders, homemakers, religious workers, government workers, athletes, farmers, scientists, and factory workers.

African Ancestored Genealogy
P.O. Box 4906
Blue Mountain, AL 36204
Phone: (256) 820-8794
Fax: (256) 820-8339
Web site: http://www.afrigeneas.com

AfriGeneas.com is a site devoted to African American genealogy, to the research of African ancestry in the Americas in particular and to genealogical research and resources in general. It is also an African ancestry research community featuring the AfriGeneas.com mail list, the AfriGeneas.com message boards, and daily and weekly genealogy chats. AfriGeneas.com provides resources, leadership, promotion, and advocacy for the mutual development and use of a system of genealogy for researching Africa-related ancestry. It encourages and supports all individuals and families of African ancestry to begin and continue researching their roots until all possible resources are exhausted and the results are published. It provides and maintains a searchable database of surnames; collects slave data from descendants of slaveholding families as well as from public and other private sources; and extracts, compiles, and publishes all related public records with genealogical value.

Asian and Pacific Islands American
History and Literature for K–12
Web site: http://falcon.jmu.edu/~ramseyil/asiabio.htm

This Web site is an Asian Americans page run by the Internet School Library Media Center (ISLMC). It includes history, literature, and biography of Americans of Asian ancestry. ISLMC is a metasite for librarians, teachers, parents, and students. Topics include notable Asian Americans, literature, media, history, arts and entertainment, associations, periodicals, social issues, ERIC resources, and various ethnic groups that make up the Asian American community. The site includes an *"Asian American cybernauts page"* that includes community concerns, culture and contributions of the Asian American communities, quotes, and personal home pages.

Irish American Post
301 North Water Street
Milwaukee, WI 53202
Phone: (414) 273-8132
Fax: (414) 273-8196
Web site: http://www.info@irishamericanpost.com

The *Irish American Post* is a monthly, on-line newspaper that covers contemporary issues affecting Irish Americans and persons living in Ireland.

Italian American Bookshelf
100 A Station Road
Great Neck, NY 11023
Phone: (516) 466-6352
Fax: (516) 466-6352
E-mail: Italbooks@aol.com
Web site: http://www.italianamericanbooks.com

This resource carries books that deal exclusively with Italian American issues and authors. It carries books on topics such as music, art and artists, anthologies, bibliographies, biographies, children's books, cooking, health, history, language, literary criticism, poetry, and politics.

Polish American Journal
1275 Harlem Road
Buffalo, NY 14206
Phone: (800) 422-1275
Web site: http://www.polamjournal.com

The *Polish American Journal,* a Buffalo-based monthly news journal founded in 1911, is dedicated to the preservation of Polish American culture and history. It contains editorials, news highlights across the nation and the world, literature resources, music news, and news of educational opportunities such as scholarships.

Native American Authors
Web site: http:www.ipl.org/ref/native

This Web site provides information on Native North American authors, including bibliographies of their published works, biographical information, and links to such on-line resources as interviews, on-line texts, and tribal Web sites. The scope of the project includes works by contemporary and historical Native American and First Nations authors in the geographical area of the United States and Canada. The Web site provides a place to learn about the works, lives, and achievements of Native North American authors. The criteria for including authors is that they are American Indian or First Nations by blood and are accepted as such by other Native people.

Native American Resources
BroadSat Communications
610 West Sixth Avenue
Stillwater, OK 74074
Web site: http://www.cowboy.net/native

This Web site is a gateway to various Native American organizations. It connects the user with various organizations dealing with all aspects of Native American communities, including legal services, finance and business, health, education, employment, environmental protection, politics, art, and culture.

Glossary

Affirmative action   Government intervention program designed to remedy inequality encountered by minorities and women in employment and education opportunities.

Civil rights   Legal rights held by all citizens in a given state.

Cultural pluralism   The peaceful coexistence and equal treatment of culturally diverse groups within the same population.

Discrimination   The denial of equal access to social resources to people on the basis of their group membership, for example, racial and ethnic populations.

Emigration   The movement of people out of their native land to other countries.

Ethnicity   An ethnic group is one of a common cultural identity, separating them from other groups around them.

Ethnocentrism   The tendency to judge other cultures by the standards of one's own culture.

Immigration   The settlement of people into a country in which they were not born.

Institutional discrimination   Socially and historically transmitted structures of inequality that place racial and ethnic minority groups at a disadvantage.

Institutional racism   Structured patterns of inequality associated with a person's race or ethnicity that determine access to social opportunity in social institutions.

Migration   The movement of people from one country or region to another in order to settle permanently.

Minority group (or ethnic minority)   A group of people who are defined on the basis of their ethnicity or race. Because of their distinct physical or cultural characteristics, they are singled out for unequal treatment within a society.

Prejudice The holding of unfounded ideas about a group, especially ideas that are associated with negative perceptions of racial and ethnic minorities.

Race A socially defined category of people who often share distinct physical characteristics.

Racism The practice of assigning characteristics of inferiority to a particular racial or ethnic category. Racism is a specific form of prejudice focused on race.

Scapegoating Blaming, punishing, or stigmatizing a relatively powerless individual or group for wrongs that were not of their doing.

Social forces The term refers to the fact that society and social organizations exert an influence on individual human behavior.

Social groups Two or more individuals who interact in systematic ways with one another and share a high degree of common identity.

Social institutions Major structural units in society that address a basic need, for example, education, economy, politics, etc. Institutions involve fixed modes of behavior backed by strong norms and sanctions that tend to be followed by most members of a society.

Stereotype A rigid and inflexible negative image of persons belonging to a group, for example, racial and ethnic minorities. Stereotypes attribute these characteristics to all individuals belonging to that group.

Index

About the Author

Adalberto Aguirre, Jr. is a professor of sociology in the Department of Sociology at the University of California–Riverside.